CIVILIZING THE MUSEUM

CIVILIZING THE MUSEUM

The collected writings of
Elaine Heumann Gurian

Elaine Heumann Gurian

Routledge
Taylor & Francis Group

LONDON AND NEW YORK

First published 2006
by Routledge
2 Park Square, Milton Park, Abingdon, Oxon OX14 4RN

Simultaneously published in the USA and Canada
by Routledge
270 Madison Ave, New York, NY 10016

Routledge is an imprint of the Taylor & Francis Group

Typeset in Garamond by
Newgen Imaging Systems (P) Ltd, Chennai, India
Printed and bound in Great Britain by
The Cromwell Press, Trowbridge, Wiltshire

British Library Cataloguing in Publication Data
A catalogue record for this book is available
from the British Library

Library of Congress Cataloging in Publication Data
Gurian, Elaine Heumann, 1937–
Civilizing the museum: the collected writings of Elaine Heumann Gurian /
Elaine Heumann Gurian.
p. cm.
Includes bibliographical references and index.
1. Museums – Philosophy. 2. Museums – Social aspects. 3. Museum exhibits.
4. Architectural design. 5. Cultural property – Protection.
6. Communication and culture. I. Title.
AM7.G87 2005
069–dc22   2005018536

ISBN10: 0–415–35766–7 (hbk)
ISBN10: 0–415–35762–4 (pbk)

ISBN13: 9–78–0–415–35766–1 (hbk)
ISBN13: 9–78–0–415–35762–3 (pbk)

FOR DEAN
MY PARTNER IN ALL THINGS

CONTENTS

CONTENTS

FOREWORD

I met Elaine for the first time in 1989 on a bus trip from Amsterdam to the Hague. At that time I was Director of the Children's Museum of the Tropenmuseum in Amsterdam. We were developing new ways of working with children in our museum. It was a great experiment and Elaine immediately recognized the value of the endeavor. She pointed out strengths and weaknesses and managed in that bus ride of just over an hour to provide me with enough stimulating and provocative ideas to keep me busy reflecting for years and of course put them into practice, too. Although she did not yet use the word "inclusive" at the time, the notion was certainly at the center of her arguments and has been guiding my thoughts on museums ever since.

The publication of her papers is timely because we are much in need of visionary and provocative thought within the mountain of books available on museums and management.

What we need are people who provide us with new visions and who fling forgotten truths in our faces. This book is rich in practical experience. There are few writers in the world of museums who combine such a broad spectrum with knowledge of the craft from the inside. And what a wealth of inventive museums she has left behind her!

I find it impossible to summarize Elaine's ideas. But the concept that museums and the people working there need to change from object-focused instructors to client-centered "includers" certainly comes close to one of them. I find this a crucial ingredient of our thinking about where museums need to go. And looking around me I dare say that we are only just beginning to put such a vision into practice. Elaine has written her papers over the years in an optimistic spirit, which is good because museums are sometimes slow movers.

I was lucky enough to be able to obtain a broad overview of how museums work individually and collectively during my years as Director General of the Dutch Museums Association and Secretary General of the International Council of Museums in Paris. And I noticed that while museums worldwide produce excellent results, there are only a few who take the idea of inclusiveness really seriously.

I have seen hundreds of museums worldwide and unfortunately too many uninviting ones. And I was especially disappointed to see uncomfortably few experiments in those parts of the world which have only recently come to develop museums and museum programs. Quite often classical European (or North American) concepts were (and are) simply copied. The refreshing debate on "What Museums for Africa," in the early nineties, has unfortunately produced very few practical results. And East- and South-East Asia are covered with clones of US museums developed and produced by expensive consultancy firms.

Why, for instance, have museums in many parts of the world not explored further the opportunities offered by intangible heritage? While the world is only at the beginning of massive global migration we need to acknowledge that history cannot be monopolized solely by places and objects, but that many people on the move take their history with them, and almost always in intangible form. Besides, there are many people in the world for whom, even if they don't move, intangible history is much more important than tangible objects.

Why are there so few initiatives around working more closely with the community? In 2002, ICOM-CC, the Conservation Committee of ICOM, held an excellent meeting in Rio de Janeiro, where colleagues were invited to show how working more closely with the community could be achieved. I saw the wonderful example of a village in Colombia actively taking part in the restoration of a revered statue of Christ from its church (with as an additional consequence that the people were so proud of this statue that they decided to keep it under guard continuously, against robbers and illegal traffickers). I saw an example in Buenos Aires of a whole neighborhood mobilized against the destruction of the Café dos Angelitos where the tango is said to have been born and where they managed to start a cultural center for the tango with an archive, a library, a museum, and a meeting place.

Creating an exciting and inviting museum, open to all, is not so much an issue of money as of enthusiastic and farsighted believers; believers in the ideas Elaine is providing us with in this book.

Elaine's early thinking is basically rooted in the 1960s and 1970s and the "hippie" climate of that time. And that is not a bad thing at all. There was much emphasis on social action, creativity and spirituality. Experiment was an almost sacred concept.

We have lost much of the 1960s and 1970s in our thinking. Museums have become more businesslike. They have restructured and become more professional in all respects. That has been a necessary and very positive development. Without it museums would not be as successful as they are right now.

But during that massive overhaul of the organizational structure of the institution as such, many of the essentials of that earlier time were neglected. That was and is unfortunate, because although museums have seen their visitor numbers multiply, they are still not institutions where all feel equally welcome. This book is centrally concerned with that issue: how to make museums socially responsible institutions.

A major setback occurred with the declaration in 2003 by a few large and famous museums that they were "universal museums," with a universal responsibility for the collections they owned, and that they therefore did not want to discuss issues of restitution anymore. For they were open to everybody and everybody could come and see their collections. But I wonder how inviting such a message is when people all over the world try to figure out the costs of paying for a trip to a museum in Berlin or New York.

Nevertheless, I am not at all pessimistic about future developments. In the 1970s museums were often still elite institutions where we had to fight for a proper place for education and where social action was unheard of. Museum directors at that time told me that these concerns were nonsense and not on the agenda. A decade later, some of them said in public that playing an active role in civil society was important, however late at night after a few drinks they admitted in confidence that they found much of this unrealistic and simply the flavor of the month. Currently it is hard to find a director who does not sincerely believe in some form of inclusiveness, but finds it unfortunately difficult if not impossible to put it into practice in her or his museum. The mental conviction is already there, but the physical drive to take action is still lacking. And once again, money is not the issue.

We need the people who dare to go against the tide. Like the museum director in Sweden who decided to remove an image from an exhibition because the Islamic community in the city wasn't feeling comfortable about it. In a climate of "an eye for an eye and a tooth for a tooth," nobody wanted to give in to "the demands of fundamentalists." She however resisted the call not to give in when she discovered that this was not a fundamentalist issue at all, but a deeply rooted feeling of unease from a community that felt far from welcome.

Creating a truly inclusive museum is not easy. Moreover, the arguments around it are often wrong. They remind me of the Tour de France, the great cycle race in France which I followed closely on the radio when I was young. The cyclists often complained about some notoriously difficult mountain: "Sometimes it is friendly and helpful, sometimes it is angry with you and fights against you." But we all know of course that it is not the mountain that fights, but the racer.

Manus Brinkman, 2005
1980–1990 Royal Tropical Institute, Amsterdam
1985–1990 Director, Children's Museum
1990–1998 Executive Director, Netherlands Museums Association
1998–2005 Secretary General, International Council of Museums, Paris

ACKNOWLEDGMENTS

This volume chronicles the evolution of my thinking during 35 years in the museum profession. I entered this wonderful line of work by accident in 1969 and progressed in it with the help of many. Over the years, I was often asked to speak in public. In the beginning, I spoke extemporaneously with few notes. I had carefully masked the fact that I was moderately dyslexic, did not think in a linear fashion and could neither spell nor write simple sentences grammatically. I had several assistants throughout my working career whose job it was to write my letters and who were always chosen, in part, for their ability to write and edit well. My first thanks goes to these intelligent, energetic women (Suzanne LeBlanc, Juanita Hall, Lisa Watt, Marylou Abrigo Riccio, Lisa Moskowitz Senich, and Mary Kuthy) many of whom subsequently rose to positions of leadership in the museum field and elsewhere. My current assistant, Margie Trone, deserves special thanks for collating cheerfully, cheerleading endlessly, and being undaunted by everything. I am blessed to have her on my team.

In 1981, I was invited to be the keynote speaker at the museum educator conference in Melbourne, Australia, which I accepted with pleasure, and thank Tony Preston, now the director of the Christchurch Art Gallery in Christchurch, New Zealand for choosing me, and creating what was, for me, a life-changing event.

I was alarmed when I received word that the conference organizers wanted to see a draft of my paper prior to my arrival. It was a clue that a written document was expected. The result, "Answers to the Questions I Am Asked Most Often," is the first formal paper that I had to write in my working career. When I delivered it at that conference, I noticed all other speakers were also reading from written text. It became immediately clear to me that the entire Anglophone museum world, outside the United States, writes and delivers papers at museum conferences. I began to understand that only my compatriot Americans believe that their public thoughts were acceptably delivered "off the cuff." Since that first paper in 1991, I determined that all subsequent speeches would be written, and they have been.

The newly popular personal computer allowed learning-disabled people to overcome indecipherable handwriting and misspellings. The "cut and paste" function allowed alternate ways of thinking to be subsequently realigned into a coherent paper. Knowing how to type, I set about learning to write. I have relied on friends and colleagues to suffer through the process of editing all subsequent papers. This is a volume which, perhaps unfairly, bears my name as author, because without the editors there would be no papers to anthologize. It is with the deepest gratitude that I thank them. First Sylvia Sawin, then Anne Butterfield, taught me to write over a 10-year period. For the last 17 years, my husband, Dean Anderson, scrutinizing each word with moderate disbelief and a quizzical expression, corrects every paper before I enter the public arena.

Much of my work has been published. The editors of the publications have been immensely generous to my words and they deserve my profound thanks. John Strand and Jane Lusaka of the American Association of Museums; Susan K. Nichols, Joanne S. Hirsch, and Lois H. Silverman, Former Editors of Museum Education Roundtable and their subsequent anthologies; Anne Focke, Editor of Grantmakers in the Arts; Stephen R. Graubard of *Daedalus*; and Sam Taylor and Zahava Doering of *Curator*. Ellen Hirzy gave this a final and thoughtful edit before I sent it to my Routledge editors, Catherine Bousfield and Matthew Gibbons who shepherded this manuscript through the maze of publication process. To them I am especially grateful. There are others in far away places that I wish to remember but cannot. I hope they feel properly thanked even if unnamed.

Andrew Wheatcroft of Routledge came to me many years ago to suggest that I publish a volume of my work. I demurred, but did not forget. It is to him that I owe the idea of this book. It is Eilean Hooper-Greenhill, a friend over many decades, to whom I owe thanks for making it a reality. Eilean tempers a razor-sharp intellect with a friendly generosity.

I am a woman of a time and age that needed men in higher places to voluntarily reach down and give me advice and an opportunity to succeed. I am grateful beyond measure to them – Ervin Holz, Nachum Glatzer, Joel Bloom, Kenn Starr, George Tressel, Joe Noble, Michael Botwinick, and Tom Leavitt. I have been graced with bosses that I could learn from, whose humanity and commitment to friendship exceeded even their enormous talent as visionary leaders. They are Andrew Hyde II, Michael Spock, Tom Freudenheim, Jeshajahu Weinberg, W. Richard West, Jr, and Robert Gavin.

There are women, more experienced and senior than I am – Amy Barry, Caroline Farber, Bela Holz, Anna Glatzer, Mary Bain, Olga Conway, and Elizabeth Moynihan – who served as models of excellence. Moreover, there are several younger women (and men) who have asked me to be a mentor to them. They know who they are as they remain unnamed. As they ascend as stars, they allow me to understand that the future in the museum field is extremely bright.

It is one's intellectual colleagues and friends, who think critically about ideas with you, who keep you honest, motivated, and moving forward. Those already referenced always added their intellectual input, but in addition, I counted on the following to set me straight. Chris Anderson, Nina Archibal, Leslie Bedford, Dawn Casey, Frank Ervin, Joan Farber, Stephen Feber, Diane Frankel, Ken Gorbey, Signe Hanson, Franklyn Holz, Aylette Jenness, Janet Kamien, Rex Moser, Tam Muro, Bonnie Pitman, Maureen Robinson, Jette Sandahl, Cheryll Southeran, Jim Volkert, Judith Wechsler, and Cliff Whiting.

The model for my intellectual professional life has always been Steve Weil. A meal with him has never failed to make me think harder and along new lines. Stephen's books are the models for mine. Their existence gave me courage that this one might also see the light of day.

I wish to thank my children – Aaron, Josef, Eve, Erik, and Matthew, and their spouses, Karen, Aaron, and Merideth, who always supported having a working parent they were proud of instead of a "cookie-mom" who was always at home. They have shared my daily adventures, as not only family and supporters, but also as assistants and trusted advisors. Matthew, in particular, took on some of the editing role for this book and has proven that an outsider looking in is incredibly useful.

My grandchildren (in order of their arrival) – Emily, Lowen, Kate, Helena, Sam, Gus, and Margo – have allowed me to see again how diverse, gifted, and knowledgeable even the very young are, and how kind and loving they can be.

Having thanked my life-partner, Dean Anderson, for editing everything, I wish to also say that in him, I have found someone who believes endlessly in my capacity and who has given me an inner life of peace – a rare gift indeed.

I wish to add the obligatory but truthful statement, that all errors are mine alone, despite the generosity of all those named here.

ABBREVIATIONS

AAM	American Association of Museums
AAM/EdCom	American Association of Museums Committee on Education
AAMD	Association of Art Museum Directors
AASLH	American Association for State and Local History
ACM	Association of Children's Museums
ASTC	Association of Science-Technology Centers
CMA	Canadian Museums Association
ICOM	International Council of Museums
ICOM/CECA	International Committee for Education and Cultural Action
MA	Museums Association
MA	Museums Australia
MFA	Museum of Fine Arts
MOMA	Museum of Modern Art
NMA	National Museum of Australia
NMAI	National Museum of the American Indian
PIMA	Pacific Island Museum Association
Te Papa	The National Museum of New Zealand Te Papa Tangarawa
USHMM	United States Holocaust Memorial Museum
V&A	Victoria and Albert Museum
WVMA	West Vancouver Museum and Archives

INTRODUCTION

Reflections on 35 years in the museum field[1]

> I believe that if we really want human brotherhood to spread and
> increase until it makes life safe and sane, we must also be certain that
> there is no one true faith or path by which it may spread.
> (Adelai E. Stevenson Jr, US diplomat and Democratic
> politician (1900–1965))

Rereading my work for this book has allowed me to see how I have changed through
experience while remaining a person consistently affected by my background. I wrote
these essays with no sense that they might accumulate into a coherent whole. Each
was intended for a specific occasion, with the topic often coming from those who had
invited me to speak or publish.

Framing each piece was an optimistic sense of an unending personal future. I had
no vision of myself ever growing old. I certainly had very little sense that I was gifted
with any particular foresight. My writing came in episodic pauses in the otherwise
busy life of a working administrator. In retrospect, this interplay between being
a museum practitioner and being a writer–reflector gives my work whatever grounding
it has.

I have divided this collection into five sections organized around these themes:
museum definitions, civic responsibility and social service, architectural spaces,
exhibitions, and spirituality and rationality. I updated many of the original pieces
with more current data and references. In a few cases, I rewrote significant portions
or included an afterword to reflect my current thinking. I sometimes begin a piece
with a quotation that I hope is provocative, illuminating, or even oppositional to the
work that follows. In each essay, I seek to parse various ingredients that, if combined,
would make museums more inclusive. These elements include exhibition technique,
space configurations, the personality of the director, the role of social service, power
sharing, types of museums, and the need for emotion, humor, and spirituality as part
of the mix.

Writing this introduction, I have looked for overarching themes and tried to tease
out the unexpressed but consistent assumptions underlying these sporadic writing
endeavors. I discovered that the essays sometimes build on each other and sometimes

1

veer off on a new tangent, but they share a core idea: that museums should welcome all because they house the collective memory of all. The staff of the National Museum of New Zealand Te Papa Tangarawa got it right when they rebranded their museum as simply "Te Papa," which in Maori means "Our Place."[2]

My writings are based on some basic conceptions, which are informed by the learning gleaned from my museum positions and invigorated by my continued exposure to the truly wonderful museums I consult with today. These conceptions include the following:

- All "truth" (even seemingly immutable fact) is synthesized in the eye of the beholder and is therefore subject to changing interpretation.
- All humans have history and should have access to it. Museums are part of a set of institutions that house such histories, or "institutions of memory."
- Humans can, and do, hold more than one worldview simultaneously and have the ability to differentiate among them. They choose, often unconsciously, which worldview they will use for each occasion. They do not seem confused by the inconsistencies or contradictions that are involved.
- Ambivalence – believing in two equal and opposite positions – is not only possible; it is our predominant mental state. The notion of winning and losing, while inculcated into all of us in the Western world, is not the way we live our lives. I am persuaded of the prevalent importance of "and."
- No society can remain civil without providing places where strangers can safely associate together. I have called such civic places – which include museums – "congregant spaces."
- The generic museum does not have boundaries it can call its own. On every border, there are abutting, even overlapping, institutions. I find this a good thing. Such blurring of the boundaries, taken to its logical conclusion, might ultimately lead to the collapse of museums as unique structures. I do not advocate that, but neither do I fear it.

The reader will find that:

- I believe in the importance of pushing for change and that everyone, no matter where they fit within the organizational hierarchy, has power to alter their collective situation.
- I favor action over inaction by using methods congruent with ideals.
- I remain committed to trial and error and think approximations, as the best we can hope for, should be celebrated.
- I think hand-crafted logical next steps beat ideological dogma.
- I remain persuaded of the importance of multiple answers over the victory of the single response.

In some sense, all the essays in this volume seek answers to a single question: "Why do railway stations have a broader spectrum of users than museums; and could

2

museums, if they did everything right, welcome the same demographic mix through their doors?" If I believed that museums were now universally hospitable, I would have happily concluded that the writings in this volume were no longer pertinent, and this book would not have been published.

I have found, however, that most museums are *not* as inclusive as they could be, and almost none of them have comprehensively readjusted their systems in order to become so. While diversity is often advocated, it is only sporadically evident. There are some encouraging exceptions, though not as many as I would like. It has been my honor to work with some extraordinary institutions that have implemented a mission of comprehensive service.

In places I have never visited, there is evidence on the Internet that essays from this book are used in training young people and that museum personnel use some of them for guidance and company. I hope that all the writings collected here are helpful, no matter when they were written or for whom. I especially hope that they are useful to museum personnel (both old friends and younger colleagues) who chafe under an uncomfortable philosophy awaiting a more hopeful time, and to those who have emergent opportunities for positive change.

My writings arise from a personal viewpoint that could be called progressive and liberal – a label often disparaged in the United States by those of other persuasions. More specifically, these papers express a liberal point of view at a time (2005) when much of the world is turning elsewhere. We seem no longer to be in a cycle where gains hold and change builds on previous attainment. Rather, the world seems reactionary and interested in reinstating old positions.

My concern in this more polarized world is that museums are more subject to political pressure than I used to think. The governmental mood in many places seems to veer in cycles from left to right and back again. Museums, in response, seem to move from being object-focused instructors (right) to client-centered includers (left) in a congruently rotating pattern. This is, of course, not always true. Other factors – like the politics of the founders and the strength of current museum leadership – play a part. Yet many museums, in the face of political opposition, real or imagined, become tentative and cautious.

The institutions I have most often been associated with were led by directors whose personal politics was more left-wing, and even radical, than the majority culture of the time. Most of these institutions flourished when the government was also more left-leaning. When more right-wing governments came to power, cultural institutions that were more interested in established canons and saw their role as the preservers and inculcators of traditional values were rewarded with attention and increased funds. Interestingly, when more liberal governments came to power, these same established institutions tried to learn the processes of inclusion and became better for the attempt. Sadly, few of these changes remain after more conservative governments return.

I now speculate that three factors prevent museums from becoming universally accessible. One is the force that many in authority (political and economic majority stakeholders) use to retain their influence. They sometimes see museums (but not libraries)

3

as a social escalator for their own enhanced power. This unfortunately is true as well for some staff members, who assert "museum tradition" to solidify the status they acquired from their position. They mimic the trappings of the power structure that surrounds them regardless of their personal origins. Museum collections often began as physical expressions of personal authority of their former owners, and sometimes museum staff aspire to the same aura when they take on responsibility for these possessions. I fear it was ever thus and ever will be.

The interaction between the individual cultural institution and its external political climate is a second element that mitigates against inclusive change. Staff are generally unobservant of the direct or implied demands that government at any level places on their museum leadership. They are further surprised by the impact that the political climate has on museum policy. Government officials (to the extent that they think about museums at all) are interested in translating their political philosophy into tangible exhibition form. Further, they are often actively averse to public controversy they have not planned themselves. To avoid politicians' ire, many museums reflexively choose to stay out of policy debates by self-censorship and moderation.

I have often underestimated the personal courage museum directors (and their senior associates) need to create institutional change. They often must deplete whatever charisma and willfulness they can muster to produce any gains at all. Directors have to be willing to risk dismissal to withstand pressure to violate their own principles, while finding pathways to justifiable compromise. Such leadership supports and encourages unexpected solutions to seemingly intractable problems. These courageous directors are nuanced negotiators and willing buffers between their staffs and the dissenting powerful. Without them, change by the rank and file is exceedingly difficult. By contrast, directors fearful for their jobs are understandably timid in the face of political pressure.

I am not an academician, as some university-based critics have noted. I do not have a doctorate, nor was I formally trained in museum work. I was not trained to manage large budgets or construction – all things I have been responsible for. I learned from the work itself, apprenticing to experienced others and reading the writings of those within and outside the museum field who have illuminated my path.

Members of this field have long debated the qualifications required for assuming certain jobs. Some posit that to gain legitimacy, staff must be academically trained with advanced degrees either in a content area or in museum studies of some variety. There are currently many (perhaps too many) university venues in museum studies, museology, and museum management – all working from the assumption that training has value. I concur and am an occasional lecturer in many of these programs. I find that passing on thoughtful experience to a class can be helpful in moving both the individuals and the overall profession forward. I disagree only with making museum-based advanced degrees a prerequisite for leadership positions.

A review of some of the foremost museum innovators of the last half century puts the lie to that need. Their backgrounds and life experiences prepared them exactly, albeit inadvertently, for their positions as heads of paradigm-changing institutions. They caused the changes they did because they arrived on the scene with the seemingly unrelated but extraordinarily useful experiences, education, and training they had accumulated.

Michael Spock, the long-time director of the Boston Children's Museum and son of a famous doctor, was a reluctant dyslexic who finally graduated college and became an exhibition creator and fabricator before becoming a director. His focus on learning for those who were educationally challenged colored all his work.

Frank Oppenheimer, the brother of J. Robert Oppenheimer, was a noted physicist in the Manhattan Project and a political radical who was forced out of his government position under McCarthyism to teach high school, and then brought both his scientific expertise and the instructional hands-on curriculum he had created to the founding of the Exploratorium.

Jeshajahu Weinberg, the founding director of the United States Holocaust Memorial Museum (USHMM), never completed high school, spoke five languages fluently, was a founding pioneer of a kibbutz in Israel at the age of 17, a fighter in the Jewish Brigade during the Second World War, an early exponent of technology within the Israeli government, and the long-time head of a theater repertory company. He (and others) used all those experiences in conceptualizing the Museum of the Diaspora in Tel Aviv, a revolutionary museum that told a story without using any authentic objects. All this background proved relevant, perhaps instrumental, to his work at the USHMM.

Dawn Casey, an Aboriginal woman who was prevented by policy from acquiring the degree she wanted and from attending the four-year university of her choice, worked her way up through the Australian civil service, starting as a bookkeeper and becoming assistant to the prime minister on matters of cultural affairs. She took a step down to become the chief executive of the National Museum of Australia (NMA) and withstood for a time, as only an experienced government official could, the unrelenting opposition in creating a fascinating museum.

W. Richard West Jr, the son of an important American Indian artist, was a noted Washington lawyer specializing in Indian affairs when he decided to direct the founding of the National Museum of the American Indian, Smithsonian Institution (NMAI). His sophistication in the politics of Washington, combined with his deep dedication to his forebears, was essential to the successful realization of the museum.

I knew all these directors and had the pleasure of working with most. They did not feel constrained by the traditions of the museum field, though they were eager learners who brought views from other fields to enrich ours.

On a more modest scale, my story is the same. I came to the museum world by accident and without planning. My former work was as an artist, an art teacher in a Jewish parochial school, and the parent of three children, one of them severely handicapped. My parents were German-Jewish immigrants who came to the United States just before the era of the Holocaust. From them I learned about apprehension in the presence of members of the majority culture and their institutions. My earliest childhood experiences were mainly in a voluntarily ghettoized section of Queens in New York City. In the way others treated us when we ventured outside our home territory, I learned that external trappings (skin color, clothing, facial characteristics, accents, and behavior) mark one as an outsider in the mainstream world. I also learned that assimilation was possible only by abandoning the culture of my family and unlearning the regional accent, word choice, and hand motions that marked my origins. In retrospect, I have unconsciously dedicated my career to making museums safe and inviting enough so that my reluctant mother, now dead, might have chosen to enter.

The experiences of my childhood, where I felt personally unwelcome in institutions that were supposedly for all, has influenced my entire professional life. But these institutions held treasures I so much desired to see that I felt the risk was worth taking. It is interesting to me that libraries, since the time when they imposed reverential silence, have worked hard at becoming friendlier, more welcoming, and useful. Museums have been more hesitant to follow suit and remain unevenly successful in broadening their appeal.

When I began working in museums during the 1960s and 1970s in Boston – first at Summerthing (1969),[3] then at the Institute of Contemporary Art (1969–1971), and for 16 years at the Boston Children's Museum (1971–1987) – I worked on access for all. I considered especially the novice learner, the shy, the anxious, and those who believed that when entering a museum they had come to the wrong place, a place that did not value them, make allowances for what they did not know, or offer them images to which they could intuitively relate. I wrote about welcome and love, experimented with hands-on and hands-off exhibition techniques, and talked about enfranchising visitors. I wished to make sure these visitors felt not only at home but refreshed by the experience and eager to come back.

I still believe in the value of these things, but 35 years later, I understand that the three institutions of my early career were rare communes of Nirvana affected deeply by the "hippie" political climate of the age. Young people in Boston in the 1960s (and we were all young then!) believed in the effectiveness of social action, the value of love, and the courage of the naive. Luckily for us, the world mostly took no notice of our Children's Museum experimentation until we were more fully formed and self-assured. Then, to our collective surprise, the museum world descended on us to study and try out what we had intuitively and unself-consciously created.

In the late 1980s, I commenced on a professional trip through the US federal museum landscape of the Smithsonian,[4] where I met sophisticated and intelligent people who worked hard and wanted the best for their museums and the public. But their opinion of what constituted "good" was far different from that of the world I had come from. I learned a lot about strategy, but action was measured in geologic time. The Smithsonian has daring folk of noble intention who often are thwarted by less noble folk well entrenched to stifle actions that might prove (to them) destabilizing. I felt I had lost my way. The lessons learned, however, have been most useful in dealing with the politics of the frustrated and the unempowered.

When I joined the staff of the fledgling NMAI,[5] I came face to face with proud and tenacious Native people. I learned that most positions I held – overtly or unconsciously – found honorable counterparts in opposite positions held by my Indian colleagues. The negotiations between these worlds are not easy and require both good will and tenacity.

Thankfully, they didn't give up on me. And mercifully, one year later, I could intuit and represent their positions without compromising my own. My time on staff began the part of my museum journey that most changed my intellectual life.

I then went to work for one of the true geniuses of the museum world, Jeshajahu Weinberg, who made it possible for all of his staff to participate in the creation of a masterpiece, the United States Holocaust Memorial Museum.[6] This institution fundamentally changed the way museums could tell stories, present ideas, and interpret information in an exhibition format. Most important, the museum inspired and provoked reactions from its various publics – from school groups to foreign heads of state – that changed all my notions about visitor behavior. The transformation of individual museums into icons, as this one illustrates, can become influences on the world stage.

Throughout my career, I have felt that publicly expressing my perception of the situation using personal terms adds to others' understanding. The use of personal experiences as a medium has also been a valuable teaching tool. Accordingly, I do not apologize for the autobiographical nature of the writing in this volume and the intertwining of myself in the ideas presented. In fact, I assert to students that being self-conscious and unapologetic is one of the main requirements for successful cross-cultural negotiation. The others include affection for the human species, insatiable curiosity, intolerance for incivility, lack of preformed outcomes when listening, and endless optimism for finding solutions that fit each unique situation.

I despair more often now, 35 years later, than I did when I began writing these essays. I find open-mindedness in meetings, in text, and in museum exhibitions in shorter supply than I used to. I am mindful that some museums have been and could again be misused to engender fear-based discrimination and new justifications for hate. Yet in my enthusiasm for action and our collective delight in the new, I do not advocate that we discard the traditional elements of museums – collections and their preservation; contemplation; and excellence – and the methods of presentation these values represent. We must treasure the old and honor the elder while steadily integrating the new to make museums more central and more relevant to a society in which we want to live. However, we cannot allow tradition to cover for intractability. We must acknowledge that we as professionals are the ones who have permitted exclusionary practices in our institutions, and we are the ones who can change them.

That said, I continue to believe that museums are important institutions, perhaps more so than we insiders understand. I continue to find brave people, many of them young, ready to take on new and difficult problems. I sense that there are people waiting in the wings who believe in balance and complexity. I acknowledge them and hope that this book keeps them company along their journey.

Notes

1 This introduction incorporates parts of two autobiographical pieces published earlier (Gurian 1998, 1999a).
2 The National Museum of New Zealand Te Papa Tangarawa is the official name of the museum, given to it by statute. Before the museum opened in 1998, the senior staff, working with Saachi and Saachi NZ, decided on the new logo (a thumbprint taken from the

Treaty of Waitangi), brand name "Te Papa," and tagline "our place." The official name has not changed, but the museum is known as Te Papa by all.

3 Summerthing was a summer program of mobile units originated by the newly elected Mayor of Boston, Kevin White, to make the summer of 1969 a more tranquil one than the riot-torn summer after the death of Martin Luther King in 1968.

4 From 1987 to 1990, I served as deputy assistant secretary for museums at the Smithsonian Institution. Our office, under Assistant Secretary Tom Freudenheim, had oversight of 14 museums and an annual budget of about $150 million.

5 While deputy director for public program planning in 1990 and 1991, I was chief negotiator for the Custom House in New York on behalf of the Smithsonian and moderated 12 consultations with American Indian people around their desires for a museum on the National Mall.

6 I became deputy director of the United States Holocaust Memorial Museum in early 1991 during the run-up to opening and remained in that post until 1993 when the museum was fully operating and I had completed my task.

Bibliography

Gurian, E.H. (1998) "Continuous, Unexpected Joy and Fascinating, If Demanding Work," in *Museum News*, 77:4, 36–37.

Gurian, E.H. (1999a) "Thinking About My Museum Journey," in Pitman, B. (ed.) *Presence of Mind: Museums and the Spirit of Learning*, Washington, DC: American Association of Museums.

Part I

THE IMPORTANCE OF "AND"
About opportunities, possibilities, taxonomy, and definitions

Museums are more varied than casual observers assume – not only in size and subject matter but, more interestingly, in intention and motivation. Museum directors may choose from many programmatic and organizational options while still pursuing missions that remain legitimately within the museum community. The choice of mission and the means of accomplishing it follow from the museum leadership's underlying philosophy about visitors, objects, citizenship, and civic responsibility. The politics and worldview of the board and staff governance team will determine museum policies and procedures, and thus the nature of the museum experience. The essays in this section review some of the options that museum leaders can consider when choosing the kind of museum they wish to run.

1

THE CONCEPT OF FAIRNESS

A debate at the American Association
of Museums, 1990

The following essay is based on notes I used for a debate presented at the American Association of Museums (AAM) Annual Meeting in Chicago on May 5, 1990. Brett Waller, then the director of the Indianapolis Museum of Art, and I had engaged in spirited debate in many informal settings in the past, and we were urged to make it a public discourse, which we did on this occasion. We sparred over the question of whether an immutable canon exists, forming an objective standard for aesthetic judgments, or instead if all things are relative and change based on the culture and objects in question. Brett always took the objectivist position, and I always took the relativist position.

The AAM session was organized using formal academic debate rules. Joallyn Archambault, director of the American Indian Program of the National Museum of Natural History, Smithsonian Institution, and an enrolled member of the Standing Rock Sioux Tribe of North and South Dakota, agreed to be my second in speaking for the issue. Speaking against was Brett Waller, seconded by Katharine Lee Reid, then the director of the Virginia Museum of Fine Arts.

The other team (and my second) did a creditable job, and in all fairness their remarks should be here too, but alas they are absent. A recent volume of essays by art museum directors is a good reflection of the objectivist point of view (Cuno 2004).

***

Let me begin by asserting that I believe there is no absolute *truth*. There is only opinion, deeply held and often subconsciously influenced by many things, including facts, events, and tangible objects. Among these opinions are scientists' closer and closer approximate descriptions of nature. The notion that the world's natural forces are governed by discoverable and, therefore, ultimately predictable patterns is under question. "The rest is commentary," my forefathers would say.

Commentary is shaped by the times, politics, life experiences, ethnicity, and social class of the commentator. For each belief sincerely presented there is often a countervailing belief, and many intermediate positions in between, no less sincerely held.

Commentary (also known as interpretation) exists in all forms of discourse and disciplines. I know that my distinguished opposition will speak of immutable canons, allowing one to distinguish "good" from "bad," and facts, separating "actuality" from "invention." But I do not believe in such absolutes.

11

Our confidence in the infallibility of our leaders has waned and been replaced by an acknowledgment of their human failings. We no longer believe automatically in the kind teacher, the all-knowing president, the protective policeman, the infallible physician. Fairness means (among other things) teaching the audience to adopt a skeptical approach to "knowledge" and to learn to ask for a second opinion. We owe no less to our visitors.

The glories of the machine age and our belief in better lives through technology were founding principles of many science museums, but are now muted by our understanding of the world's finite resources and the global caring that must prevail if we are to survive. Fairness suggests we include within our technological exhibitions a balancing concern for the environment and its long-term implications for our economy.

The appearance of many vocal ethnic groups gaining power in many places around the globe reminds us that presentations of history, art, and anthropology reflect the presenter as much as the presented. Having been voiceless in the past in the preparation of our exhibitions, minority people find themselves absent, or unrecognizable, in our museums. Their growing unhappiness with this situation is causing us to rethink our collections and presentation strategies. We are more often including the views of the interpreted. That seems only fair to me.

Anthropologists no longer believe in an unchanging culture, if they ever did; rather, they believe that all cultures evolve over time. Thus, more and more of our cultural exhibitions are including contemporary material of evolving cultures rather than period pieces statically presented in a frozen moment in time. And that seems fair to me.

Today there is a growing appreciation within academia that the presenter, the interrogator, the commentator, and the collector of data and objects all affect the information they are working with through the mediating influence of their own experiences and beliefs. Since we in the museum field play many of these roles, what responsibility do we have to understand and then reveal our own personal biases?

Let me state two of my own personal aspirations for fairness within the museum field:

- All exhibitions and public programs should encourage viewers to evaluate, perhaps even with skepticism, the content presented in order to make use of it within their own personal frameworks.
- All producers should overtly reveal their personal identities, backgrounds, and points of view and place them publicly for all to see.

Let me go further. Exhibition creators have often written their label copy with an amalgam of centrist generalizations presented with a dispassionate authoritative voice. They prefer that conflicting ideas and contrary evidence remain the responsibility of others, such as college courses, scholarly journals, evening programs attended by few, and, occasionally, the exhibition catalogue. I believe that is unfair to the visitor.

Fairness demands that we present our audiences with the broadest range of conflicting facts and opinions within the exhibition – or alternatively, having taken a single viewpoint, reveal ourselves (the authors) by name, bias, class, education, and opinion.

To do otherwise suggests that audiences are children unable to think for themselves. To continue in our old practices is to believe in the right of a nonelected power elite to transmit its values untested and unexamined. Our audiences are not our children; our audiences are our friends and potential colleagues. We owe them respect. Anything else is unfair.

But, you ask, in the world of the relative, how will we know what is good? We won't. We never did. In my former life, I owned a picture that was deaccessioned by the Museum of Fine Arts, Boston, around 1930. They refocused their collection then and continue to do so now because their notions of good and value have constantly changed. Reassessment is not new within the field of aesthetics; art historians have always done so. What is new is the claim that more than one voice, one class, one tradition might deserve to be part of the decision-making process; that in fact many voices might need to be heard, and often simultaneously; that we significantly broaden our profession's understanding of authority and of worth. To do this we must also broaden our staffs and expand our collections to include multiple viewpoints from within our own organizations.

Finally, and not surprisingly, this debate is, in the end, a political conversation about power and control. It is about the transmission of values and an argument for sharing authority.

We ought to believe in good common sense. At the edges of this argument we must remain conciliatory and not fundamentalist. I am not advocating the replacement of one dogma with another. I am advocating the replacement of hegemony with multiple viewpoints. For me, the term "fairness" brings with it a requirement for balance, and for equity.

Bibliography

Cuno, J. (ed.) (2004) *Whose Muse? Art Museums and the Public Trust*, Princeton, NJ, Cambridge, MA: Princeton University Press and Harvard University Art Museums.

2

THE IMPORTANCE OF "AND"

A comment on *Excellence and Equity*,[1] 1992

In tennis, at the end of the day you're a winner or a loser. You know
exactly where you stand... I don't need that anymore. I don't need my
happiness, my well-being, to be based on winning and losing.

(Chris Evert (1992) in *The Columbia
World of Quotations* (1996))

We Americans have consistently believed in the importance of winning. "There is no
such thing as second place" is an adage we have all heard. The childhood game of
"King of the Mountain" has trained our youngsters to believe that at the top of the
pyramid there is only one "king."

This simple idea – that there are only single winners – affects our intellectual life
as well. The idea that two equally weighted ideas could both be "primary" has not
often been tolerated; one must be supreme. A group discussion in which more than
one competing idea is presented usually leads to a discussion of priorities.

"And" is a word we learned to read in the first grade and one we have used orally
much earlier. We all know the meaning of "and" – it is a word that links things
together. Yet in the arena of ideas, we consistently behave as if "and" means "or."

The American Association of Museums report *Excellence and Equity: Education and
the Public Dimension of Museums* uses "and" in the title (AAM 1991). This report made
a concerted attempt to accept the two major ideas proposed by factions within the
field – equity and excellence – as equal and without priority. The equity faction of the
task force that prepared the report advocated for attention to previously underserved
visitor groups and cultural sensitivity when consulting with them. The excellence
group felt that scholarship was primary and should not be "dumbed down" in order
to accommodate new audiences. After much discussion in which each proponent
attempted to "win" the group over, the task force decided to go forward with both
rather than one or the other. These ideas, which were seen as conflicting, were instead
linked with "and."

However, for the museum field to go forward, we must do more than make
political peace by linking words. We must believe in what we have written, namely
that complex organizations must and should espouse the coexistence of more than

14

one primary mission. That restatement should include attention to public service even when the results are potentially conflictive with other mission priorities.

The intent of the task force was to promote real inclusion – the acceptance of multiple ideas and the sharing of power with those who hold them – within the institutions and the professions that we love. For example, we can have both ethnically focused museums and generic museums that are inclusive in their respective presentations. We can simultaneously be citizens of the country, even the world, and be functioning members of our specific community. There can be an intellectual canon of the Western tradition that is valuable for all of us to learn, and we can simultaneously learn about the glories of the rest of the world using the appropriate canons associated with each culture. Research and public service can both be primary if the museum administration wishes it. Can equity and excellence exist side by side without one diminishing the other? Of course!

One can postulate that the internal fight for idea primacy within the task force was not only intellectual but one of implicit resource allocation. In all candor, to have a museum hierarchy that includes more than one primary idea – more than one department at the top – assumes that the institution plans to fund the work associated with these fundamental ideas more or less equally.

The report raises the issue of money rather obliquely, but the task force intended that fundamental ideas should have dollars commensurate with their place in the mission hierarchy. Realistically, to fund ideas equally is either to garner lots of new money or to reallocate what funds there are among programs according to the new pecking order. That step will diminish the monetary hegemony of the former winners and engender anxiety and anger among the previously funded.

An implied requirement to shift resources is probably the most uncomfortable consequence of the report. The haves will argue that to give up anything is to diminish the quality and thereby the excellence of their work. And in fact, some diminution of quality or scope may occur temporarily in response to an altered resource landscape. But we cannot proclaim the report a success without acknowledging that implementation – even including difficult budgetary actions – should follow. In public service, both excellence and equity can occur in each of our museums if we so wish it, and public service itself can become one of the primary missions of each of our museums if that becomes our collective intention. The task force hopes it has persuaded the field and that there will no longer be only single winners.

Afterword

In 1989, Joel Bloom was president of the American Association of Museums as well as director of the Franklin Institute. He had always been a supporter of museum education. Furthermore, he was a supporter of women's equity in the workplace. The majority of museum educators at the time, like teachers in the public schools, were women. Given the prevailing organizational hierarchy, which has long favored research and curatorial functions over those of public service, it was rare that educators held positions of power within their own organization. Combining these two advocacy positions (education and women's rights), Joel established the Task Force on Museum Education and charged the group with producing a policy paper for consideration by the AAM council.

The individuals who were asked to participate were high-profile members of the museum education community, representatives of private foundations and government grant-making agencies, and sympathetic directors and deputies of museums. I was a member of the group.[2]

Excellence and Equity, the result of the group's work, became a museum touchstone worldwide. That it had such an impact was a surprise to many, myself included, who had served on the committee.

The report gave prominent voice to the premise that museums should, at a minimum, have a mission that balanced the focus between the audience and the objects. It stated that museums had not only an important public dimension but a public responsibility:

> Museums can no longer confine themselves simply to preservation, scholarship, and exhibitions independent of the social context in which they exist. They must recognize that what we are calling the public dimension of museums leads them to perform the public service of education – a term we use in its broadest sense to include exploration, study, observation, critical thinking, contemplation, and dialogue.
>
> (AAM 1991)

The report moved the discussion of equity from the voluntary and charitable position it had in many institutions to one of obligation: "We believe in the potential for museums to be enriched and enlivened by the nation's diversity. As public institutions in a democratic society, museum must achieve great inclusiveness" (AAM 1991).

The recommendations within the report, while widely accepted as good and fitting rhetoric, continue to be debated to this day and have not been universally implemented. I have learned over the years that acknowledgment is very far from action. Notwithstanding the unevenness of implementation, it is clear that an underlying change has taken place. Today the audience is always considered in some form in every museum, and the role of the educator within the museum has broadened.[3] But I would assert that museums have not gone as far as Steven Weil contends when he says that they have moved from "being about something to being for somebody" (Weil 1999). One might say almost cynically that that particular phrase has become a widely used mantra without as much empirical evidence as one might wish.

The influence of *Excellence and Equity* can hardly be underestimated even without evidence of universal action. For example, the proposals within *Excellence and Equity* became the underpinnings for a similar discussion in Great Britain, which resulted in the publication of *A Common Wealth* (Anderson 1997) just a few years later.

16

Together, these two reports are used extensively in many museum studies courses as foundation documents, affecting the viewpoints of a generation of museum workers.

As the AAM task force thought out the contents of *Excellence and Equity*, their discussion was filled with tension, which often played out as a semantic exercise. As a result, the publication reads like the work of Solomon, and occasionally the text makes no grammatical sense at all. The choice of title reflected the deep schism that occupied us. Was excellence analogous or antithetical to equity? And if they were companion ideas, which should come first in the title, given the inherent priorities of sequence? How could education be listed as "a primary responsibility of museums" (Pitman 1992), given the meaning of primary?[4]

The sentence "Museums must fulfill both elements of this dual responsibility – excellence and equity – in every aspect of their operations and programs"(AAM 1991) is an example of the lengths to which the chair (Bonnie Pitman) went to keep peace. It is patently unrealistic to believe that museums would immediately (or ever) do anything within "every aspect of their operations and programs," but it soothed our souls to say so.

I was (and remain) a very vocal partisan of the equity side of the argument. However, having looked at the dictionary meaning of "eq·ui·ty: The state, quality, or ideal of being just, impartial, and fair," that is not what I meant when I argued on its behalf. I was arguing for passion within our museum exhibitions, not "impartiality." And had I known that the definition included the term "fairness," I might have asked who was being fair to whom? Fairness implies "consistent with rules, logic, or ethics," which in turn suggests that there are rule makers – not the more even playing field that I was advocating.

I believed then in equity in a context closer to the meaning of the word "welcome." Welcome is, to my knowledge, not mentioned in *Excellence and Equity*. And I mean it in the sense of the common synonyms for welcome: "accept, accept gladly, accost, admit, bid, welcome, embrace, entertain, flag, greet, hail, hug, meet, offer hospitality, receive, salute, show in, take in, tumble, usher in." Welcome is a word of action.

The other word I am likely to use to emphasize equity is "inclusion." Like so many other words, inclusion has meanings that were certainly not intended. The dictionary definition is: "The process by which a foreign or heterogeneous structure is misplaced in another tissue."

The AAM task force's internal debates centered on the imprecision of word choices and the nuances each member placed on the words chosen. It seemed to me that the most important word in the title and perhaps the whole document was "and." It has occurred to me that perhaps my whole career was metaphorically about "and." I originally wanted the title of this whole volume to be "The Importance of 'And'." The editors concluded, quite rightly, that it might be too obscure.

Jerome B. Wiesner – one of the American negotiators of the nuclear non-proliferation treaty during the Kennedy administration – once explained to me the process they used to negotiate with the Russians: "We write out a draft document. We have it translated into Russian by a native Russian speaker. A native English speaker translates it back into English having not seen the original version. If the first English version matches the last one, then (and only then) do we show it to our negotiating counterparts. It is how we can predict where the misunderstandings will be within each of our cultural contexts" (private conversation).

In the end, language matters. The words we use in attempting to change museum directions matter. We need translators within each cultural context. We do not yet have precise words or even uniform understanding of the words we use. But we do have "and." And a good thing, too.

Notes

1 The original version of this essay was published in the *Journal of Museum Education* 16:3 (Fall 1991): 3–17 for Museum Education Roundtable, an association of museum educators in Washington, DC. This journal was distributed to the members of the Education Committee of the American Association of Museums (AAM/EdCom). The article was published among a series of articles written by committee members to commemorate the publication of the AAM report *Excellence and Equity: Educaiton and the Public Dimension of Museums*. A revised text was published as (Gurian 1992a).

2 I was deputy director of the United States Holocaust Memorial Museum in Washington, DC at the time.

3 To see a more optimistic view of the expansion of the role of the educator and to see the consequence of *Excellence and Equity* and other position papers on Francophone Canada, see (Blais 2000).

4 Primary: "First or highest in rank, quality, or importance; principal."

Bibliography

AAM (1991) *Excellence and Equity: Education and the Public Dimension of Museums: A Report*, Washington, DC: American Association of Museums, Task Force on Museum Education.

Anderson, D. (1997) *A Common Wealth: Museums and Learning in the United Kingdom*, London: Department of National Heritage.

Andrews, R., Biggs, M., and Seidel, M. (eds) (1996) *The Columbia World of Quotations*, New York: Columbia University Press.

Blais, J.-M. (2000) "Museum-Related Education in Quebec: An Historical Survey," in *Musées*, Montreal: Société des musées québécois. Volume 22, issue December.

Gurian, E.H. (1992a) "The Importance of 'And'," in Nichols, S. (ed.) *Patterns in Practice: Selections from the Journal of Museum Education*, Washington, DC: Museum Education Roundtable.

Pitman, B. (1992) "Excellence and Equity: Education and the Public Dimension of Museums, an Introduction," in Nichols, S. (ed.) *Patterns in Practice: Selections from the Journal of Museum Education*, Washington, DC: Museum Education Roundtable.

Weil, S. (1999) "From Being About Something to Being for Somebody: The Ongoing Transformation of the American Museum," in *Daedalus*, Cambridge, MA, 128:3, 229–258.

3

THE MOLTING OF CHILDREN'S MUSEUMS?

An observation,[1] 1998

> Children's museums are "continually exploring the boundaries of what is meant by a museum and by a museum experience. At this point, we are not sure that anybody really knows."
>
> (Michael Spock in *Museums, the Story of America's Treasure Houses* (1967))

Children's museums may be facing a dilemma. It can be argued that they have exhausted the potential bequeathed them by the experimentation of the 1970s without developing fresh approaches for the new millennium. In the face of rising attendance and the numbers of contemplated and completed new museums, this may come as a surprising statement.[2] In an attempt to find potential directions for a new time, this essay reviews the changes in direction that children's museums have taken, the audiences they now serve, and the needs of each audience segment.

The fundamental short-term question seems to be, is the still useful, beloved, and increasingly imitated foundational exhibition technique – hands-on interactivity – enough to sustain the children's museum?

In asking themselves this question, children's museums are seeking new pathways to enlarge their subject matter, expand their service to different age groups, and broaden their relationship to the educational and social service systems in their environments. In discussing an art exhibition at the Manhattan Children's Museum in 2002, a reporter asserted:

> It is symbolic of the new territories children's museums are taking. Not content to just let kids romp around amid science exhibits, they are now tackling subjects such as contemporary art and cultural identity while positioning themselves as community gathering places.
>
> (Burghart 2002)

What is interesting about this comment is that it is inaccurate in almost all its details. Children's museums have never been only places to romp in, or exclusively science exhibitions. They have, almost since their inception, included art of all types and cultural material as topics. However, the perception that they are all the same is embedded in this journalist's response and makes the case that the public may perceive them to be similar.

I would contend that the long-term sustainability of children's museums is not based on tweaks in strategy, subject matter, or audience mix, but on fulfilling the deeply held and often unexpressed aspirations of parents and teachers. The essay will attempt to show that, throughout their history, children's museums' approaches have consistently reflected contemporary assumptions of child rearing, educational philosophy, and learning theory; were seen as progressive; and were often understood in the intelligent popular press. Changes in children's museums' strategies, when they occurred, resulted from dissatisfactions with long-held assumptions about child rearing or educational philosophy that were thought to be no longer working. The history of children's museums is the history of making visible the contemporary yearnings of adults, on behalf of children, and offering a physical venue that expressed those aspirations.

It may be time again for children's museums to review trends in contemporary literature (and the concomitant academic research) on children's well-being, with a view toward creating a new museum paradigm.

A review of children's museum history

The first children's museums were founded between the turn of the twentieth century and the end of the First World War. The world's first children's museum, in Brooklyn, was established in 1899. Its objectives were:

> To form an attractive resort for children with influences tending to refine their tastes and elevate their interests; to create an attractive education center of daily assistance to pupils and teachers in connection with school work, and to offer new subjects of thought for pursuit in leisure hours.
>
> (Gallup 1907)

Based on philosophies attributed especially to John Dewey, but including Johann Pestalozzi, Johann Herbart, Joseph Rice, and Friedrich Froebel, these museums believed that children were not small adults but developmentally different, requiring educational instruction based on their specific needs (Dewey 1975, first published in 1938). To educate youngsters optimally, the theory went, one needed tangible material to experiment with, touch, observe, and examine. "There must be more actual material, more 'stuff'," Dewey said, "more appliances, and more opportunity for doing things" (Dewey 1977).

So hands-on philosophy was embedded in these institutions right from the start. By some accounts, Anna Billings Gallup, the first curator at the Brooklyn Children's Museum, unlocked cabinets so that children could touch specimens (Zervos 2002).

In the beginning, and quite within Dewey's teachings, the perfect subject matter for instructing children was natural history, and almost all children's museums or children's rooms in larger museums focused on natural specimens. Many also produced loan kits for schools and community institutions, and some even had loanable material for homes.

The First World War ended with the hope that the League of Nations would provide a forum for discussion that would end acrimony forever. The underlying assumption was that inexperience with other cultures allowed for fear, hatred, and violence and that to know each other better would aid in world peace. Children's museums (as well as schools) broadened their focus to include cultures from around the world. They began expanding their collections to include cultural material and used these items in exhibitions. This interest fit within the earlier traditions of general museums, which began as cabinets of curiosities, but the inclusion of cultural material in children's museums now had a social objective.

By the 1940s educators believed that Dewey had been too restrictive in his subject matter choice, so the arts and physical science were given increased expression in schools. Museums, too, began to offer creative arts programs for children concentrating on individualized expression. In Israel children's art classes started in Betzalel in the 1940s, later migrating to the Ruth Youth Wing in the Israel Museum in Jerusalem, in the hope of healing traumatized youth. During the same period, "self-expression" classes for youngsters were held in such august institutions as the Museum of Modern Art. Gradually, new and existing children's museums emphasized children's creative nature.

At the end of the 1960s the Boston Children's Museum under Michael Spock, the Exploratorium under Frank Oppenheimer, and the Barnesdale Junior Art Center under Claire Isaacs independently began experiments in creating experiential exhibition environments. These new techniques of open-ended problem-solving experiences had kinship with the materials found in the progressive schools of a slightly earlier age, the teaching materials needed for the "open classroom," and unstructured individualized instruction centers set up in the corners of classrooms. These experimental exhibition techniques were not so much a radical departure philosophically from the past as a new interpretation consistent with the hands-on philosophy laid down by the original children's museum creators. What they added was the underlying theory that experiences based on open-ended unstructured self-directed exploration would allow children to intuitively understand things that would be recalled later on when the theories were named and explained.

The big departure for the museum world was that this work was not based on, nor even in some cases referenced to, the central characteristic of traditional museums: collections-based objects. In fact, the Boston Children's Museum, then more than 50 years old, put all its collections in storage and made what had once been the heart of the presentation off limits to visitors while the staff worked on new active presentation methods. Neither the Barnesdale Junior Art Center nor the Exploratorium had collections.

The museum world, which up to that point had acknowledged children's museums as colleagues (though maybe of a lesser order), began to believe that these non-artifact-based institutions were not, and should not be called, museums. That was okay with the directors in question, who went on with their experiments.

In fact, only one of these three institutions had the word "museum" in its name. In the 1970s, the Boston Children's Museum applied for museum accreditation and told the AAM they were prepared to fail if the accreditors decided that the museum was not really a "museum." The accreditors, upon full review, decided Boston was indeed a museum! The impact of this decision was wide-ranging, giving rise to a feeling that a potentially radical breakthrough had occurred.

Lack of collections use was not the only threat to mainstream museums. The other anxiety most often expressed was about the permitted, even encouraged, explorative conduct of the visitor. The behavior appeared undisciplined, and the museums seemed to engender "fun" and thus had to be without educational value, said the most vocal detractors.

These hands-on places were clearly influenced by learning theory and the progressive "open classroom" school experiments of the time, which held that children learned best when allowed to select what personally interested them and could explore that interest using handleable material in their own sequence and timeframe. Theories of child psychology, which espoused the development of well-adjusted, individuated children, reinforced the work.

Educators referred to museums as "informal education" sites and compared them to more regimented schools around them. Frank Oppenheimer was often quoted as saying, "No one ever failed a museum." The philosophy underpinning the museums mirrored the emphasis found in parenting literature on raising children as individuals, conscious of their needs and gifts. The most famous writer of such material at the time was Michael Spock's father, Dr Benjamin Spock.

The intended audience

From the inception of children's museums, the intended audience included teachers of children, with all manner of services being provided to enhance their role. In the 1970s, the audience was consciously expanded again to include parents and caregivers as direct recipients of services and as important learners on the exhibition floor (Gurian 1993).

The original children's museums targeted middle-school and late-elementary-school children and were started during the time when elementary school ended at the 8th grade, often the end of school altogether for many youngsters. But by the 1940s, child labor laws were in place, and mandatory school reached 16 years of age. Junior high schools were established exclusively for grades 7 through 9, and by the 1960s middle-schools were created for a slightly different mix of grades 6 through 8.

As schools gave increasing attention to this older age group, children's museums started attending to a younger mix: infants, preschoolers, and primary grade students. By the mid-1970s, these youngsters became the bulk of the attendees of US youth museums (much to the surprise of children's museum administrators). Children's museums created in the 1970s, 1980s, and 1990s were intended primarily for very young children, even though these new institutions were based on the hands-on experiments of Boston and the Exploratorium. The content embedded in these established museums did not seem developmentally appropriate for these younger visitors. So new content was designed that included environments of daily life, such as the shop, fire station, and boats.

Some children's museums tried to encourage the return of the older child, with only partial success, and many science museums (based on the Exploratorium interactive model) began to be the successor family institutions for those formerly known as "children" and now known instead as youth and "kids." Youngsters who viewed themselves as having outgrown childhood did not want to be associated with a place that had the word children in its title.

The drop in the age of attendees was caused in part by trends in the prevailing philosophy of child development. In the late 1960s and 1970s, the work of Jean Piaget and his stages of cognitive development (begun in the 1930s) began to be joined with other theorists concerned with stages of human development, including Erik Erickson and Abraham Maslow, Harvard psychologist Jerome Bruner with his colleagues, Burton White and Jerome Kagan. These theorists emphasized the importance of early stimulation of children as an explanation for the difference in school performance between the affluent and the poor and disabled. Their work fostered the early introduction of enriched environments for the less successful. This notion of early intervention was translated by middle-class parents who, wanting the best for their children, began bringing babies as visitors to children's museums.

That is where most children's museums find themselves in the United States at the start of the twenty-first century: hundreds of new or newly refurbished institutions with the interactive hands-on approach as their touchstone and very young children as their audience.

Many recent programmatic expansions – infant play spaces, resource areas, parent information centers, climbing structures with an educational focus – have been copied and embedded into museums for the general public, in social service centers, and in even more recent times by commercial venues.[3] The once-distinctive niche of the children's museum is no longer so clearly defined.

Audience segments in children's museums

Today, children's museum professionals find themselves serving three disparate audience segments – family, school, and community. While museums sometimes use different rhetoric when describing the needs of each group (and our reasons and hopes for serving them), more often they use the rationale for service to one group to describe work with another. Upon reflection I contend that each group cannot be lumped with the others, nor is language used for one segment suitable or interchangeable with another. A further, but common, problem occurs when spending priorities vary considerably while the rhetoric of service suggests parity.

Even though they use the same facility, each of these groups often come at different times. They have different needs and require different supervision, intervention, and even different content. The sources of programmatic revenue associated with each group are distinctly different. Furthermore, negotiating and securing funding for each source requires specific expertise. Let me describe each of these groups and their desires with some specific detail.

In the United States, the admission base generated by family visitors is generally the largest single source of earned income. These visitors come on weekends and school holidays, and they also use and pay for all kinds of ancillary services (food, parking, parties, programs). They are highly educated people who are usually affluent or else temporarily poor by virtue of a current life choice, such as studying or participating in lower-paying but socially responsible work. Having been steeped in popular early childhood literature, they have learned that stimulation at a very early age makes for the most successful adults. Thus, they see children's museums as highly desirable institutions in their pursuit of age-appropriate stimulation for their very young children.

The adult in the general visitor segment often demands a steady flow of changing exhibitions, a clean and aesthetic environment, and new, interesting programs. As a group they share child-rearing practices and expect the staff to relate to their children in certain ways, including encouragement for endeavors great and small with a gentle insistence on sharing and "taking turns" in a civil manner. They want their children to be protected and expect the museum to be safe, albeit challenging. They remember their own childhood fondly and recall (sometimes inaccurately) being able to leave the house freely and explore the neighborhood by themselves and with their friends without adult supervision. The families in the general visitation group are usually urban or suburban and middle-class regardless of their ethnicity, religion, race, or country of origin.

To serve this important (and revenue-producing) population best, the museum encourages, wittingly or unwittingly, certain class-determined attitudes toward children. For example, in most museums there is an expectation that these children have leisure time, access to technology, experience with travel, enough nutrition, and familiarity with movies and books. It is assumed that they come from homes where learning is encouraged and success is expected.

The children of this population usually have had a more protected upbringing than their own parents. They are carted around from one safe environment to another, have constant supervision or even interference from adults, and have less exposure to the consequences of their decisions than do their less affluent counterparts.

Because this audience is the bedrock of most of the admissions income stream, it has many advocates within the staff. If catered to properly, attendance and income rise and the museum prospers. The consequence of doing otherwise is bleak.

The second group is the school group. Teachers need curriculum justification to take their classes to the museum because field trips are expensive and because there is considerable pressure for every teacher to produce measurable academic achievement in every class. The teacher who determines to go on a school trip needs to be selective. For its part, the children's museum needs to provide an experience that is educationally useful and needs to distinguish itself from its general-audience reputation as a "play place." The underpinnings of individual choice embedded in the physical exhibits are often anathema to the teacher who needs every child to have learned the same thing. Children allowed to travel in school groups tend to be slightly older than the general visitor and include a wider economic stratum, language skills, and experiences. Depending on the school, this may be the first museum experience of any kind for some of the children.

Programmatically, the teacher requires the museum to provide a "class" where the group members each receive the same material in some orderly manner. Because the teachers demand more content, the museum provides more instructional personnel, both paid and volunteer, and more attention to curriculum development, often using carry-on props rather than the exhibition as the focus. If the exhibitions have been designed for individual choice, they work less well for school groups. Accordingly the group is often relegated to spaces that look a lot like the classrooms they have just left.

The dynamics that surround the school group visit are also different from those of the volitional family social group. The children are surrounded by fewer and less attentive adults, and the children themselves are conscious of and bonded to each other. Their social interaction becomes part of their agenda. When large numbers of groups (such as summer camp groups) share the building with families, they often annoy and interfere with each other, causing dissatisfaction from both sides.

While the family audience pays admission on an individual basis, the school (and sometimes the community group) often receives a subvention from educational or other governmental authorities. In the United States this audience numbers between 20 percent and 50 percent of the annual attendance and is artificially limited by the museum administration; in Europe, especially if the subvention allows for free entrance, the percentage can be much higher.

While exhibits are primarily designed for the family audience, the salaried staff is hired primarily to work with school groups. Trained teachers on the staff find school groups easier to predict and easier to prepare for than the general audience. Without attention by the administration to the balance of program offerings, more school programs and school-like programs are provided than any other. School-like programs do not necessarily work well for the general audience or the community population without modification, and often these programs do not work well within the exhibition space.

The third group is referred to euphemistically as "community" – children and their caregivers in the lower economic strata. No matter what their ethnicity, race, or language, they have different expectations than other visitor groups. They come, for example, from different cultural or ethnic backgrounds than the more affluent who live around them, often have more than one language spoken at home, and are not fluent in the majority language. They may have an uneasy status in society as guest workers or immigrants, both legal and illegal. They are skittish about authority and venturing out into unfamiliar environments that have clearly been organized for others. They generally are not trusting of those who offer good deeds and who might be well meaning but appear patronizing or irrelevant. Most of this population never visits a museum. The adults' lives are more stressed, and they are more focused on issues of immediate need. The audience is not waiting around hoping to be invited in. Serving this group is not as simple as providing increased access.

Without a knowledgeable and experienced staff advocate in a senior position, and without consistent funding streams such as endowment or government funding infusions, this group is talked about regularly but served only minimally and intermittently. The rhetoric of inclusion is often used and is included in mission statements. The desire to serve the underserved is repeatedly expressed, but lack of practice and difficult economics make real service to this group inconsistent and intermittent.

Why does anyone bother with this population of largely nonusers? Because there is an important fourth group to be considered – people of influence (politicians, policy makers, foundations and charities, corporate sponsors, and grant makers). These authority figures with access to financial resources are often concerned with the underserved and school-based community. They are rarely interested in funding the more affluent. So every well-meaning (and even cynical) children's museum wishes to serve the underserved community and be funded by one of these agents. To be economically successful requires museum leadership that is adroit in the political arena and persuasive with the foundation community. These skills are different from those necessary to raise money from affluent individuals.

In the United States, many successful grants are product oriented – exhibitions and curriculum material, for example. This funding is therefore episodic and short term and tends to set up a cycle of cynicism within the less affluent community because contract staffs for one project or another are always arriving or being phased out. Successful work with the less affluent audience requires, by comparison, long-term advocacy and constant community presence, and that type of economic stability is extremely difficult to get.

If children's museums genuinely wish to serve all three segments, there needs to be an advocate for each group within the staff hierarchy. Each must be armed with different skills, experiences, and passions. In most cases, the advocate for the poorer segment of the community, such as outreach coordinator, is often of a lesser stature than the advocates for the other groups, and the work they do is often performed at sites outside the museum proper. So while the museum can justify its work with this community, it is often neither advocated for internally nor affects the staff or program within the building. If we really want to serve children in the areas of least affluence and opportunity, then we must create budgets, staff structures, board representation, and long-term strategies that allow for the needs and differences of these families.

Newly created children's museums are popular with the affluent general audience, I would contend. Middle-class parents are installing them to fit within their homogenous suburban communities so that they do not have to travel to the inner city, interact with children distinctly different than themselves, and seemingly jeopardize the safety of their children. They are, unintentionally, reinventing ghettoization. Discordant with this, the Association of Children's Museums (ACM) has an expressed mission to become "the town square" for the whole community. This lack of convergence happens, I think, because the economic base of children's museums rests squarely on these privileged users who pay only lip service to the notion of inclusion, while the desire of children's museum leadership is more all-encompassing. In the future that economic base may be spread thinner and thinner as more and more children's museums spring up competing for attention and other museums and for-profit institutions create competing attractions.

What parenting books are currently advocating

An important clue to the possible future directions of children's museums might be found by reviewing the contemporary popular press in the areas of parenting, education, and learning theory.

A cursory review suggests that some of the underlying experiences and philosophies of child rearing are changing. One can still find books on enhanced individualism, such as multiple intelligences and inherent personality types (Gardner 1983). But these now compete with books that concentrate less on the exploration of individualized creativity and more on the common needs and responsibility of family and community. Words juxtaposed – like individualism and collectivism – invade many sociological treatises. Like most previous parenting books, research-based scholarly journals form the underpinning of parenting material.

Politics in the United States, both from the left and the right, currently stress "family values." Accordingly, there is an increased interest in interrelatedness, nonviolent problem solving, delayed gratification for the common good, disciplined accomplishment, and interpersonal caring. A new emphasis on citizenship permeates child development books. In response, one begins to see exhibitions in children's museums that enhance group problem solving and the sharing of resources.

An even newer category of parenting books stresses spirituality and specific religious training as central to rearing successful children. At least in the United States, given the political climate, the intermixing of values with religion is noted everywhere in the press as a new frontier of interest. There has been a recent spate of Jewish children's museums that might fit within this category.

The explosion of agritourism, ecotourism, and rural vacations suggests an increased interest by families in experiencing nature.[4] Embedded in that trend is nostalgia for the imagined small town of yesteryear, hence the explosion of town-like play environments in children's museums.

The expansion of petting zoos into zoos that once had only exotic animals speaks to parents' interest in giving children access to the domestic animals the parents knew in childhood. Looking at currently expanding children's museums, one can see increased use of outside exhibition spaces with plantings as well as inside themed areas of artificial apple orchards, forests, and other natural spaces.

The difficult world situation with its religious polarization has brought home to us that simple attention to cultural difference, promoted so earnestly in children's museums of the past, does not necessarily make a safer society. Cultural exhibits based on our League of Nations past, which stressed commonality – we all eat, we all sleep, but we use different and intriguing products to do so – seem no longer adequate as the message for children's museum exhibitions.

27

Is increased technology good for interactivity?

The term "hands-on" used to mean tactile involvement of all kinds. Now it has been expanded to mean interaction with technology, which is increasingly available in children's museums. A growing literature, both pro and con, explores the meaning of children's interaction with technology. On the one hand, an explosion of knowledge is available to children, and because they are taught computer use at an early age in school, they can access information on their own very early. On the other hand, there is a certain mesmerizing lack of sociability found in sitting in front of a screen. A deep discussion will have to commence about the role of technology within the children's museum exhibition palette. In fact, a new children's museum in Pittsburgh has eliminated high-tech access for children. Their explanation is interesting food for thought:

> Our own research suggests that in some cases, while enhancing an individual's experience, "interactives" – in particular those relying on computing and information technologies – inadvertently impoverish the social interaction that can arise with and around exhibits in museums and galleries. There is a danger that we are confusing interactivity with social interaction and collaboration.
>
> (Heath and Vom Lehn 2002)

What's to become of children's museums?

Readers will take exception to many of the specifics in this article because the European children's museum scene differs markedly from that in the United States. Many, though not all, children's museums in Latin America and in the Middle East, however, resemble American children's and science museums more than do those in Great Britain and on the continent. For example:

- Some European children's museums successfully cater to older children.
- Some social service agencies in Great Britain create children's museums specifically for underserved populations and their parents. In those cases, the less affluent and more deprived become the majority attendees.
- Some museums have special focuses like modern art or child psychology and special modalities like theatrical interpretations.

At the outset of this essay, I suggested that the prototypical children's museums may have exhausted the potential of the paradigm, even as their numbers continue to grow, and other museums continue to borrow from children's museums strategies and poach (appropriately) on their audience. I remain unconvinced that a viable new paradigm is waiting in the wings.

USA Today published an article entitled "Struggling to Raise Good Kids in Toxic Times," which included the following:

> A pervasive unease grips many people when they look at children in this country. Crime may be dropping and the economy thriving but

28

Americans sense something is going very wrong in the way we raise our young.

American parents complain that there seems to be difficulty in: limiting exposure to popular culture, instilling values consistently, sharing sufficient unprogrammed time together, offering daily models of useful work and community help, while there seems to be too much: negative influences from the media, emphasis on materialism and pressure for achievement and appearing grown-up.

(October 1, 2001)

For me the current modalities within children's museums have too much "doing" and too much stimulation. There is no time to smell the flowers, walk in the woods, see the sunset, or practice skills to one's own satisfaction.

There is a pervasive lack of silence for children, of satisfying examples of doing nothing, of fostering and teaching children the pleasures and repose of an internal reflective life.

So as we try to envision new models let us try to have the broadest perspective. Museums have not paid enough attention to imagination and fantasy, examples of meaningful work, idealism and beauty, religion and spirituality, handwork and kindness, silence and inner lives, and creativity.

My hope for the next generation of children's museums would include the following:

- A celebration of the watcher as learner. We need more passive computers to watch the action (slave monitors), viewing platforms, scanning areas to prepare the shy for what's next. Holding back is not just shyness, and even if it is, why do we not value reticence, moderation in response, soft talking?
- Respect for the modulated visit. We need more quiet spaces, spaces for calming down.
- Spaces that foster loving interaction between generations. We need more holding and rocking, sitting still and listening to lullabies.
- A focus on group enterprise that requires cooperation.
- Rewards for experimentation that arise from within rather than through external approbation, allowing for joy and flow (Csikszentmihályi 1990).
- More discipline and less judgmental overlay. Children need to understand that practice is its own reward without having to appear to be practicing for the Olympics.
- Apprenticeships where learning by doing is not faked but real, and with real consequences.
- More belly laughs, less accomplishment testing, and more rolling around.

In order to continue evolving, children's museums need to begin a dialogue that puts the various issues raised throughout this paper squarely on the table. If we are to be responsive to new theories of child rearing where are the programs and models that reflect new thinking and should be replicated? If we wish to continue to be teaching sites, what are the curriculum-based issues that fit within our institutions? How can we build the same exhibitions that work both for the volitional and the group audience? Can we invent new business plans that make us less dependent on admissions for our financial well being? And if we plan to include underserved populations, are we willing to embed programs of social service, different hours, guides from the community, positions with authority within the museum structure, and enough ways of securing funding so that useful programs can be sustained?

If children's museums do not succeed in answering all of these questions, we may witness a waning movement even as museums grow in number.

Conclusion

To review, I hope that this article makes useful points for everyone who deals with children in their museums. They are:

- Underserved audiences, school groups, and volitional family groups are very different one from another. For a children's museum to be successful, it should consider each group separately and program accordingly. Programming opportunities need to be embedded within the design of the physical environment. It is not enough to build for one of the audiences, supplementing that program for other groups by keeping them together, putting them in a classroom, or layering on additional material.
- Without overturning the current business plan, acknowledge that the fantasies and aspirations of middle-class parents do affect the direction of children's museums. It is wise to be cognizant of popular parenting material for the educated and affluent parent and adjust accordingly.
- Appropriate content for the very young is different from that for the middle-aged elementary school child (who reads, has skills, and has considerable independence). Yet even that content needs to be expanded to accommodate what we increasingly know about learning in the very young.
- Technology needs to be used sparingly and in ways that involve, not isolate, children.
- Finally, museums have a civic responsibility to help create citizens who are attuned to the needs of the group, more so than is displayed by our overly supervised, secluded middle-class children or their unsupported cousins in the inner cities in the United States. There is value in encouraging group responsibility, even for the very young.

Finally, in the exploration of theories – new views on child rearing, curriculum development for young school children, and the needs of a very different underclass – and translating them into physical environments that work and meet the unmet and often unexpressed needs, children's museums could again regain their place as the most exciting and innovative part of the museum community.

Notes

1 The chapter has a long history. The most recent version originated as a speech to the "Hands On" Conference in Lisbon in May 1998. It was subsequently presented at the Association of Children's Museums conference of the same year. It has been updated and modified for this publication. However the basis of this paper was written first with Anne Dobbs Tribble as (Gurian and Tribble 1985) and revised as (Gurian 1995b). Underpinning it all is a debt of gratitude to Gregory Baeker for his master's thesis written in 1981 and to Anne Dobbs Tribble (now Butterfield) for all the work we have done together (Baeker 1981).

2 The museum website of the Association of Children's Museums (ACM) reproduces a 2001 *Chicago Tribune* article that puts the attendance figures of US children's museums at 33 million, up from 8 million in 1991, the number of institutions at almost 300, up from 200 in 1990 and 38 in 1975, with 80 in the planning phase, and many existing children's museums in the process of expansion (Dean 2001 in http://www.childrensmuseums.org/Chicago_Tribune.htm).

3 Almost all fast food restaurants in the United States have indoor climbing structures offered to their customers for free. Almost all commercial bookstores have children's book centers with hands-on equipment, and toy stores and other educational venues specialize in allowing children to interact with their products.

4 "Ceballos-Lascuráin (1993) reports a WTO estimate that nature tourism generates 7% of all international travel expenditure (Lindberg 1997). The World Resources Institute (1990) found that while tourism overall has been growing at an annual rate of 4%, nature travel is increasing at an annual rate between 10% and 30% (Reingold 1993). Data which supports this growth rate is found in Lew's (1997) survey of tour operators in the Asia-Pacific region who have experienced annual growth rates of 10% to 25% in recent years (Lindberg 1997)" (The International Ecotourism Society 2003).

Bibliography

Baeker, G.G. (1981) *The Emergence of Children's Museums in the United States 1899–1940*, Toronto: University of Toronto.

Burghart, T. (2002) *Children's Museum Invites Youngsters to Step Inside Contemporary Art*, Naples, Florida.

Csikszentmihályi, M. (1990) *Flow: The Psychology of Optimal Experience*, New York: Harper & Row.

Dean, T.L. (2001) "Children's Museums Exhibit Attendance Leap over Decade," *Chicago Tribune*, Saturday, May 5, 2001.

Dewey, J. (1975, first published in 1938) *The Need of a Theory of Experience. Experience and Education*, 18th edn., Kappa Delta Pi Lecture series. New York: Collier Books.

Dewey, J. (1977) in Peters, R.S. (ed.) *John Dewey Reconsidered*, London: Routledge and Kegan Paul.

Gallup, A.B. (1907) *The Work of a Children's Museum*, Washington, DC: American Association of Museums.

Gardner, H. (1983) *Frames of Mind: The Theory of Multiple Intelligences*, New York: Basic Books.

Gurian, E.H. (1993) "Adult Learning at Children's Museum of Boston," in Strand, J. (ed.) *Selected Reprints from Museums, Adults, and the Humanities, a Guide for Educational Programming*, Washington, DC: American Association of Museums.

Gurian, E.H. (1995b) "A Draft History of Children's Museums," unpublished, Cleveland Children's Museum.

Gurian, E.H. and Tribble, A.D. (1985) "Children's Museums, an Overview," unpublished manuscript.

Heath, C. and Vom Lehn, D. (2002) *Misconstruing Interactivity, Interactive Learning in Museums of Art and Design*, London: King's College.

The International Ecotourism Society (2003) *Ecotourism Statistical Fact Sheet*. Available http://www.ecotourism.org/index2.php?research/stats (accessed February 26, 2005).

Schwartz, A. (ed.) (1967) *Museums, the Story of America's Treasure Houses*, New York: E.P. Dutton and Co., Inc.

Zervos, C. (2002) *Children's Museums: Edu-Tainment for Young Learners*, Adelaide. Available http://www.museumsaustralia.org.au/conf02/Papers/zervosc.htm (accessed February 17, 2005).

4

WHAT IS THE OBJECT OF
THIS EXERCISE?

A meandering exploration of the many meanings
of objects in museums,[1] 1999

> Philosophically speaking, an object is a thing external to the mind or
> perceiving subject, it is also an obstacle, a hindrance, as in the verb *to
> object*, meaning to interrupt or propose changing directions. I want us
> to consider objects in museums – and the object of museums – as
> things that exist outside, in themselves, and resist the common-
> place.... Objects as resources, as the means by which we are re-*sourced*,
> re-oriented, and renewed.
>
> (James Cuno 2004)

Introduction

"Why did the Serbs and Croats shell each other's historic sites when they had so little
ammunition and these were not military targets?" I routinely ask my museum
studies graduate students this question when I lecture. "To break their spirit,"
is always the instantaneous answer. Museums, historic sites, and other institutions of
memory, I would contend, are the tangible evidence of the spirit of a civilized society.
And while the proponents of museums have long asserted that museums add to the
quality of life, they have not understood, (as the graduate students did, when
confronted by the example of war) how profound and even central that "quality" was.

Similar examples reveal the relationship between museums and "spirit" in sharp
detail. Why did Hitler and Stalin establish lists of acceptable and unacceptable art
and then install shows in museums to proclaim them while sending the formerly
acclaimed, now forbidden, art to storage? Why did the Nazis stockpile Jewish
material, force interned curators to catalogue and accession it, intending to create
a museum to the eradicated Jews? Why, when I was in the rural mountains of
the Philippines, was I taken to hidden closets that served as museums, holding the
material of the tribe's immediate past, secreted from the dealers who were offering
great sums for the same material?

In adversity it is understood, by antagonists and protagonists alike, that the
evidence of history has something central to do with the spirit, will, pride, identity,
and civility of people, and that destroying such material may have led to forgetting,

33

broken spirits, and docility. This same understanding is what motivates cultural and ethnic communities to create their own museums in order to tell their stories, in their own way, to themselves and others.

Yet neither the museum profession, nor its sibling workers in the other storehouses of collective memory (archives, libraries, concert halls, and so forth), makes – nor, I would contend, understands – the case clearly about its institutions' connectedness to the soul of civic life. In cities and states under duress, you can hear mayors and governors making the case better. Dennis Archer, mayor of Detroit, said recently in a radio interview, "Detroit, in order to be a great city, needs to protect its great art museum, the Detroit Institute of Art." It was Archer and his predecessor, Coleman Young, who championed and underwrote the creation of Detroit's Museum of African American History. And it was Teddy Kolik, the fabled mayor of Jerusalem, who was the chief proponent of the creation of the Israel Museum (and who placed one of his two offices within the building). Mayors know why museums are important. Citizens, implicitly, do too. A recent survey in Detroit asked people to rate the importance of institutions to their city and then tell which they had visited. The Museum of African American History was listed very high on the "important" list and much lower on the "I have visited" list. People do not have to use the museum in order to assert its importance or feel that their tax dollars are being well spent in its support.

The people who work in museums have struggled collectively over the proper definition and role of their institutions. Their struggle has been, in part, to differ-entiate museums from other near relatives – the other storehouses of collective memory. The resulting definitions have often centered on things – on objects and their permissible uses. I believe the debate has missed the essential meaning (the soul, if you will) of the institution that is the museum.

Objects are not the heart of the museum

The following discussion will attempt to capture that soul by throwing light on the shifting role of museum objects over time. It will show how elusive objects are, even as they remain the central element embedded within all definitions of museums. This essay will also postulate that the definition of museum object – and the associated practices of acquisition, preservation, care, display, study, and interpretation – have always been fluid and have become more so recently. Objects did not provide the definitional bedrock in the past, although museum staffs thought they did. I will show that museums may not need them any longer to justify their work.

But if the essence of a museum is not to be found in its objects, then where? I propose the answer is in being a place that stores memories and presents and organizes meaning in some sensory form. It is both the physicality of a place and the memories and stories that are told therein that are important. Further, I propose that these two essential ingredients – place and remembrances – are not exclusive to museums. And, finally, I contend that the blurring of the distinctions between these institutions of memory and other seemingly separate institutions (like shopping malls and attractions) is a positive, rather than negative, development.

Not meaning to denigrate the immense importance of museum objects and their care, I am postulating that they, like props in a brilliant play, are necessary but not sufficient. This essay points out something that we have always known intuitively: that the larger issues revolve around the stories museums tell and the way they tell them. When parsed carefully, the objects, in their tangibility, provide a variety of stakeholders with an opportunity to debate the meaning and control of their memories. It is the ownership of the story, rather than the object itself, that the dispute has been all about.

This essay suggests what museums are not (or not exactly) and, therefore, continues the dialogue about what museums are and what makes them important, so important that people in extremis fight over them.

What is an object?

"Ah, but we have the real thing," museum professionals used to say when touting the uniqueness of their occupation. When I began in museum work, in the late 1960s and early 1970s, the definition of museums always contained reference to the object as the pivot around which we justified our other activities.[2] Although there were always other parts of the definition, our security nonetheless lay in owning objects. With it came our privileged responsibility for the attendant acquisition, its preservation, safety, display, study, and interpretation. We were like priests and the museums like our reliquaries.

The definition of objects was easy. They were the real stuff. Words were used like *unique, authentic, original, genuine, actual*. The things that were collected had significance, and were within the natural, cultural or aesthetic history of the known world.

Of course, real had more than one meaning. It often meant *one-of-a-kind*, but it also meant *example of*. Thus, artworks were one-of-a-kind, but eighteenth-century farm implements may have been examples. Things made by hand were unique, but manufactured items became examples. In the natural history world, almost all specimens were examples but had specificity as to location found. Yet some could also be unique – the last passenger pigeon or the last dodo bird. Objects from both categories, unique and example, were accessioned into the collections. Museums owned the objects and took on the responsibility of preserving, studying, and displaying them.

Yet even in these seemingly easy categories there were variations. In asserting uniqueness (as in made-by-hand), specific authorship was associated with some objects, such as paintings, but not with others, most especially utilitarian works whose makers were often unknown. Some unique works were thought of as art and some as craft; with some notable exceptions, art was individualized as to maker and craft was not. This practice, which is now changing, made it possible to do research and mount shows of the work of particular artists in some, but not all, cultures.

What are collections?

In the early 1970s, the American Association of Museums (AAM) established an Accreditation Commission. As its members deliberated, they discussed whether groups of living things could be called collections or whether institutions that so "collected" should be classified as museums. Heretofore, "museums" were conserving things that had never been alive or now were no longer alive. The field debated if the living things of botanical gardens, fish in aquaria or animals in zoos were collections and if so, those institutions were, de facto, museums. It was decided that, yes, at least for funding and accreditation purposes, they were museums, and the living things they cared for were likewise to be regarded as collections, and hence objects.[3]

Yet there were other institutional repositories that cared for, protected, preserved, and taught about "objects" but were not called museums nor necessarily treated by museums as siblings. Archives and libraries, especially rare-book collections, were considered related but not siblings even though some museum collections contain the identical materials. There were also commercial galleries and private and corporate collections that were considered by museum professionals to be different and outside the field, separated supposedly by underlying purpose. A legal distinction of not-for-profit was considered an essential part of the definition of a museum. It was clear that while objects formed the necessary foundation upon which the definition of museum might rest, they were not sufficient in themselves.

Can noncollecting institutions be museums?

The AAM Accreditation Commission next sought to determine if places that resembled collections-based museums but did not hold collections (i.e. places like not-for-profit galleries and cultural centers) were, for purposes of accreditation, also museums. In 1978, they decided that, in some instances, galleries could be considered museums because, like museums, they cared for, displayed, and preserved objects even though they did not own them. Ownership, therefore, in some instances, no longer defined museums.

There was also the conundrum brought to the profession by science centers and children's museums, mostly of the mid-twentieth century. Earlier in the century, these places had collected and displayed objects, but by mid-century children's museums and science centers were proliferating and creating new public experiences, using exhibition material that was built specifically for the purpose and omitting collections objects altogether. How were these "purpose-built" objects to be considered? They were three-dimensional, often unique, many times extremely well made, but had no cognates in the outside world. Much of this exhibit material was built to demonstrate the activity and function of the "real" (and now inactive) machinery sitting beside it.

The Adler Planetarium, applying to the AAM for accreditation, also caused the AAM to reconsider the definition of a museum. The planetarium's object was a machine which projected stars on a ceiling. If institutions relied on such "objects" were these places museums? Had the profession inadvertently crafted a definition of objects that was restricted to those things that were created elsewhere and were then transported to museums? That was not the case in art museums that commissioned site-specific work. Certainly the murals of the depression period applied directly to museum walls were accessionable works of art – an easy call! Portability, then, did not define objects.

In 1978, the AAM Accreditation Commission, citing these three different types of noncollections-based institutions (art centers, science and technology centers, and planetariums) wrote specific language for each type of museum and, by amending its definition of collections for each group, declared these types of organizations to be...museums! They elaborated: "The existence of collections and supporting exhibitions is considered desirable, but their absence is not disabling."[4] In response, many museums set about creating more than one set of rules – one for accessioned objects and another for exhibitions material – and began to understand that the handleable material they used in their classes (their teaching collections) should be governed by a different set of criteria as well.

Nevertheless, there were often no easy distinctions between the handleablity of teaching collections' objects and those others deserving preservation. The Boston Children's Museum loan boxes, created in the 1960s contained easy-to-obtain material about Northeast Native Americans. But by the 1980s, the remaining material was retired from the loan boxes and accessioned into the collections because it was no longer obtainable and had become rare and valuable.

Even purpose-built "environments" have, in cases such as the synagogue models in the Museum of the Diaspora in Tel Aviv, become so intriguing or are of such craftsmanship that, decades later, they became collections' objects themselves. So, too, have the exhibitions created by distinguished artists, such as parts of Charles and Ray Eames's exhibit, *Mathematica: A World of Numbers and Beyond*.

Dioramas were often built for a museum exhibition hall in order to put objects (mostly animals) in context. These display techniques, which were considered a craft at the time they were created, were occasionally of such beauty, and displayed such special artistic conventions of realism (and seeming realism), that today the original dioramas themselves have become "objects," and many are subject to preservation, accession, and special display. The definition of objects suitable for collections has, therefore, expanded to include, in special cases, material built for the museum itself.

What is real? Is the experience the object?

In the nineteenth century, some museums had and displayed sculptural plaster castings and studies. The Louvre and other museums had rooms devoted to copies of famous sculptures that the museum did not own. The originals either remained *in situ* or were held by others. People came to see, study, and paint these reproductions. They were treated with the respect accorded the real thing. For a long time, museums and their publics have felt that though there were differences between the "original" and reproductions, both had a place within their walls.

Similarly, reconstructed skeletons of dinosaurs have long appeared in museums. They usually are a combination of the bones of the species owned by the museum plus the casting of the missing bones from the same species owned by someone else. Sometimes museums point out which part is real and which is cast, but often they do not. "Real," therefore takes on new meaning. Curators recognize that the experience of seeing the whole skeleton is more "real," and certainly more informative, than seeing only the authentic unattached bones that do not add to a complete or understandable image.

Likewise, multiples or limited editions were always considered "real" so long as the intention of the artist was respected. Thus, the fact that Rodin and many others authorized the multiple production of some pieces did not seem to make each one any less real or less unique. The creation of additional though still limited copies – using the same etching plates, but after the death of the artist – caused more problems. But often, while acknowledging the facts of the edition, such works also hung in museums, and if the quality was good, were accessioned into their collections.

Is the image the object?

The twentieth century's invention of new technologies has made multiples the norm and made determining what is real and what that means much more difficult. While original prints of movies, for example, exist, it is the moving image that the public thinks of as the object rather than the master print of film. Questions of authenticity revolve around subsequent manipulation of the image (e.g. colorization, cutting, or cropping) rather than the contents of any particular canister.

Printed editions of identical multiples are considered originals and become more valuable if signed; unsigned editions are considered less "real" and certainly less valuable. In such cases one could say that the signature, rather than the image, becomes the object. Photographs printed by the photographer may be considered more real than those using the same negative but printed by someone else. With the invention of digital technology, many identical images can be reproduced at will without recourse to any negative at all. So the notion of authenticity (meaning singularity or uniqueness) becomes problematic as images indistinguishable from those in museums are easily available outside the museum. It is the artist's sensibility that produced the image. It is the image itself, therefore, that is the object.

Is the story the object?

Of the utilitarian objects of the twentieth century, most are manufactured in huge quantities and therefore could be termed "examples." Which of these objects to collect often depends not on the object itself but on the associated story that may render one of them unique or important.

The objects present in the death camps of the Holocaust were, in the main, created for use elsewhere. There is nothing unique in the physicality of a bowl that comes from Auschwitz-Birkenau. These bowls could have been purchased in shops that sold cheap tableware all over Germany at the time. However, when the visitor reads the label that says the bowl comes from Auschwitz, the viewer, knowing something about the Holocaust, transfers meaning to the object. Since there is nothing aside from the label that makes the bowl distinctive, it is not the bowl itself but its associated history that informs the visitor.

Does the cultural context make the object?

As Foucault and many others have written, objects lose their meaning without the viewer's knowledge and acceptance of underlying aesthetic or cultural values. Without such knowledge, an object's reification even within its own society cannot be understood. Often the discomfort of novice visitors to art museums has to do with their lack of understanding of the cultural aesthetics that the art on display either challenges or affirms.

By accessioning or displaying objects, the creators of museum exhibitions are creating or enhancing these objects' value. Further, society's acceptance of the value of museums themselves likewise transfers value to their objects. When museums receive gifts or bequests from a major donor's holdings, they are inheriting – and then passing on – a set of value judgments from someone who is essentially hidden from the visitor's view. A particular aesthetic pervades such museums because of the collections they house and the collectors who gave the objects to the museum in the first place.

This issue of values determining choice comes into sharper focus when museums begin acquiring or presenting collections from cultures whose aesthetic might be different. When installing a show of African material in an American art museum, should the curator show pieces based on the values inherent in the producing culture (i.e. focusing on the objects that attain special aesthetic value within that culture), or should the curator pick objects that appeal more to the aesthetic of his or her own culture? This question, the source of much debate, arises when museums attempt to diversify their holdings to include works created by a foreign (or even an assimilated) culture quite different from the culture that produced the majority of the museum's holdings. For example, the choice of which African or Latino art to accession or show has to do not with authenticity but with quality. And the notion of quality has been sharply debated between the scholar in the museum and the peoples representing the culture of the maker. So the question becomes: Who selects the objects and by what criteria?

In material created by indigenous artists, the native community itself some-times disagrees internally as to whether the material is native or belongs to a modern tradition that crosses cultural boundary lines. Some within the native population also argue about the birthright of the artist; blood quantum, traditional upbringing, and knowledge of the language sometimes have considerable bearing on whether artists and their creations can be considered native. In such cases, the decision about what is quality work that should be housed in a museum may have little to do with the object itself and more to do with the genealogy of the producer.

What if your story has no objects or doesn't need them? Is the absence of objects the object?

Most collections were created by wealthy people who acquired things of interest and value to themselves. The everyday objects of nonvalued or subjugated peoples were usually not collected. Often the people in the lowest economic strata could hardly wait to exchange their objects for those that were more valued, giving no thought, at the time, to the preservation of the discarded material. So it goes for most peoples during their most impoverished historical periods. Accordingly, their museums must choose among a narrow band of choices: do not tell that part of their history, re-create the artifacts and environments, or use interpretive techniques that do not rely on material evidence.

The Museum of the Diaspora in Israel, struggling with this issue more than 25 years ago, decided to tell the complete story of five thousand years of Jewish migration without using a single authentic artifact. It elected to create tableaux that reproduced physical surroundings in an illustrative manner based on scholarly research into pictorial and written documentation of all kinds. The museum did so because its collection could not accurately or comprehensively tell the story, and a presentation of settings that appeared "like new" honored the history of Jewish migration more than an assortment of haphazard authentic artifacts showing their age and wear. The experience, wholly fabricated but three-dimensional, became the object. It presented a good public experience, many argued, but still did not qualify as a "museum." Ultimately this total re-creation was accepted as a highly distinguished museum. The Museum of the Diaspora also presented movies, photos, and recordings in a publicly accessible form, arguing that a comprehensive presentation required material that was nonartifactual.

The African American and Native American communities in the United States have suggested, in the same vein, that their primary cultural transmission is accomplished through the ephemeral vehicles of oral language, dance, and song. Their central artifacts or objects, are not dimensional at all, and museums that wish to transmit the accuracy of such cultures, or display historical periods for which material evidence is not available, must learn to employ more diverse material. The performance may be the object, and the performance space might need to be indistinguishable from the exhibit hall. As museums struggle to do this, one begins to see videos of ceremonies and hear audio chanting. Such techniques, once thought of as augmentation rather than core interpretation, have increasingly taken on the role and function that collection objects played.

Even in museums like Cleveland's Rock and Roll Hall of Fame or Seattle's Experience Music Project, the sound and performance of the artists is the artifact, much more than the stationary guitar that, say, Jimi Hendrix once used. Indeed, musical instrument archives at the Museum of Fine Arts, Boston, and other places have long struggled with the proper presentation of their "artifacts." "Silent musical instruments" approaches an oxymoron.

How is the object to be preserved? Is the object to be used?

The museum, in accepting an object for its collection, takes on the responsibility for its care. In doing so, collections managers follow rules organized for the safety and long-term preservation of the objects. Climate control, access restrictions, and security systems are all issues of concern to those who care for objects. Institutions devoted to music or performance transform the notion of collections and certainly the notion of preservation, because while it is true that most things are preserved better when left alone, some musical instruments are not among them. They are preserved better if played, and so, for example at the Smithsonian's National Museum of American History, they are.

Likewise, many native people have successfully argued that accessioned material should be used in the continuance of ceremony and tradition. Rather than being relinquished to isolated preservation (and losing their usefulness), artifacts are stored in trust waiting for the time when they must again be used. In the 1980s, when native people from a specific clan or group asked for an object to be loaned for a short-term use, this was a radical notion for most natural history museums. That request now is more common and often accommodated. For example, at the end of the 1980s, the Dog Soldiers of the Northern Cheyenne requested their pipe, which the Smithsonian's National Museum of Natural History holds, and used it in their ceremonies, after which it was returned to the museum.

Now native museums and, less commonly, some general museums that hold native material accept objects into their collections with the express understanding that they will be lent and used when needed. The notion of a museum as a storehouse in perpetuity has, in these instances, evolved into the museum as a revolving loan warehouse. A long-standing and easily understood example predates this relatively new development. The Crown Jewels of the British monarchy, which are displayed in the Tower of London, are worn by the monarch when he or she is crowned. And so it has been for many centuries.

Whose rules are used for object care?

Other fundamental rules of collections care are being challenged successfully worldwide by native people's involvement. Collections care has been predicated on the basic notion that objects are inanimate. Though some objects were once alive, they now are no longer, and most had never been alive. Thus, collections care policies proceeded from the assumption that objects should be preserved in the best manner possible, avoiding decay from elements, exposure, and use. Protective coverings and storage cases were designed to do just that. Extremes in the exposure to light and temperature, and all manner of pest infestation, were to be avoided. But when the museum was recognized to be neither the only nor the absolute arbiter of its material holdings, accommodation to the beliefs of the producers of the materials or their descendants became necessary.

These beliefs often included a lack of distinction between animate and inanimate. Thus, spirits, "mana," fields of power, and life sources could live within an object regardless of the material from which it was made. And that being so, the care of these living things, it was argued, is and should be quite different from the care of dead or never alive things. So, for example, bubble wrap, while an excellent protector of objects, does not allow for breathing or "singing and dancing at night." Those working in good faith with native populations have come to respect their own objects and now provide for the appropriate life of the object. Some objects need to be fed, some need to be protected from their enemies, some need to be isolated from menstruating women. Collections are no longer under the absolute province of the professional caregivers. Storage facilities that accommodate the native understanding of their objects require new architectural designs that allow access for some and isolation from the curious for others.

Who owns the collections?

This change in collections use and care alters the notion of the museum as owner of its collections and opens the door to multiple definitions of ownership. These new definitions have far-reaching implications. If tribal communities can determine the use, presentation, and care of objects "owned" by museums, can the descendants of an artist? Can the victims or perpetrators of a war event? In the recent Smithsonian National Air and Space Museum's Enola Gay exhibition controversy, the veterans who flew the plane and their Second World War associates ultimately controlled the access to, presentation of, and interpretation of the object. Ownership or legal title to an object does not convey the simple, more absolute meaning it did when I began in the museum field.

The notion that if you buy something from a person who controlled it in the past, then it is yours to do with as you wish is clearly under redefinition in a number of fields. What constitutes clear title? Under what rules does stolen material need to be returned? What is stolen in any case? Do Holocaust victims' paintings and the Elgin Marbles have anything in common? The issue is so complex and varied that countries forge treaties to try to determine which items of their patrimony should be returned. Similarly, museums in countries like New Zealand, Canada, and Australia have developed accords that, in some cases, give dual ownership to collections. Museums and the native populations then jointly control the presentation, care, and even return of the objects, or museums give ownership to the native populations who, in turn, allow the museum to hold the objects in trust. Ownership has developed a complex meaning.

If I own it may I have it back, please?

Some of this blurring of ownership began with native people maintaining that some items should not be in the hands of museums, regardless of their history. It was easy to understand why this would be claimed for human remains held in collections. Almost all cultures do something ceremonial and intentional with the remains of their people: in almost all instances, they do not leave bodies for study in boxes on shelves. So when native people started to call for the return of their ancestors' remains, there was an intuitive understanding of the problem in most circles. This, however, did not make it any easier for the paleontologists and forensic curators whose life work had centered on the access to these bones, nor for the museum goer, whose favorite museum memories had to do with shrunken heads, mummies, or prehistoric human remains. The arguments that emanated from both sides were understandable and difficult to reconcile. It was a clear clash of world views and belief systems. To the curators it seemed that removal of human remains within museum collections would result in the unwarranted triumph of cultural tradition and emotionalism over scientific objectivity and the advancement of knowledge.

As it turned out, the Native American Grave Protection and Repatriation Act (NAGPRA)[5] made clear that Native American tribes had rights to the return of their sacred material and to their ancestors' remains and associated grave goods regardless of the method by which museums had acquired the material. However, the emptying of collections into native communities, as predicted by the most fearful, did not happen. Rather, museums and native communities working together in good faith moved into an easier and more collegial relationship, as between equals. In most cases, the objects returned are carefully chosen and returned with due solemnity. Some tribes have chosen to allow some forensic samples to be saved, or studied prior to reburial, and some have reinterred their ancestors in ways that could allow for future study should the native community wish it.

NAGPRA struck a new balance between the world view of most museums and their staff (which endorsed a rational and scientific model of discourse and allowed for access to as much information as could be gathered) and the spiritual interests of traditional native peoples. A variety of museum practices were broadened, and visitors began to see the interpretation of exhibitions changed to include multiple side-by-side explanations of the same objects. For example, *Wolves*, an exhibition created by the Science Museum of Minnesota, presented scientific data, native stories, conservation and hunting controversies, and physiological information together in an evenhanded way. An argument for multiple interpretations began to be heard in natural history museums whose comfort level in the past had not permitted the inclusion of spiritual information in formats other than anthropological myth.

How old is an object?

The scientific dating of artifacts used in religious practices often holds little relevance to the believers. When an object such as the Shroud of Turin, for example, is carbon dated and shown to be insufficiently old, the problem of writing its museum label becomes complex. An object held in Te Papa, the Museum of New Zealand, was returned to an iwi (tribe) that requested it, with all the solemnity and ceremony appropriate. So, too, went records of its age and material composition, at variance with beliefs held by the Maori people. But if, as the Maori believe, spirit or mana migrates from one piece to its replacement (rendering the successor indistinguishable from its more ancient equivalent), then how relevant is the fact that dates or materials are at variance? The object's cultural essence is as old as they say.

Similarly, when restoration of landmarks includes the replacement of their elements (as is routinely the case in Japanese shrines), the landmark is said to be dated from its inception even though no material part of it remains from that time. That does not upset us. So even something so seemingly rational and historical as dating is up for interpretation.

The object is off-limits. It is none of your business.

Museums, even in their earliest incarnations as cabinets of curiosities, were available to all interested eyes, or at least to those allowed to have access by the owners of the cabinets. In fact, part and parcel of conquest and subjugation was the access to interesting bits of the subjugated. This assumption that everything was fair game held currency for a long time. Though the notion of secret and sacred was also understood (e.g. no one but the faithful could enter Mecca), this concept did not attach to museums or their holdings. If a museum owned it, the visitors could see it if the staff wished them to.

So it came as a surprise to some curators that contemporary native peoples began to make demands on museums to return not only human remains but material that was sacred and once secret. Accommodations negotiated between museums and native people sometimes led to agreements to leave the material in the museum but to limit viewing access. The notion that one people, the museum curators, would voluntarily limit their own and others' access to material owned by museums initially came as a shock to the museum system. But under the leadership of sympathetic museum and native people and, further, under the force of NAGPRA, museums began to understand that all material was not to be made available to all interested parties.

This new understanding was the beginning of the "It is none of your business" concept of museum objects. It held that the people most intimately concerned with and related to the material could determine the access to that material. In many cultures sacred ceremonies are open to all, and the objects used are available for view in museum settings, but that too may change. For example, in Jewish tradition, Torahs once desecrated are supposed to be disposed of by burial in a prescribed manner. Yet some of these are available for view, most notably at the United States Holocaust Memorial Museum. There may come a time when such artifacts will be petitioned to be removed for burial even though the statement they make is powerful.

Who says all objects need to be preserved?

Ownership is not always at issue; sometimes the preservation of the object itself needs examination. Museums have felt their most fundamental responsibility extended to the preservation of the object, yet in returning the human remains to the earth, artifacts are being intentionally destroyed. That was difficult to reconcile by those trained in preservation. Even more difficult was the belief that not all things made by hand were intended to be preserved; perhaps some should be allowed to be destroyed. The Zuni war gods, preserved by museums, were returned to the Zuni tribe when it was proven successfully that they could only have been stolen from grave sites. But even more difficult to understand was the Zuni's assertion that these objects were created to accompany the dead and that preservation of them was therefore anathema. The war gods were returned to the Zuni so that they could watch over the gradual decay of these objects as they returned to the earth. In effect, the Zuni were entitled to destroy the objects that the museums had so carefully preserved.

The notion of preservation has, therefore, also been blurred. Museum personnel began to wrestle with the notion that all people do not hold preservation of all objects as a universal good. The Tibetan Lamas who create exquisite sand paintings only to destroy them later would certainly understand this.

The object speaks.

I would be remiss if I did not also acknowledge the power of some objects to speak directly to the visitor, for example, in the sensual pleasure brought about by viewing unique original objects of spectacular beauty. But the notion that objects, *per se*, can communicate directly and meaningfully is under much scrutiny. The academicians of material culture, anthropology, history, and other fields are engaged in parsing the ways in which humans decode objects in order to figure out what information is intrinsic to the object itself, what requires associated knowledge gleaned from another source, and what information is embedded in cultural tradition.

In some ways, it is because of this parallel contemporary inquiry into the "vocabulary" of objects that I can inquire into the object's changing role in the definition of museums.

What are museums if they are less object-based?

Museum staff intuitively understand that museums are important – an understanding that the public shares. However, especially for the public, this understanding does not always revolve around the objects – though objects are, like props, essential to most museums' purposes, making an implicit thesis visible and tangible. The nature of the thesis can range from explanation of the past, to advocacy for a contemporary viewpoint, to indication of possible future directions – in each case through a medium that presents a story in sensory form.

Museums will remain responsible for the care of the objects they house and collect, but the notion of responsibility will be, and already has been, broadened to include shared ownership, appropriate use, and potentially removal and return.

The foundational definition of museums will, in the long run, I believe, arise not from objects, but from "place" and "storytelling in tangible sensory form," where citizenry can congregate in a spirit of cross-generational inclusivity and inquiry into the memory of our past, a forum for our present, and aspirations for our future.

45

Coming back to definitions, the current definition of museums used by the AAM Accreditation Commission encompasses all museums and no longer separates them by categories. Museums, in this definition, "present regularly scheduled programs and exhibits that use and interpret objects for the public according to accepted standards; have a formal and appropriate program of documentation, care, and use of collections and/or tangible objects" (American Association of Museums 1997).

For the visitor, it is the experience of simultaneously being in a social and often celebratory space while focusing on a multisensory experience that makes a museum effective. Virtual experiences in the privacy of one's home may be enlightening but, I think, are not part of the civilizing experience that museums provide. It is the very materiality of the building, the importance of the architecture, and the prominence that cities give to museum location that together make for the august place that museums hold. Congregant space will, I believe, remain a necessary ingredient of the museum's work.

The objects that today's museums responsibly care for, protect, and cherish will remain central to their presentations. But the definition of "objectness" will be broad and allow for every possible method of storymaking. These more broadly defined objects range from hard evidence to mere props and ephemera. I hope I have shown that objects are certainly not exclusively real nor even necessarily "tangible" (even though the AAM uses that word). For it is the story told, the message given, and the ability of social groups to experience it together that provide the essential ingredients of making a museum important.

Museums are social-service providers (not always by doing direct social-service work, though many museums do that) because they are spaces belonging to the citizenry at large, expounding on ideas that inform and stir the population to contemplate and occasionally to act.

Museums are not unique in their work. Rather they share a purpose with a host of other institutions. We need museums and their siblings because we need collective history set in congregant locations in order to remain civilized. Societies build these institutions because they authenticate the social contract. They are collective evidence that we were here.

Notes

1 This essay was previously published in 1999 by the American Academy of Arts and Sciences in *Daedalus* (Gurian 1999b).
2 "For the purposes of the accreditation program of the AAM, a museum is defined as an organized and permanent non-profit institution, essentially educational or aesthetic in purpose, with professional staff, which owns and utilizes tangible objects, cares for them, and exhibits them to the public on some regular schedule" (American Association of Museums 1973).
3 "...owns and utilizes tangible things animate and inanimate" (ibid., 9).
4 An art center "utilizes borrowed art objects, cares for them and maintains responsibility to their owners... [its] primary function is to plan and carry out exhibitions" (ibid., 12). A science and technology center "...maintains and utilizes exhibits and/or objects for the presentation and interpretation of scientific and technological knowledge.... These serve

primarily as tools for communicating what is known of the subject matter..." (ibid., 12). A planetarium's "principal function is to provide educational information on astronomy and related sciences through lectures and demonstrations" (ibid., 11).

5 Native American Grave Protection and Repatriation Act (25 U.S.C. 3002) (NAGPRA 1990).

Bibliography

American Association of Museums (1973) *Museum Accreditation: Professional Standards*, Washington, DC: American Association of Museums, 8.

American Association of Museums (1997) *A Higher Standard: The Museum Accrediation Handbook*, Washington, DC: American Association of Museums, 20.

Cuno, J. (ed.) (2004) "The Object of Art Museums," in *Whose Muse? Art Museums and the Public Trust*, Princeton, NJ, Cambridge, MA: Princeton University Press and Harvard University Art Museums.

Gurian, E.H. (1999b) "What Is the Object of This Exercise? A Meandering Exploration of the Many Meanings of Objects in Museums," in *Daedalus*, Cambridge, MA, 128:3, 163–183.

NAGPRA (1990) *Native American Graves Protection and Repatriation Act*, 101 Congress, US. Available http://www.cr.nps.gov/nagpra/SITEMAP/INDEX.htm (accessed October 6, 2005).

5

CHOOSING AMONG THE OPTIONS

An opinion about museum definitions,[1] 2002

> There is a serious crisis of institutional identity and a crisis of concept.... The truth is, we do not know any more what a museum institution is.
>
> (Sola 1992)

Introduction

Throughout my more than three decades in the museum business, people have debated the definition of museums. I have been among them, arguing that the boundaries of museums are expanding and that expansion can be seen as a positive development. Much of my writing has been about the importance of museums in the building and rebuilding of community. I steadfastly believe that museums can foster societal cohesion and civility. Taking museums' community-building role seriously is not easy and requires multifaceted and consistent commitment.

Yet even if we agree that museums have an overarching public responsibility, they are not and should not be programmatically uniform. Museums should choose among the many possible emphases and carefully define their vision so that their stated mission and direction are accurately articulated and achievable. That accomplished, staff will know what direction to go in, and the public will know from the outset what they might experience.

Here, I propose five different museum categories: object-centered, narrative, client-centered, community, and national. Each category was formed from legitimate but different directions and by different pressures, and each has contributed different areas of excellence to the museum field. But museums always borrow ideas from each other, and the result has been that through borrowing all museums are now a mixture of some or all of these types, and almost no museum is wholly one kind or another. But parsing museums into this taxonomy of archetypes offers a filter for viewing institutional intentions, allowing for future possibilities, and celebrating the gifts that each type of museum has brought.

I write partly because rhetoric most appropriate to one noble mission is sometimes grafted inelegantly and even inappropriately onto a museum with another purpose. Frankly, this can lead to a facile expression that is often unexamined and, at its worst, might be termed expedient and even cynical. I am hopeful that if we use a new taxonomy of terms – a sorting language – then maybe we can measure, respect, and celebrate each museum for what it actually is.

If museums' missions were examined with more precision, one outcome would be an acknowledgment of what we always knew – that museums are, should be, and always were, positioned along on a broad continuum.[2] To state the obvious, "no museum can do what the whole range of museums can do any more than one college can cover the whole breadth of college possibilities...." (Weil 2002).

Let us maintain our overarching commitment to public service, but let us declare the search for definitional homogenization over. Let us make it safe for museums to narrow their direction, to specialize. At the same time, let us celebrate museums that truly aim to be broad in their approach and can do so successfully. Then, collectively, let us hold each museum accountable to put its money where its oratory is.

The object-centered museum

Object-centered institutions are the "treasure-based" museums that concentrate on the material they own or borrow. The objects are the source of research and scholarship and the basis for public exhibition programs. The extant collections inform subsequent acquisitions.

Since the 1960s, object-centered museums have been under the greatest pressure to diversify their approach and have undergone the most change. Commentary had centered on these institutions' lack of responsiveness to a wider, less informed audience. Today, decades of critique and pressure have led to many forms of interpretative materials that can be understood by the novice. Object-centered museums now routinely include interpretation in many forms – glossaries, introductions, overviews, films, multimedia kiosks, and extensive labels – their exhibitions.

Lack of conceptualization was another critique of object-centered museums, which often displayed objects with no indication of the object's place in its surroundings, its uses, and its meaning. But object-centered museums are now much livelier. Many have reinstalled their collections in a more understandable format and have incorporated exhibition techniques piloted by other kinds of museums. For example, many art museums have created reading alcoves and hands-on locations, techniques that originated at children's museums.

It may be time, however, to say that some of these object-centered museums might proudly remain what they wish to be: displayers of objects for their own sake, unabashedly and without apology. Without meaning to offer a "hidey-hole" to museums too lazy to invigorate their displays, it may be time to allow stunning objects to take their place as just that. And if that is the intention of the museum, then the institution should say so, and we will all understand.[3]

The consequences of such a decision would be that some few institutions might remain the provinces of the initiated, the repositories of many treasures viewed just for their beauty or their mystery. These museums would remain "temples of the contemplative." Let us hope that the Frick and the Pitt Rivers will resist change; or when changing they will remember to let us wander down the aisles bathed in the riches of the things on view. Such object-driven museums will proclaim proudly that their focus is on installations of "stuff." That, I hope, is what the new installation of British material at the Victoria and Albert Museum is intended to signal (Ricketts 2001).

The questions that would lead experimentation at such museums include: Are there interpretive models that can help the beginner by augmenting but not interfering with contemplation? Does contemplation need to be a silent and antisocial activity, or is there a mix of furniture and activities (such as more seating, desks for writing, conversation pits) that will encourage social and joint contemplation without interfering with others? Can visitors have access to information that will allow those who wish it to learn more without visually disturbing others? And as always, in the area of scholarship, what is the interesting juxtaposition of objects that will bring new, unexpected surprise to the visitor?

Given the pressure on object-centered art museums to expand their collection base to include objects made by artists of equal quality but from different cultural aesthetics, the issue of object selection and purchase will need to be taken on within the context of the maker more forthrightly than before. Who is choosing the objects? What constitutes aesthetics from the maker's standpoint? How will the viewer understand these choices?

The narrative museum

Object-centered museums of old told "stories" primarily to the extent that their available collections might relate. The pressure to tell stories regardless of available material gave rise to narrative museums, of which the Jewish Museum Berlin and the United States Holocaust Memorial Museum are important recent examples. The narrative museum bases its primary focus on the explication of a story, recognizing that objects have important but limited use. In these museums, objects serve primarily as evidence. Narrative museums specialize in contextualization.

These institutions are interested in making the nonvisible visible and are comfortable with including emotions (pathos, humor, and dramatic tension) if they fit the story.[4]

Some narrative museums are created by cultural groups who wish to tell their story to themselves and to outsiders and find that they do not have or cannot find the necessary collections. This is especially true in museums that present information about formerly subjugated or repressed peoples.[5]

Narrative museums focus on telling a story using any interpretative means possible and have been the most willing to use all exhibition strategies (whether found in commercial, attraction, or museum settings). They have had little difficulty with including objects, reproductions, technology, and anything else, as long as it is in the service of moving the narrative along. They have been eager to embrace technology in as many forms as possible.

While social history museums are foremost among the narrative museums, narratives can also be found in natural history museums to impart the notion of geologic or biological evolution through time, whether or not they have access to the most telling physical specimens. Historic houses, open-air museums, and art museums, like the Picasso Museum, can be narrative museums when they wish to tell a visual biography. To support the story, the collecting policy of narrative museums often focuses on examples or classes of things rather than, or in addition to, unique items.

In all such cases, the storyteller has a viewpoint, and much has been written about the lack of objectivity in these presentations. While it is generally understood that no exhibition is "objective," narrative museums' curatorial bias can be seen more forthrightly and less apologetically than in any other museums.

New exhibition techniques should come in the future from narrative museums as they experiment further with non-material evidence. Sound, smell, live performance, and interpretation have all been demonstrated to enhance parts of stories, yet each of these avenues of presentation is still in its infancy.

Often, especially in large encyclopedic museums, there are some object-based galleries and some that are primarily narrative. This combination has sometimes confused the critics and the audience (Cotter 1994). If the distinctions of this essay have any use, it may be to allow directors to declare which strategy they are using so that their critics may then follow suit by utilizing the appropriate differentiated criteria.

Client-centered museum

Client-centered museums,[6] most especially children's museums and some science centers, have audience as their priority rather than content. They often have no collections at all. The museum's main focus is on ways of promoting learning among their targeted visitors (such as children and families) (Borun et al. 1995). The staffs of these institutions view themselves primarily as educators and are interested in child-rearing norms and learning theory. They continue to seek out and embed this theory in improved approaches to their programs and exhibitions.

The principal visitors to client-centered museums include novice learners of all ages. Exhibitions and programs are structured to reduce any apprehension to learning. Since these museums are focused on the audience, their concern includes the nonachiever, the nonliterate, and the handicapped.

Client-centered museums piloted many approaches that other museums have since adopted. Their great strengths are in creating hands-on environments, placing visitor services personnel on the floor, and establishing special preschool environments. These museums also piloted hands-on discovery boxes, label copy experimentation meant to turn adults into willing learners, and resource centers within exhibitions.

Client-centered museums are the biggest creators of purpose-built environments that allow participation to enhance understanding. Creators of these exhibitions borrow freely from strategies used in educational and playground toys, public attractions, and industrial design. They have been accused of being playgrounds and not museums, and as the level of activity gets more vigorous, critics have posited that no learning is going on at all. These institutions are often labeled "Disneyesque." They are noisy rather than contemplative and seem chaotic rather than predictable and orderly. Since the early 1970s, when interactive museums became accepted into the pantheon of accredited museums, it has become even harder for museum associations to create acceptable inclusive definitions of museums.

A strength of client-centered museums is "free-choice learning."[7] Rather than working with school groups as groups, they often allow individual exploration, and they are interested in enhancing socializing behavior between individuals. These museums often intentionally provide psychologically supportive environments to parents, caregivers, and their children.

Community-centered museums

Similar to client-centered museums in that they are also interested in service, community-centered museums differ in emphasis. Their primary concern, no matter what the subject matter, is the well-being of their communities rather than the interactions of each individual social unit (a family, a group of friends, a school class). "They generally arise from a community's desire for self-expression, rather than being created by or aimed at an elite group" (Tirrul-Jones 1995).

An editorial in an *ICOM News* issue devoted to community museums put it this way: "In many cases, community museums are the only way that local traditions – crafts, religious rites, language – survive" (Hogan 1995). These institutions, to underscore Pacific Island Museum Association's (PIMA's) vision of cultural nurturing,[8] often teach traditions such as drumming or native language as part of their offerings, host community events, feasts, and celebrations, and provide information and community assistance on issues, such as health education and conflict resolution.

Community museums look the least like museums and are often named cultural or community centers. They are often a mixed-use space of affiliated organizations and functions, with a blend of meeting spaces, gathering spaces and stages, offices, food service, and teaching spaces. They mix social service, day-care, performance, and community events with exhibitions. The target audience is often those who live in the neighborhood, who do not traditionally use museums, and whose group collectively is under stress or in great transition.

There have been community-centered museums in many countries and over many decades. Tribal museums of indigenous peoples often concentrate on the societal needs of their people as their primary agenda. Eco-museums are a kind of community-centered museum started to preserve, in living history fashion, the work, crafts, or information known only to the elders of the community. Controlled by the community itself, they hope to create a new economic reality by turning this knowledge into a tourist attraction. Community-centered museums often make their objects available for ceremonial use and study as a matter of course.

Because of the higher social status typically accorded to object-based museums, community-based museums have often been fragile. They tend to evolve toward more traditional institutions in order to achieve greater recognition and funding. Many times, they have failed for lack of consistent funding. The community museum movement in the United States in the late 1960s included the creation of the

Anacostia Museum by the Smithsonian Institution, with *Rats* being its most famous exhibition. Much was written about Anacostia; today it looks undifferentiated from other small museums. If community-centered museums were accorded some primacy in the museum pantheon, perhaps they would be less likely to become diffuse, discarded, or unrecognizable.

Ironically, the history of museum finance reveals the insistence of funders that object-centered and narrative-based museums become more community focused, while these same funders have often ignored those small handcrafted community centers that were already the leaders in this field. A contemporary resolve that museums function as "meeting ground," "forums," and "town square"[9] coincides with the mission of community-centered institutions. If other museum sectors intend to take on these important social roles, they would do well to study the close community relations, long-standing staff commitment, and targeted programming that community museums have practiced and that their missions entail. Building community is difficult, nuanced, and must be sustained over time. It is not for everyone.

National (and government) museums

Museums created by a nation are themselves a distinct category. Powerful actors – government officials, politicians, and pressure groups – outside the scope of the museum profession often wish to be involved in content and exhibition strategies. If you work in a national museum, you may have to begin with "national" as your primary mission. The most heated museum-related press coverage is often associated with national museums and their presentation of nationhood.

Governments, large and small, build museums to celebrate their achievements. In government-sponsored museums cultural policy comes into play. Totalitarian governments often attempt to control their public image by dictating the content of museum exhibitions and programs. But in democratic societies, museums are one of the visible arenas within which the rightness of belief is debated freely but publicly.

Exhibition designers working within government museums must consider the balance between celebratory stories and social criticism, the percentage of space given to minority and indigenous groups, and the difficulty in displaying the avant-garde. They must carefully walk the boundaries between pornography and free speech.

Governments, national and local, have also been proponents of tourism as an economic driver for financial growth. National capitals, sometimes thought of as cultural backwaters, have become must-see tourist destinations when new government museums have been built. This is true of Washington, DC; Ottawa, Canada; Wellington, New Zealand; and Canberra, Australia. Indeed, a successful array of national museums in national capitals changes the tourism pattern of a country, enhances the flow of money to the capital city, and incites jealousy from the other cities' museums. This is why government-sponsored museums have given architects opportunities to create prestigious buildings, and governments have invested large sums of public funding in new institutions.

Part of the reason that the tourist patterns change is that the citizen visitor's motivation for seeing these museums leans more to patriotic pilgrimage than ordinary museum-going. People visit who otherwise would never go to a museum in their home-towns. The iconic nature of the national museum becomes its most important aspect.

Subject matter choice

The museum categories outlined earlier are not based on subject matter. A museum can fit into any, some, or many of these emphases regardless of content.

Let me illustrate this with five art museums and note their different primary direc-tion. The Metropolitan Museum of Art in New York is mainly object based. Zoom (the German children's art museum) is client centered. The Picasso Museum in Paris is a narrative museum. The National Gallery of Canada is a national museum, and the art gallery in Soweto, South Africa is a community museum. They are all art museums. And while these definitions are inexact of necessity, a person working in each of these would make choices based on different criteria when presented with similar works of art and would, I suspect, write quite different labels for display.

The mission statement, if precise, allows staff to know what basic direction they are to take. And when the primary directions are understood, the next choices about audience, topic, and exhibition strategies can be intelligently tackled.

For museum leaders, then, the first aspect of defining mission is to decide which of these categories on a continuum of possible mixes and tendencies the museum is to be – object based, narrative, client centered, community focused, and/or national. Then, work through the possible combinations that would be most effective and compatible in meeting other specific objectives.

What do we know about audience?

Since museums are often discussed as an undifferentiated whole, the non-museum-going public may not know what they're missing. If we were more fine-grained in our self-descriptions, certain segments of the public might make different choices and start to come.

Marilyn Hood (1983) looked at people's motivations in choosing leisure-time activities. Grouping her subjects into frequent, occasional, or not-at-all users of museums, Hood found that people who visited museums only occasionally, or never, looked primarily for the following attributes when choosing to participate in an activity: "being with people, participating actively, and feeling comfortable and at ease in their surroundings." They visited museums infrequently or not at all because they believed that their primary recreation criteria would not be fulfilled by museums. However, one can think of some kinds of museums – especially highly interactive children's and science museums – where the desired criteria would have been satisfied. Clearly, differentiating museum types one from another might also change the demographics of their users and might encourage the occasional user and nonuser to choose to participate in certain museum activities.

Funding and rhetoric

A dilemma for museums lies in the fact that much of the targeted funding available in the grant-making marketplace is temporary. If a grant-funded project or program is not firmly embedded in the museum's mission as a first or second priority, it will disappear when the funding expires, exposing the lack of commitment to the activity and its audience regardless of the promotional language used previously.

In many private museums, admission fees from the general public provide the largest single source of income. The requirement to pay for entry, however, skews the composition of the audience. Demographic studies show that museum visitors tend to be middle- or upper-income and highly educated. They are trained to go to museums and can afford them. Thus attendance fees are incompatible with the target audiences of some of the museum categories described earlier and are a hindrance to all museums where the audience might be more diverse if admission was free. This result can be seen in the free national museums whose audience diversity is slightly broader than in private or civic fee-required museums. It will be interesting to see the evolution of audience demographics in the United Kingdom (both in overall numbers and demographics), where admission charges in the major museums have just been dropped.[10]

Notes

1 This essay was previously published in *Curator* (Gurian 2002).

2 Weil writes, "We have too often chosen to ignore the very rich ways in which museums differ and to focus instead on their then margin of overlap" (Weil 1990) p. xiv.

3 Gopnick (2001) wrote "Hence the growth of wall texts: They provide an experience that everyone feels comfortable with – reading a hundred words of simple explanation – as a replacement for a properly artistic one that many people find quite tough. But if visual art means anything at all, we have to imagine that its purely visual component can be eloquent all by itself, without the help of words – that long looking will unlock more of the secrets of an art museum's holdings than hours in the library."

4 Jeshajahu (Shaike) Weinberg, the founding director of both the Museum of the Diaspora and the United States Holocaust Memorial Museum, was quoted as saying he wanted to make "hot" museums.

5 The Museum of the Diaspora in Tel Aviv, Israel, opened with only reproductions and tableaus in order to tell the complete story of the Jewish Diaspora because many important objects just did not exist.

6 Michael Spock, then director of the Children's Museum, Boston, coined this phrase when speaking about the history of children's museums in the late 1960s.

7 Falk, director of the Institute for Learning Innovation, John favors this term to describe the learning behavior in most museums. The website uses the expression multiple times, that is, "Established in 1986, the Institute for Learning Innovation is a non-profit organization committed to understanding, facilitating, and communicating about free-choice learning."

8 "The Pacific Island Museum Association (PIMA) brings together museums and cultural centres in Pacific Islands to develop their capacity to identify, research, manage, interpret and nurture cultural and natural heritage" (Pacific Island Museum Association 2001).

9 The Association of Children's Museums' (ACM) vision is "to bring children and families together in a new kind of 'town square' where play inspires lifelong learning" (The Association of Children's Museums 2001).

10 It appears that while the actual numbers of visitors have substantially increased in Great Britain with the return of free admission, the demographics have not changed appreciably. "...although there has been a rise in visiting among those who might be described as being 'socially excluded', the most significant impact on visiting appears to have been among those groups who traditionally have always gone to museums and galleries" (Martin 2003).

Bibliography

The Association of Children's Museums (2001) *Strategic Framework*. Available http://www.childrensmuseums.org/strategic_framework_2001.htm (accessed January 27, 2005).

Borun, M., A. Cleghorn, and C. Garfield (1995) "Family Learning in Museums: A Bibliographic Review," in *Curator*, 39:2, 123–138.

Cotter, H. (1994) "New Museum Celebrating American Indian Voices; Museum Celebrates American Indian Art," *New York Times*, C1.

Gopnick, B. (2001) "With Explanatory Labels Papering Museum Walls, Are We Still Looking at the Pictures They Explain?," *Washington Post*, December 9, 2001, Section G, p.1.

Gurian, E.H. (2002) "Choosing among the Options: An Opinion about Museum Definitions," in *Curator*, 45:2, 75–88.

Hogan, T.E., Editor (1995) in *ICOM News*, Paris, 48:3, 1.

Hood, M. (1983) "Staying Away: Why People Choose Not to Visit Museums," in *Museum News*, 61:4, 50–57.

Martin, A. (2003) *The Impact of Free Entry to Museums*, London: MORI, 10.

Pacific Island Museum Association (2001) *Constitution (Charitable Purpose)*. Available http://edtech.mcc.edu/~mfulmer/pima/cst-intro.html (accessed March 3, 2005).

Ricketts, A. (2001) "Ingenious Panache," *Spectator*, December 7, 2001.

Sola, T. (1992) "Museum Professionals: The Endangered Species," in Boylan, P. (ed.) *Museums 2000: Politics, People, Professionals and Profits*, New York: Routledge.

Tirrul-Jones, J. (1995) "Regional Museums Serve Their Communities," in *ICOM News*, 48:3, 3.

Weil, S.E. (1990) *Rethinking the Museum and Other Meditations*, Washington, DC: Smithsonian Institution Press.

Weil, S.E. (2002) "Your Paper," personal e-mail, January 23, 2002.

6

TIMELINESS

A discussion for museums,[1] 2003

Joy Davis, Elaine Heumann Gurian, and Emlyn Koster

When I was young and casting about for ways to deal with the dark
atmosphere of the then raging Second World War and the stupefying
news of the annihilation of European Jewry that had begun to drift into
our New York apartment, I discovered, among other marvelous things,
the exquisite world of museums.... Those surroundings became for me
a kind of second home, places in which to calm the troubled heart.
> (Chaim Potok, United States Memorial
> Holocaust Museum Brochure)

Consider a world in which every museum, either as an extension of its mission or as
its raison d'être, is geared to respond to contemporary events and issues. Such a
scenario would be transformational for the image of the museum as a socially or
environmentally responsible player in mainstream society. The museum's learning
experiences would encompass timely dialogues about salient related news, thereby
causing the community to perceive the museum as a contemporary resource.
Currently, though, while some museum leaders have responded in very interesting
ways to external situations as they arise, it is rare to find a museum in which
"timeliness" has become a central tenet of its modus operandi.

Why would a museum bother to become more timely – or timely at all? When is
it appropriate? And what new skills and structures do we need to provide timely
responses? Such questions brought together a diverse group of museum and heritage
professionals, along with specialists from the world of journalism, to the University
of Victoria's Dunsmuir Lodge in British Columbia, Canada, to explore their pertinent
experiences and philosophies, trends in the field, and a more thorough understanding
of the implications of timely approaches to museum practice.[2] After three days of
discussions, the participants were united in the belief that timeliness, flexibility, and
responsiveness could be seen as tools in making these institutions more useful to
society. A premise of societal usefulness pervaded the deliberations. This essay,
written by three of the facilitators at Dunsmuir Lodge, is both a report of the sessions
and a commentary on the issues that arose.

If museums aspire to be relevant, then why do so few museum missions specifically include timeliness? The answer may lie in the evolving history of museums. The museum community has long felt that its mission was to share timeless truths and well-researched facts from a platform of seasoned experience within its core subject matter. The field has reasoned that museums were a refuge of authority and stability. For the past two decades or so, this assertion of authority has been challenged, both internally and externally. Museums have come to accept the importance of "inclusion" and "public accountability" and have become uncomfortable with the notion that they can portray anything close to "objective truth."

Recognition of museums as part of a pantheon of civic institutions that together provide a resource for the public good has been accompanied by the fledgling notion that being responsive in a timely way to important external events may add an effective new strategy for our common and collective education. Words such as "forum" and "town hall" have been added to museums' missions, but without a widespread understanding of their weighty operational implications. In order for museums to include responsiveness in their programming, they must create new systems and reinvent their internal ethos.

Although the group of discussants readily agreed that an exploration of the issue of timeliness might yield useful insights about museum and community interactions, the parsing of the meaning of timeliness and its many close cognates – relevance, flexibility, responsiveness – proved to be an elusive and imprecise process. The conclusion was that it would be valuable to explore further the concept and the subsequent structural changes that participants' museum organizations would need in order to put it in place – notwithstanding the imprecision of the definition.

The definition of timeliness in a museum context

In the absence of a commonly accepted understanding of timeliness in museum practice, discussions began with an examination of how the term "timeliness" is used in other fields. Internet searches by all participants revealed many definitions and varied motivations for timely actions. The examples from other industries tend to fall into two allied and often intertwined definitions: timeliness as a unit of measure (as in the speed of the response); and timeliness as the inclusion of contemporary (and sometimes faddish or trendy) issues:

- The fields of medicine and pharmaceuticals tend to frame timeliness as rapid and appropriate interventions of benefit to patients.
- In law, timeliness in research and action is seen to provide a winning edge in adversarial negotiations.
- Theater embraces timeliness as a means of staying on the leading edge of artistic expression by addressing current and emergent issues.
- The courier and transportation industries value timeliness in terms of speed and punctuality, for the competitive advantage these provide.

- Politics relies on timely research to understand trends and determine public positions.
- The investment industry relies on timely information as the basis for strategic decision making.
- Government and business sectors use timeliness as a measure of efficiency and performance in the delivery of products and as a basis for accountability in customer service.
- The environmental sector responds to and seeks to influence public values and attitudes in timely campaigns to further its cause.
- The education sector evaluates the quality of scholarly information on a continuum of timeliness, moving from immediacy and currency to reliability and timelessness.

While all these sectors provide interesting parallels for exploring timeliness in museums, the central role of timeliness within the broadcasting and communications sectors prompted the greatest range of useful reflection on both the radical changes experienced in this sector and their implications for museums. Just as communication technologies have dramatically expanded the media's capacity to accumulate, store, manipulate, and share information, so the desire of people for immediate access to multiple forms of information has increased, along with their capacity to seek, process, and use information for personal fulfillment.

In a world of immediate and accelerating access to information of all kinds, museums may feel pressure to keep pace in terms of the speed, relevance, and variety of information they provide. At the same time, the capacity of museums to offer thoughtful perspectives, to hold collections that convey "timeless" meaning, and to serve as venues for contemplation is increasingly valued in times of growing dissonance between real and virtual time (Franklin 1998). Similarly, an inherent tension surrounds the use of timeliness for each of the aforementioned sectors. They all wish to temper speed with accuracy, immediacy with reflection, access to a plethora of information with a need for integrating commentary, and the need for creating systems of trustworthy reliability in a time of general upheaval.

For museums, the obligation to be reflective and considerate, and the seeming imperative to react to emergent issues, were recurrent themes in the workshop. Some participants noted that many museums are so inclined to base their responses on meticulous research and analysis that they altogether miss the opportunity to be timely or relevant. Others noted that the museum's key strength is its capacity to assemble thoughtful analysis and to introduce material at appropriate times in order to "include the event, the contemplation and the finding of meaning." This form of timeliness is based on the museum's ability to make a judgment about what constitutes the appropriate topic at the appropriate time. Timeliness, in this instance, is related to the fit between the message and the "teachable moment."

In an effort to position the relative importance of this topic, the group engaged in a writing exercise that produced a variety of statements, including these: "The opportunity of a museum is to respond to current life issues." "Given the problems we face, the obligation of museums is to be responsive, relevant, and engaged with the community." "The purpose of museums is building understanding of contemporary concerns and current issues."

It was acknowledged that since every museum has unique resources, contents, and community relationships, its mission will be unique and tailor-made. Nevertheless, the group sought to define a range of characteristics that a museum would ideally entrench in its mission: service to community; a commitment to social responsibility; contribution to the common good; appreciation of the nature and value of its unique content (subject matter, objects, and so on); resources (including its building and history); effective stewardship of both cultural and natural heritage for the present and the future; and leadership in both celebrating human accomplishments and confronting difficult issues. Out of this wide-ranging list (and with considerable editing), the group distilled an overall role statement for museums that integrates the notion of timeliness within the larger potential purpose of museums in society, as follows: "A responsibility of museums is to use their unique resources in timely ways to build understanding of the challenges and opportunities we face, locally and globally."

Examples of museums behaving in a timely manner

It was generally recognized that museums can play important roles in support of their communities when disaster strikes, particularly if they have policies and an organizational culture that allow for quick and empathetic responses to human needs. The ways in which museums respond to crises tended to be a recurrent topic, particularly since the terrorist events of September 11, 2001, were still fresh in the minds of participants. A distinction was made between facilities-based and content-based responses to crisis, and it was generally agreed that the former were entirely appropriate actions for a public institution, particularly if they are coordinated with other emergency response strategies across the community. Advance planning and rapid decision making were seen as key elements in effective museum responses to emergencies. In addition to the obvious public benefits that timely emergency actions deliver, museums such as Liberty Science Center – which turned its attention to the immediate and longer-term aftermath of the World Trade Center disaster, when it found itself in full view of the falling towers – found that a deeper understanding and support of its mission and values ensued among a broadening group of stakeholders. (Liberty Science Center's experience with the aftermath of the World Trade Center attacks and the implications of such an event on the museum field are profiled in Koster (2002), and in Koster and Peterson (2002).) It was also noted that museums that find themselves in the midst of crises must attend to the needs of their staff as well as the community they serve, not just during the crisis but in the aftermath as well.

At a more passive level, making their facilities available as public gathering spaces was seen as an important role for museums. The public perceives museums as multi-generational gathering spaces – like churches and shopping malls – that allow people to seek both refuge and company as they contemplate the crisis and its implications in a safe, perhaps inspirational, setting. Extended hours and specific services to support gatherings of people in the museum space are among the institutional responses needed to make museums available for public gatherings.

A poignant example of the museum as an intentional congregant space at a time of local crisis came from Kimberly Camp, a former director of the Detroit Museum of African American History, who described making this institution's public rotunda available to the laying-in-state of Coleman Young, a former mayor of Detroit. This timely response to a community need strengthened the museum's ties to the community and extended its connections among people who had not visited the museum before. In another example, the Art Museum of Grand Forks, South Dakota, invited a local church to use its space for six months when the church had been demolished in the aftermath of flood and fire.

Museums can also act quickly to provide the public with information on breaking news. The National Air and Space Museum acted in a timely manner during and right after the Columbia Shuttle explosion of February 1, 2003, by bringing a television set on the floor and stationing an expert to interpret the information for the public in real time.

It was in this realm that participants recognized the greatest philosophical and practical difficulties for museums. The capacity of the Newseum, for example, to respond quickly to breaking news is integral to its mission and organizational structure. This innovative museum – which is part of the Freedom Forum based in Washington, DC, and dedicated to the history of current news and the process of reporting the news – is committed to providing immediate coverage (both online and within its galleries) of issues of concern to its audiences. As the events of September 11, 2001 – both nearby at the Pentagon and at the World Trade Center – unfolded around them, Newseum staff took on the dual tasks of recording news as it came in through the networks and of finding ways to present it immediately to the public.

Because of the Newseum's relationship to the Freedom Forum and Gannett Publishing, the owners of USA Today, the Newseum has precleared instant access to documentation of events as they are published. Its infrastructure has been built to be responsive.[3] By working through the night, staff were able to mount an exhibition of images and text that opened on the morning of September 12 and remained on view, with minor revisions, for several months. The staff who produced the exhibition were journalists who share a specialized background in publishing the results of one's efforts overnight. The museum-trained staff learned from this experience that exhibitions can be done overnight and subsequently joined in doing so.

Museums that seek to provide timely responses to longer-term issues and social dynamics – for example, AIDS or global warming – tend to approach this task with a higher degree of confidence, but with mixed degrees of success in sustaining such initiatives. The Quick Response Team (QRT) initiative of the Royal British Columbia Museum sought to provide a program or exhibition on a contemporary issue within a month after it was highlighted in the media. Although the series was well received by the public, QRT was eventually cancelled due to lack of curatorial resources and issue-related expertise, combined with shifting institutional priorities. A similar initiative known as the Current Science and Technology Center at the Museum of Science in Boston has been developed to help people understand contemporary science and technology through a frank examination of associated successes, drawbacks, and implications. To overcome internal staff reservations about the institution's capacity to balance this timely program with other museum programming, a separate coordinator was brought on so that ongoing priorities could continue without interference. This initiative is strongly partnered with external academic and corporate partners and has proven to be very popular with the public.

Museums that exist specifically to address major social issues – Holocaust memorial museums, human rights museums, and so on – learn to deal with new developments in a timely fashion, often because the press expects it of them. Looking for expertise, the media assumes that the United States Holocaust Memorial Museum in Washington, DC, is an authority on all atrocities. To respond to external requests, this institution has set up systems to anticipate and accommodate the challenges inherent in dealing with difficult, but seemingly related, topics. When all parties are pre-conditioned in this way, the challenges encountered in timely responses seem to be less pronounced. Indeed, for such museums, responsiveness is likely to be a key element of success.

Some museums that are less mission-focused on breaking news are challenging themselves to find an appropriate balance between covering an event as news in an immediate and timely way and providing a reflective context that allows for thoughtful perspectives. Individual museums have successfully employed strategies to be responsive through the process of identifying the range of timely content and social roles they can undertake. The group recognized that the concept of timeliness in museums varies significantly and noted many examples tried by individual museums:

- Framing an issue by providing background information needed to understand immediate concerns – such as fundamental scientific information necessary to understand such things as global warming, cloning, and genetically altered food.
- Appropriately timed program series that build understanding on a particular topic.
- Creating forums for balanced presentations of contested information.
- Collecting objects and information contemporaneously with current events.
- Reorientation of collecting to focus on materials currently deemed relevant but previously overlooked.
- Measuring performance in terms of a quantification of achievement within a given period.
- Programming that matches time-related cycles – seasons, holidays, and community anniversaries.
- Rapid response to a breaking issue or event.
- Providing space for group activity related to external organizations or events that have previously been seen as outside the museum's mission and content – such as team victories, funerals and memorials, and blood drives.

- Offering counseling support in the presence of a related exhibition on a difficult subject.
- Building separate spaces or allowing existing gallery spaces to be used for reflection and contemplation in the light of societal trauma.
- Altering open hours and fees in order to make museums more available during disturbed times.

The internal ingredients necessary to be timely

Margaret Engel, director of the Newseum, emphasized the role that organizational systems, including mission and values, play in creating both a framework for purposeful action and organizational culture that is positioned for rapid response. She also emphasized the importance of having prearranged information sources and templates in place, along with exhibition and programming facilities to enable staff to inject content efficiently. Others noted the value of the journalistic mindset in setting institutional and individual expectations for gathering, interpreting, and sharing information on contemporary issues. Leadership that is committed to relevant and responsive programming, streamlined decision-making processes, capacity for independent staff action, flexibility in resource allocation, and a clear understanding of the nature and implications of the museum's commitment to timely responses were also identified as critical success factors. In order to create swift response, the following factors need to be in place:

- A fast and clear internal decision-making process.
- Both the policy and courage to confront complex or controversial issues, including, specifically, governance that has comfortably and clearly delegated immediate decision making to the executive level.
- Staff who are deployed or trained to implement exhibitions and programs quickly.
- Internal systems that are designed and formatted to rapidly gather, process, present, and interpret related information.
- An acceptance that works in progress can be publicly viewed and altered rather than fully rationalized prior to opening.
- Prearranged collaborations with external organizations whose information base is deep and who are also organized and committed to be timely.
- A public relations department with an ongoing cordial relationship with the media.

Perhaps the most significant dilemma that confronts museums seeking to be timely is the capacity and willingness of staff to sustain such a commitment. While many staff embrace the notion that museums must be relevant, and therefore timely, their professional education and training, skill sets, disciplinary specialization, commitment to thorough, well-researched exhibitions and programs, and lengthy work processes all mitigate against rapid responses to emergent concerns. In some situations where rapid response is within the museum's mission, a rapid response team has been constituted whose responsibility and work ethic remain quite distinct from those of the rest of the staff. Clearly, it takes time to assuredly develop the right culture and capability to address the challenge of timeliness in a museum.

The community's role in enabling the museum to be timely

Vital to the success of many timely initiatives is the sustained engagement of communities, both specialized and general, as partners with the institution and its programming. Such involvement has multiple benefits. It ensures that programming is meaningful to the museum's constituents; builds a broad base of public support; draws in more diverse audiences; and directly contributes to the good of the community. Just as many see community-based programming as inherently relevant, it was recognized that relevant programs are inherently timely and responsive to community needs.

Since different kinds of institutions have varied capacity for timely programming, and their communities have varied expectations about the nature, quality, and format of information they like to receive, a broad-ranging discussion ensued on the ways in which the institutional mission sets a context for timely action. Many missions tend to specify functional activities as they relate to particular topics and audiences, rather than a clear social purpose that connects directly with contemporary and future concerns. Such statements of mission fail to create frameworks that enable timely response to contemporary issues.

It seemed clear to the group that in order to be timely and responsive there needs to be a fair amount of shared authority among interested parties within the museum. The more authoritarian the internal structure of the museum, the less flexible it seemed to be. Furthermore, museum staff who are interested in the choice of relevant and timely topics need to ask: "Relevant to whom?" For some participants, this very question of timeliness and relevance had to do with shared authority among partners, creating a standing relationship with members of the community, and breaking the traditional relationship between staff as authority and visitors as recipients.

Programming that supports a selection of exhibited contemporary issues can be challenging for museums as they seek to provide diverse, balanced, often multidisciplinary perspectives on complex issues, offer accurate information on evolving topics, involve appropriate external voices, deal with the controversy associated with difficult topics, and explore the current and future implications of the issue, all while ensuring that the exhibition or programming is accessible, palatable, and engaging for varied audiences. Timely museums may find themselves dealing with disaffected external stakeholders who feel empowered to utter public criticism, accusing the museum of taking sides and relinquishing its neutral position, often unfairly. But as Dawn Casey, director of the National Museum of Australia, said, "I don't enjoy being attacked, but it's a whole lot better than being irrelevant" (Casey 2001).

There is, in fact, a surprisingly large amount of timely, responsive programming going on in museums around the world. Such programs often seem remarkable as they are grafted on museums whose core work is defined quite differently. There are also many instances when the public has superimposed timely uses that the staff finds surprising and unexpected.

Final thoughts

The conversation held at Dunsmuir Lodge was an attempt to understand timeliness more fully and then describe the ingredients necessary for intentionally integrating relevant activities into museums in the future. The group was persuaded that timeliness was an important and increasingly useful element in the pantheon of museum possibilities. In the end, however, we recognized that it will be museum staff and their leadership who will have to think that timeliness is valuable to their institution and their community in order to become more flexible and adaptable as they respond to contemporary issues.

Afterword

After the three-day conversation had ended, the three co-facilitators – Joy Davis, Director of the Cultural Resource Management Program at the University of Victoria; Emlyn Koster, President and CEO of the Liberty Science Center; and I – decided that the topic was worthy of future discussion within the museum field. As a way of implementing that further conversation, we wrote this article as a "Forum" piece for the journal *Curator*. I am grateful to my colleagues, Joy and Emlyn, for agreeing to allow me to include it in this compendium of my work. The article is certainly the work of all authors and furthermore a report on a conversation to which all participants contributed.

It was our collective hope that further examples of institutional and individual timely use of museums would result from such a publication. But we were more interested in the discussion that we hoped would follow around the following question: Are museums to be reflective of past thinking only, or are they civil organizations that have, as part of their missions, the promotion of contemporaneous discussion on matters of importance and urgency. Further, do they wish to proactively offer their museums as locations that "calm a troubled heart" (Potok) in a troubled time?

Notes

1 This essay was written with Joy Davis and Emlyn Koster and previously published in *Curator* (Davis *et al.* 2003).
2 The three-day conversation on the subject of timeliness in museums took place April 3–5, 2003, at Dunsmuir Lodge, near Victoria, British Columbia, and was jointly sponsored by the Cultural Resource Management Program of the University of Victoria (www.uvcs.uvic.ca/crmp) and the Museum Group, an association of senior museum consultants (www.museumgroup.org).
3 Longer-term responses to this crisis included collecting objects related to reporting the news of September 11, 2001, development of more reflective interpretations of the news, and publication of a book on the journalistic response to this terrorist attack.

Bibliography

Casey, D. (2001) "Museums as Agents for Social and Political Change," in *Curator*, 44:3, 230–236.

Davis, J., Gurian, E.H., and Koster, E. (2003) "Timeliness: A Discussion for Museums," in *Curator*, 46:4, 353–361.

Franklin, U. (1998) "Le Bistro Des Idées," in *Muse*, 15:4, 9.

Koster, E. (2002) "A Disaster Revisited," in *Muse*, 20:5.

Koster, E. and Peterson, J. (2002) "Difficult Experiences: A Museum Forum on the Lessons of September 11," in *ASTC Dimensions*, Washington, DC, May/June.

Potok, C. (2005) United States Holocaust Memorial Museum. Available http://www.facinghistorycampus.org/Campus/Memorials.nsf/0/DE9B4E8C4798B95385256ECF0070413E?OpenDocument (accessed January 18, 2005).

Part II

A SAFER PLACE
Museums in a civil society

The argument has been made that museums should be treasure houses, elaborate storage facilities, and temples of the contemplative. Less has been written about museums as lively, funny, noisy, inclusionary places that offer human interactions, civic discourse, and social service in addition to their more expected exhibitions and programs. The writing in this section advocates for expanding the list of legitimate activities – extending beyond the old core activities of preserving, protecting, studying, and educating about objects. Museums, I argue, are important civic spaces and should gladly accept this often unacknowledged responsibility.

7

THE MUSEUM AS A SOCIALLY
RESPONSIBLE INSTITUTION,[1] 1988

> There is a tradition in European museums, once strong and now
> growing strong again, that museums should be agents of social and
> political change.
>
> (David Anderson 2000)

When I asked a friend to comment on the title of this paper, her immediate flip response was, "Of course, they are social. Museums hold cocktails, teas, and dances." The answer, while funny, is also worth reflecting upon. She's right, of course. They do have cocktails, teas, and dances. But for whom?

It is clear that no museum has ever been "value neutral." Museums are, and always have been, products of people's work, collectively and individually. Those people have always been influenced by their class, ethnicity, religion, sex, time period, and region. Their imaginations and limitations have determined the shape of the institutions we call museums.

In academia, a revolution is taking place. The fields of history, art history, and anthropology, among others, are reexamining their foundations. The historic search for objective reporting about objective truth is no longer dominant. Academics now acknowledge that objective reporting never existed, only reporters who attempted to remain impartial. Complete impartiality was never an achievable or realistic goal. Today academic researchers are trying to acknowledge their own social context and then consciously report from within it.[2]

It used to be fashionable to think of museums as having an objective point of view, presenting to the world perceived knowledge (as it truly was) to the visitors for their edification. It is now fashionable to think of all presentations as representations, or the display of a certain point of view (which is either intentional or unintentional). I am sure we can all agree that no exhibition is the unvarnished truth, because we now admit that someone has varnished everything. Yet the argument goes on – justifiably – about a both/and position in which some information belongs to "an accepted knowledge base."[3]

The question implied in the statement, "Are museums socially responsible institutions?" is not, however, about the reality of knowledge. Rather, it is more fundamentally "Are museums forces for good?" The reflexive answer is "Of course!" Can we bear to ask the question in reverse: "Can museums be socially irresponsible institutions and, by extension, forces for evil?" The answer is, "It depends – on who you are and how you define responsibility."

Amplification is in order. It is clear that some museums and collections have been used consciously for coercion, for self-aggrandizement of the ruler in power or the victor in conquest, and for attempts at mind control. The museums Hitler set up and the ones he intended to set up are a straightforward example.

> Between 1933 and 1945, the Nazis confiscated the holdings of many governments and individuals that they had subjugated. Hitler and his top advisors admired traditional European art and planned a new museum in Linz, Austria, that would display the finest examples from confiscated collections. Because they considered it damaging to German ideals, the Nazis despised modern art. They labeled Impressionist and Expressionist works "degenerate" and confiscated them from national museums, publicly burning some of these works but exchanging most of them with dealer-collaborators for desirable examples of Old Master painting.
>
> (Seattle Art Museum)

The issue of museums as forces for evil is easy to understand by invoking extreme examples, but in the age of relative moral values, it is much more difficult to detect when museums cross the boundary into authoritarian imposition. When have they falsified the truth to present propaganda? When have they allowed the donor or the government to prevail over others in the citizenry? The grey area is broad. Each one of us must use our own internal moral values when working out the roles our organizations should play. Some institutional positions are the amalgam of the collective; many are not. There are struggles for control both within the institution and within the surrounding society. Moral certainty has a tendency to creep in. Rationalization of one's position is an all-too-human tendency. Attempting to build a socially responsible institution is a difficult task and one that needs constant tending.

It might be helpful if museums had a checklist that they could use collectively to ascribe a social responsibility score for their institution. There seems to be a plethora of self-study material on this subject designed for all manner of institutions, most especially universities. The museum self-study instruments that have been assembled[4] are helpful but not perfect. They do allow for a kind of introspection that may be useful for judging the internal climate of particular museums. The motivation to embark on such a self-study is usually for the sake of tangible gain – accreditation, access to grants, winning of recognition. This tends to make formal self-study episodic at best. The need for internal moral assessment is, on the other hand, constant.

The questions that need to be raised are usually not quantifiable but rather impressionistic, and the multiplicity of acceptable answers is nearly endless and certainly variable. While there may be reasons to test for a social responsibility score,

I would suggest that most museums smugly think they have already taken the test and passed it with flying colors.

Museums are institutions set up for the transmission and preservation of things we collectively hold dear. That purpose is a good one, so why is there any debate about social responsibility and how it applies to museums? The concerns might begin to reveal themselves when we ask targeted questions. Here is a selection of questions that might appear on such an internalized self-study checklist.

Given that museums:

- House, research, and preserve artifacts deemed worthy.
- Display these objects and presumably educate the public about topics thought to be important.
- Provide ancillary materials that visitors would otherwise not have access to, such as performances, books, films, and lectures.
- Provide a physical place to socialize with others, have a snack or a meal, and keep warm or cool in inclement weather.

Then, in the area of collections:

- What artifacts do we choose to keep?
- What objects do we consider acquiring? Who decides?
- Who were the collectors and what do we know about them? What were their motivations and internalized priorities when they acquired them?
- Who thinks they really own the material? What is their view on how it is interpreted?
- Do these people want the collections returned? If so, who decides?

In the area of exhibitions:

- How do we choose exhibition topics?
- What exhibition strategies do we use?
- Are the topics intended to be overt propaganda, covert propaganda, or a personal point of view?
- Does the exhibition style(s) match the needs of a whole range of learners?
- Do we use other sensory, nonliterate modalities?
- Are the exhibition creators made known to the public?
- Do they include advisors who have divergent points of view?
- What role have the funders played?
- Who decides? Who determines the proper answers to these questions?

In the area of institutional philosophy:

- What does the mission statement say?
- Is there a value statement, and what does it say?

- Do we make the public feel welcome?
- Do we have tolerance for public behaviors that are outside the upper-class norm?
- Who decides?

In the area of public programs:

- What audiences are these programs geared to?
- Where are the programs publicized?
- Does the staff reflect the diversity of the audience?
- Does the staff reflect the diversity of the local surroundings?
- Is there a range of public offerings that match a range of interests?
- Who decides?

In the area of research:

- What are the research topics? How are they determined?
- What is the target research audience?
- Does the research staff participate in public education?
- Who decides?

About the physical building:

- Do we welcome people just to be with each other in a museum setting? Should we?
- Do we have amenities that invite socialization?
- Is it easy to enter and find one's way around?
- Does the place feel like a cathedral or a clubhouse?
- Is the building located in a neutral or non-neutral environment?
- Who decides?

In administration:

- What is the management structure and style?
- How are staff recruited, advanced, and disciplined?
- What is the composition of the board?
- What are the financial stability of the organization and its sources of income?
- What are the price points for admission? For articles in the shop?
- What are the open hours?
- Who are the target audiences?
- What is the charge for use of the building after hours?
- Who decides?

Always, "who decides?" Who are the people making choices within each section of the institution? Do they have similar or different backgrounds? Do they represent multiple points of view? Are they in touch with the broadest range of our society? What is their philosophy about museums?

Historically, museums have been staffed and visited by white, well-educated folk. The staff, the audience, and the donors were mirror images of each other. They were mostly not very self-conscious, but instead appeared self-confident, even self-congratulatory. They believed that they knew what their audience wanted and/or what was good for them. It was fashionable to be certain and to some extent patronizing.

But it is no longer. It is now fashionable to be self-conscious. It is also fashionable to want to serve a broader audience and to do so in ways that are not paternalistic. But museum workers are not sure how to accomplish this just yet.

We should be afraid of fashion, since it is certain to change. What we are talking about today may seem self-evident to us, but remember that caution and skepticism are always prudent.

The question should read, "Should museums be socially responsible institutions?" And the answer should be, "yes." If the question is, "Are museums currently socially responsible institutions?" Then the answers range from "yes," to "sometimes," to "not yet," to "not always."

Afterword

The original essay was written in 1988, at a time when the issue of social responsibility was much in the air. Rereading it in 2005, I find it hopeful and certainly still useful. Reflecting on the questions listed will still enable those who have not yet questioned the internal workings of the organizations they eagerly serve to become more self-conscious.

The issues of social and political responsibility still occupy many. For example, David Anderson of the Victoria and Albert Museum wrote in 1994:

> Cultures, not objects, are our real concern. It is the cultural space around and between objects that gives them their meaning and makes it impossible for museums to avoid a social and political role. To ignore or deny this role, despite all the difficult problems its entails for us, would be to evade a fundamental public responsibility.
>
> (Anderson 2000)

In 1988, when the original piece was written, the Smithsonian Institution was headed by Robert McCormick Adams, who I served as the deputy assistant secretary for museums. Adams, a noted archeologist, was devoted to diversity and multiculturalism. He instituted new hiring practices to broaden the applicant pool, encouraged diversity, and was happy with exhibitions that were thoughtful but contentious. He had a hand in hiring me in 1987 because of the work I had done and the philosophic positions I held. He set about to change the Smithsonian and succeeded somewhat overall, but perhaps in depth only in some small ways.

Change is difficult and, I have learned, not necessarily permanent. The Smithsonian today is concerned with other matters; diversity is a minor melody, and contentious exhibitions are certainly not high on its list. In museums, people in the United States and elsewhere still speak of social responsibility but I think the responsibility they mean is different than when the term was used in 1988. Museums have new buzz words, one of them *community*, another *forum*, and still another *meeting place*. They are used imprecisely but fervently. They have replaced *social responsibility*. Some would argue, perhaps rightly, that they mean the same thing.

When you enter the term "social responsibility" into an Internet search engine, you get a list of responses: physicians for social responsibility, educators, computer professionals, behaviorists, and the list goes on. Each organization is made up of a segment of some profession that wants its particular sector to become more attuned to inclusion and to take on positions that they see as morally imperative. Some of their colleagues see these same positions as controversial, unworkable, too costly, or naive. A few of these organizations began in the 1960s and perhaps served as models for the more recent ones. A perusal of their charters indicates that they each have their own take on the meaning of the phrase "social responsibility." But all of them want to work for a better, fairer world as they see it.

The newest and potentially most influential organizations at work in this arena, at least from my point of view, are large-scale, highly successful, commercial enterprises that emphasize social responsibility as part of the way of doing business. Former polluters now highlight their nonpolluting commitment, for example. Multinational companies support the differences in the cultures they find themselves in. Collectively, these businesses assert that good citizenship is good for business. I feel encouraged by that.

I would contend that museums continue to wish to be responsible. They wish to be supportive and inclusive. They wish to be helpful to society. Each museum has a take on what that means. There is no uniformity now, but to be fair there was none in 1988 either. What feels different to me is that there appears to be no urgency now. Museums' commitment is often expressed in an "of course" mode or even as cliché statements, but the serious implementation activity seems thinner than when I wrote this piece.

I remain committed to the difficult work of social responsibility, whatever I mean by it. In the world of continued relativity, personal meaning remains our only consistent guidepost for the directions we are to take. A new generation will have to renew the fervor.

Notes

1 The initial text of this talk was presented as the keynote speech at the "Museums as Socially Responsible Institutions" conference, held at George Washington University, Washington, DC, in October 1988.

2 This is how this particular change is explained by Simon During in his introduction to *The Cultural Studies Reader*:

> To introduce the forms of analysis developed by the discipline [cultural studies] we can point to two features that characterized it when it first appeared in Great Britain in the 1950s. It concentrated on 'subjectivity' which means that it studied culture in

relation to individual lives, breaking with the social scientific positivism or 'objectivism.' The book that is often said to inaugurate the subject, Richard Hoggart's *The Uses of Literacy* (1957) is a very personal work....The second distinguishing characteristic of early cultural studies was that it was an engaged form of analysis.

(During 1993, Hoggart 1957)

3 This is a long-standing argument between acceptors of existing independent factual information and the personal construction of all knowledge. The phrase "accepted knowledge base" can be found in the following:

> Some constructivists...believe that there is no such thing as an objective reality. Rather they claim that knowledge exists exclusively in the mind of the learner....Many constructivists, myself included, believe instead that there is an objective reality by which we may judge many things. As a science educator, I feel it is important for students to construct valid scientific knowledge about the world around them....In many areas there is a currently accepted knowledge base that learners need to understand to function in and contribute to our world.
>
> (Jeffrey 2000)

4 For example the Museum Assessment Program is a grant program funded by the Institute of Museum and Library Services and administered by the American Association of Museums (AAM). It is a two-part program of self-assessment and the provision of experienced museum official on site visit. AAM also has an accreditation program in which the first part is a large self-assessment document. Each of these has community and public service sections. MEP (the Museum Excellence Program) was created by Museums Alberta in Canada. It starts with self-assessment tools and can lead to recognition of exemplary achievement. It includes a social responsibility section.

Bibliography

Anderson, D. (2000) "Museum Education in Europe," in Hirsch, J.S. and Silverman, L.H. (eds) *Transforming Practice: Selections from the Journal of Museum Education, 1992–1999*, Washington, DC: Museum Education Roundtable.

During, S. (1993) "Introduction," in During, S. (ed.) *The Cultural Studies Reader*, London: Routledge.

Hoggart, R. (1957) *The Uses of Literacy*, Harmondsworth: Penguin.

Jeffrey, K.R. (2000) "Constructivism in Museums: How Museums Create Meaningful Learning Environments," in Hirsch, J.S. and Silverman, L.H. (eds) *Transforming Practice: Selections from the Journal of Museum Education, 1992–1999*, Washington, DC: Museum Education Roundtable.

Seattle Art Museum, *Holocaust Provenance, Research on World War II History of Ownership*, Seattle, WA: Seattle Art Museum. Available http://www.seattleartmuseum.org/Collection/holocaustProvenance.asp (accessed February 3, 2005).

8

TURNING THE OCEAN LINER
SLOWLY

About the process of change in larger
institutions, 1990[1]

These are interesting times. Everything is in a state of flux. Museums, those venerable institutions, are changing their missions and their way of doing things. Large and entrenched institutions, such as the Smithsonian, are like ocean liners: turning the ocean liner (even slowly) is a ponderous and an uncomfortable affair.

In Canada, the Royal Ontario Museum has been engaged in just such a turning. And in the United States, the Field Museum and the American Museum of Natural History are currently engaged in reorganizations that will profoundly affect their ways of doing business. Each has established a leadership position in the public program arena that is equal to research, and each is engaged in integrating education and exhibitions. While seemingly innocuous, these changes represent a profound new commitment to the public side of the house.

I have just returned from a two-day meeting of an education task group for the American Museum of Natural History. Michael Spock, the vice president for public programs of the Field Museum, was part of that group. I worked with Michael Spock for 16 years at the Boston Children's Museum, before both of us went off – in all innocence and arrogance – to enter the mainstream museum community. Both of us were invited to institutions by bosses eager to promote change. Our work seemed to them to provide a promising complement to their own aspirations. We thought we were ready for the big time.

I am now the deputy assistant secretary for museums at the Smithsonian. I work with Tom Freudenheim, the assistant secretary for museums. His portfolio contains oversight responsibility for the 14 Smithsonian museums and 6 major museum-related offices, and he advises the secretary on institutional directions as related to museum issues. We have a mission; simply put, we believe that museums should be accessible to absolutely everyone and by every possible means.

Needless to say, oversight in a collegial and academic institution such as the Smithsonian is difficult at best. The museum directors do not like it and think they do not need it; they certainly are competent and professional, and used to running their own show. The tension between the directors and the central administration is palpable. They believe we are good only for getting and giving them money, and we don't do that enough.

But on the issue of setting courses, both those who agree with the changes we seek and those who disagree profoundly see us as pains in the neck.

Let me discuss background for a moment. What are the external pressures that are producing changes in the museum field? Change by itself is so uncomfortable that institutions do not do it voluntarily or for noble reasons alone. They change because they fear the consequences of not doing so, and only then are willing to override the cries of anguish from the discomforted.

I think the pressures are as follows:

- Demographics are changing. People of color are forming coalitions that are politically persuasive. Even where the attempts at power have not been entirely or ultimately successful, the specter of the Rainbow Coalition,[2] for example, induces federal legislators and others to become more assertive about civil rights.

- The middle class is becoming multicolored. Even if the number of people of color in good, well-paying jobs is nowhere near their numbers in the general population, those who are in positions of power are no longer willing to behave as if they are simply a part of the majority culture. They are assertive, saddened by their previous treatment, and clear about the changes that should take place. Most of all, they are politically savvy and know how to place pressure on central institutions.

- The academic world has discovered context and the role of the interpreter. There is no longer a belief that the object will tell its own story or that there are neutral and objective truths. In art history, in anthropology, in political and social history, it is fashionable to discuss the donor, the observer, and the museum practitioner as purveyors of biased information and narrowly influenced by their own time and class. As museum professionals, we recognize ourselves to be the captives of our own time and place and become sensitive to the affect of our actions, lest they offend people different from ourselves. Thus, we are left with uncertainty and complexity.

- As a nation, Americans seem no longer committed to the notion of a melting pot. If we were, each of us would willingly take on a new homogenized national identity, speak a single national language, and believe in a single value system, keeping our traditions around only enough to eat with cultural variety. Now we believe in multiculturalism – the conviction that each culture is equally worthy, should remain identifiable while evolving over time, and share in the power and representation of governance.

- Museums, like the governments they are often a part of, are surrounded by massive change. Collectively, we seem unable accurately to see the road in front of us. I don't know about you, but I am totally discommoded by the happenings in Germany, Eastern Europe, and the former Soviet Union. New countries have replaced old ones without a cataclysmic trace. How did that happen? If change was so inevitable and imminent, why didn't we see it coming?

- In the United States, part of our funding is related to the stock market which has a volatility that causes unease, yet we seem to go on without calamity. Are we financially safe or near economic disaster? The former signs of a comforting stability seem to be missing.
- In turbulent times, we worry about the security for our own children. We know from child development class that chaos is emotionally disruptive. Lack of familial security leads children to become socially dysfunctional. When raising children, parents must set limits (with love, conviction, and predictability) if children are to function successfully. How can we do that in a world in which we are given so few models of predictability and precious little in the way of global human kindness?

Although it may seem otherwise, my purpose is not to talk about worldwide uncertainty. It is simply to acknowledge how pervasively uncertainty affects the context in which we work. Each one of us is engaged in changing museums. If our current collective view is that there is no *one* truth and that our immediate future is uncertain, then how then can we chart a course? Only with tentative certainties and simultaneous misgivings.

And what changes are we talking about?

Natural history museums are currently the most fascinating to watch. Founded to help us understand exotic plants, animals, and people, and during a time when societies believed in "pure" cultures, this kind of museum, as a side effect, made the host country feel superior. A while ago we believed "God's" endless riches were there for the plucking, hunting, and stuffing (that's how we made dioramas), and for colonizing and collecting. Now, with cultural and biological diversity the profound issues of our day, natural history museums have in their collections the very materials most pertinent for public education.

For the peoples among us who we sometimes refer to as native or minorities (both terms probably under question), natural history museums hold material that is important to an understanding of their own history. How will we tell a contemporary ecologic or cultural story with materials that were collected for another purpose?

One of the ways to adapt to the world's new circumstance is to change profoundly the way we think about museums' relationship to the public. We must begin to think that one of the tenets of our central mission is that we are at the service of our publics. We are no longer places with a primary focus only on the object. The audiences are partners on a mutual quest to learn, not passive students to be preached to by their teacher/scholars. We must put systems into place that allow for advocacy on behalf of our audience. We must change our management and exhibition production systems so that the product, the exhibition, will become intelligible to novices and allow them to better understand issues that are germane to their lives. We are no longer preachers to the great unwashed; we are united as partners with our publics and their families. We must help our audience, which touchingly believes and trusts us, to become more skeptical and demanding.

To reflect our commitment to multiculturalism in our museums, we must (and have begun to) diversify our boards and staffs, share leadership with representatives of many communities, broaden our collections to include the ordinary objects that represent the history of the poor and disenfranchised, adopt explicit points of view within our exhibits, give up anonymity in exhibition production and reveal identifiable authorship, welcome behaviors and interests in our galleries that do not match our former assumptions about appropriateness, and think about our holdings not as a sacred preserve but as objects, some of whose very ownership may be rightfully in question.

The very preservation of some objects may be anathema to the original producers. We may be the generation that disbands parts of our collections and rewrites the rules of collecting, the very reason for which our museums were founded. And we now must change our staff compositions to reflect the many perspectives of our communities. How can we do all of that? We must, quite simply, do everything and all at once.

Each of the proposed solutions is complex. It involves:

- Retraining ourselves to be culturally sensitive, supportive of others, and more self-critical.
- Training gifted, undereducated, often minority, staff for new positions, and paying for their delayed education.
- Recruiting widely in places where we are uncomfortable. In some cases, this means selecting a promising but inexperienced person of color over more seasoned applicants.
- Promoting museum service as a viable career to those who have never considered it.
- Mentoring and setting up staff support that lasts for a long time.
- Changing the ways we are perceived by diverse communities who do not now use us but could.
- Including various perspectives within our exhibitions so that casual visitors will see that views like their own are potentially included.
- Having diverse and knowledgeable people in positions of authority and visible to the public.

Each of these changes is costly, disruptive of old patterns, and diverts resources from long-established work. Everywhere people will say no, engage in sabotage, and suggest cogent and often precise reasons why change cannot occur. Our attempts will be imperfect, sometimes inequitable, unevenly adhered to, often resisted. We wish it were logical, straightforward, and easy.

Change is a tall order. The Smithsonian – along with other institutions – is engaged in this multicoursed pattern of change. How does it feel? Uncomfortable!

Americans have been trained to hope for the quick fix. This is the sound-bite solution. We have not been prepared for multifaceted, nuanced issues. Americans believe that progress is continuous and inexorable. We are not collectively ready for slow, complex, even messy change that is capable of reversal. We wish that what is self-evident to us would be so for our neighbor, too.

Change never moves fast enough for the aggrieved, who see it as grudging or done in bad faith. In a bureaucracy, it is easier to stop action than to start it. The sentimentalist yearning for the past and the idealist pursuing the future are equally condemned. Expediency carries the day and is often at war with principle. One always wishes that it is not only behavior that is changed but hearts and minds as well. One has to get used to "victory" by coercion (all this while knowing quite clearly that there is no universal truth).

And as for me – the person who came from the isolated, hippie, uniformly politically correct Boston Children's Museum where I lived on the right wing of a far-left organization – this three-year journey has been fascinating but searing. I have had to remember that I used to be liked. I used to believe that all decisions were made on the basis of some previously held moral principle, and I have since discovered that there is no uniformly accessible person or system to believe in. My feelings are easily injured, and I did not (and still don't) understand the phrase, "Don't take this personally." My arrogance born of moral certainty is gone.

I am, however, left with the belief that chaos is not good for us individually or collectively. To reassure others, I put on a face of certainty even as my inside voice is saying, "Are you kidding?" I have learned to consult my innards for direction. If it feels right, it must be useful. If it feels wrong, I should avoid it if I can. I look for opportunities to compromise, but they are difficult to find – almost right and almost wrong are so close together. I still find that passion is essential to my work, but I have discovered that others' passions do not match mine. In fact, they are often passionately opposed. This, in turn, reminds me that the world is complex and that there is more than one honorable position to be held on every subject.

I think we are on a profound adventure. I am committed to doing it all. My work is more scattered than before because I cannot easily pick my targets. I want it all to end right and be done right now. The way down the road is certainly not clear to me anymore. I hope the few next steps are.

Afterword (as seen in 2005)

Fifteen years later, I am struck by the passion of the piece, at how much I predicted accurately and how much I didn't. The most striking thing I did not anticipate was losing. It did not occur to me then that the world might veer to the right, that civil liberties might be eroded even while the comforting rhetoric remained. That a new enemy (terrorists) would be named even as the old ones (former communists) were becoming our friends. I did not predict that the pressure to change museums would waver and die down, even though the conversation would continue. I did not predict that the changes that were made would be fundamentally small except in a few places. And I certainly did not predict that change could be eroded and stepped back from. I should have anticipated the possibility of failure.

I had gone to college during the cautious 1950s and seen my politically active left-leaning professors excoriate our apathy. I had seen my middle-class seeking generation evolve into hippie social activists. Yet even though I had lived through the cyclic cultural policy of Nixon to Carter to Reagan and Bush to Clinton, I did not understand the worldwide implications.

These implications are to be seen in this piece if one looks for them. Change is slow and always resisted. The Smithsonian 15 years later is the same resistant place it was in the 1990s, with a huge visible exception: the National Museum of the American Indian (NMAI) is completed, open, and has mostly held on to its ideals. It has successfully ridden the wave of the progress made at its founding. The National Museum of African American History and Culture looks like it will be created within the Smithsonian after 20 years of gestation. It might, however, only inch along, with many trying to push and pull it around. Given the current climate, it could become a traditional museum when it is finished. It will take an extraordinary director with fearlessness and vision to create something otherwise. The newly appointed Lonnie Bunch might just be that director.

In the meantime, Te Papa (the National Museum of New Zealand) and the National Museum of Australia (NMA) have opened to huge success. Each represented new triumphs of inclusion and welcome only to be prodded by new, more right-leaning governments to change directors and alter course to become more predictably conservative. The major British museums have instituted admission fees and then taken them off again so that the old, numerically larger audience could return – but without an appreciable change in social demographics.

The museums in question are still the wonderful places I always loved. They are highly visited but not highly altered. Everybody involved must be doing something right because these institutions have survived and been well used. But I am tired. Tired that the effort to make them more egalitarian, more inclusive, and more representative remains episodic and sporadic. While there are some overarching trends that we can celebrate since the original piece was written – most museums are more visitor focused than in the past, many more museums think cautiously about the cultural material they hold, and there continues to be a small number of experimental museums taking risks – most institutions remain fundamentally unchanged. Perhaps I must look to my younger colleagues with fire in their bellies and a mixture of naiveté and idealism to take up the cause. I am ever hopeful that they will succeed, and I am ready to support them wholeheartedly.

Notes

1 The initial text of this talk was presented under the title "How change proceeds within a very large and complex organization, as seen in 1990" at the Canadian Museums Association annual meeting in Toronto, Canada, on March 12, 1990. Subsequently the title was reflected upon and changed to the present one.
2 A political action group formed in the United States by Jesse Jackson in 1984 to include members of different minority groups.

9

THE OPPORTUNITY FOR SOCIAL SERVICE,[1] 1991

When I was approached to give a speech on programs for special audiences –
adolescents, preschoolers, families, elderly, handicapped, and others – I telephoned
a range of colleagues to find out if anyone was creating new programs in the
United States. By "new" I did not mean inventive for the particular museum, but
innovative for the profession at large. I didn't uncover major new programs, but in
following a variety of leads I came across a new way of thinking about museums that
intrigues me.

Programs for special audiences, I found, generally break into two categories: first,
programs that help groups make better use of the facility, and second, offerings that
attempt to meet social needs expressed by the community itself. This essay will focus
on the latter category – programs that position museums as social support centers.
I will suggest reasons why some institutions choose to accept and even accentuate
that role, while others choose to reject it.

The introduction of PlaySpace at the Boston Children's Museum in 1975 led me to
explore this topic of social concern. PlaySpace, a preschool crawling and discovery center, was intended to serve a social purpose, yet it was placed within the exhibition area,
a location traditionally reserved for displaying collections related to the museum's
mission. It was designed to allow preschoolers a physically safe yet challenging environment to play in as well as to provide comfortable seating for the adult caregivers
who supervise the activity. The physical set-up is not unique. Spaces quite like it can
be found in playgrounds and preschools everywhere. Rather, it is the underlying purpose that was revolutionary at the time: PlaySpace was designed expressly to facilitate
parenting, to acknowledge the presence of a heretofore invisible museum visitor, the
baby, and make both parent and child feel welcome (Robinson and Quinn 1984).

Parents of young children, isolated in an urban environment without traditional
multigenerational family support and living in often inclement weather, were
covertly beginning to assemble in many indoor public places (libraries, museums,
shopping malls) seeking human companionship and simultaneously learning how to
parent by watching and talking to others. The Children's Museum staff argued that
this covert use of potentially inappropriate facilities should be turned into occasions
for overt support by as many places as could afford and were willing to build what
were, in effect, indoor playgrounds.

As part of the PlaySpace mission, other nonmuseum gathering places were investigated as appropriate sites for this social need. Today, in many places worldwide, PlaySpace copies and analogues are found in airports, hospitals, train stations, women's prisons, and homeless shelters, as well as in other museums. The proposal to establish such a social support system, for a specific target audience within institutions of divergent missions, was successful.

Of course, museums are and have always seen themselves as instruments of social responsibility as well as transmitters of cultural values. But the term social responsibility, as our trade uses it, has rarely been construed to cover the provision of direct service to some element of the community. Instead, social responsibility has most often meant a rather passive imparting of knowledge to a willing and self-selected visitor audience. By contrast, social service recipients might be described as clients rather than visitors, and the intended outcome for programs of social service is more direct, more activist.

Let me suggest other examples of activist social service in museums. In the field of employment assistance, some museums have offered apprenticeships, preprofessional and professional training programs, and special employment opportunities for the poor, the court-adjudicated, the adolescent, the mentally ill, the physically disabled, and women returning to the workforce.

In the field of education, museums have offered literacy programs, after-school homework assistance, alternative schools for school dropouts, professional schools, charter schools within the museum, and classes in prisons and hospitals.

In the field of economic assistance, there have been schemes designed to provide direct markets for craftspeople. Museums have set up shops that allow for profit sharing, started or assisted cottage industries, and offered apprenticeships to ensure the transmission of craft skill from one generation to another.

In the field of health care, dental and medical caregivers have been invited to museum sites to deliver health education information, screenings, and direct clinical service.

To support the museum and community workforce, museums have set up formal day care centers and more informal drop-in day care for infants, the elderly, and latch-key children.

To provide service to special communities, mobile museum units have gone to outlying districts, old age homes, and prisons.

And in the ecomuseum and the native museum movements, people have gained power over their own things, their own presentations, their own finances, and their own information (Davis 1999).

Museums routinely allow their meeting spaces to be used by social service and civic organizations. Some museums distribute their excess food to segments of the hungry community, and I suspect that somewhere there are museum programs for the homeless that allow the museum's facilities to be used for toileting, washing, and shelter in emergencies.

The delivery of social service is neither new nor confined to a single nation or kind of museum. I imagine that each of our museums has offered some of the aforementioned programs. But very few museums, when talking of their missions, include this kind of direct service to their community as a stated priority. Further I would suggest that many of the museums that provide some of the programs listed here would be reluctant to have their leadership acknowledge such a role.

Some would argue that the decision to become part of the social support system violates, or at least dilutes, the museum's other (perhaps more central) functions of collection, preservation, display, and education. Detractors would contend that many other kinds of institutions deliver social service better than museums, but without the reverse being true – that these social service institutions cannot, in turn, provide the service that is unique to museums. Folks opposed to this use of museums would maintain that each type of institution should concentrate on what it does best.

Let me begin another line of reasoning that will lead, I hope, to an understanding about who sees museum social service programs as central, and why (and who does not and why not).

From 1989 to 1991, I helped organize conversations with the American Indian community in order to ascertain what kind of institution they wished the Smithsonian to build as the National Museum of the American Indian.[2] This new museum was to be the inheritor of approximately one million Indian objects in what is reputed to be the finest and most comprehensive American native collection in the world. To a person, these native advisors were not interested in establishing a museum in the conventional sense. Quite the contrary, they felt they had been ill served by the museum establishment. What they did want to build was an institution that would be directly useful to their own tribal members, especially their youngsters. The Indians wanted access to their specific objects not out of acquisitive desire, but to use them in ceremonies that sustain their spiritual identity and to reinforce a feeling of pride and enhanced self-esteem for their tribal members. They were not interested in the objects as objects. The native people I spoke with were interested in direct service programs. They wanted, for example, development of curriculum material for their schools, recording of their stories in the native language, training for their young people in traditional dances, and use of objects in the continued practice of their spiritual traditions.

No consultation went very long before members spoke about the primary importance of their unique languages, the thought patterns associated with speaking their native tongue, and the imperative of teaching that language to their children. I learned that members passed on their heritage through stories, songs, dances, and ceremonies and wished their museums to integrate these methods of communication.

The institutions they were creating for themselves were often called cultural centers rather than museums. But like museums, the purpose of these centers was the direct transmission and continuity of culture for their own people.

I learned from my Indian colleagues that they were not governed by the Western view of private ownership of cultural property. They did not distinguish between the worlds of the spiritual and the secular or between the worlds of the animate and the inanimate. The value museums place on the preservation of objects was, in some cases, hostile to their own world view. Most important, they believed in a person-to-person transmission of cultural practice and values. The usual mission of museums – acquisition, preservation, and protected display – was not congruent with their need. The Indians understood and were always quick to say that their culture was not Western. And their new museum will likely be, from a Western viewpoint, unconventional.

This would not surprise Edwina Taborsky, who wrote a paper in 1982 entitled "The Sociostructural Role of the Museum." She begins her article by asking: "Why is it important to the existence and development of culture, knowledge and social development to have objects and images kept apart from daily life, in a separate building, which some people conserve and analyze, and others visit and look at?" (Taborsky 1982)

> The assumption that societies without museums are deprived of any of their supposed functional results must be questioned. Are there no other social systems in a society that can perform these same services? Is there nothing else that can gather, store and provide a sense of social heritage, a fund of social knowledge, a sense of development, other than a museum? It has to be acknowledged that other social systems have done so in the past and continue to do so. Myths, poetry, songs, stories, dance, rituals, religion, social rites, kinship structures, are all strong systems which have provided societies with such services. . . . That is, all societies seem concerned with the preservation and production of social images and with the generation of knowledge about these social images. But they use different methods for dealing with these social needs.
>
> (1982)

Is it possible that museum professionals worldwide have been struggling toward a common paradigm for museums from an inaccurate vantage point: namely, that all people, regardless of cultural experience, want and need to preserve and transmit the traditions and values of their cultures through an object-centered, preservation-based organization?

Taborsky asserts:

> Museums are a *specific method* for dealing with images of social heritage and social consciousness, and this method is particular only to one specific logical pattern of comprehension of and behavior in the environment.
>
> (1982)

As a result of working on this paper, I am persuaded that institutions of cultural transmission take many forms, and each arises from different and, in some cases, quite opposite fundamental intentions. The useful conclusion I have come to is that societies in which the transmitted medium of culture is person-to-person oral exchange – and where objects, no matter how elegant, have little currency as personal treasures for hoarding or display but rather are valued primarily for their narrative use – will be more likely to create museums whose central programs will be offerings of social support.

Conversely, societies that place crucial importance on objects of property and view those as fundamental to cultural transmission will create museums that emphasize collection, storage, and display, and only secondarily educational offerings for the visitor. These institutions will be less inclined to deliver direct service to the community. Interesting and sometimes acrimonious debate happens when museums established as object-based institutions hold material belonging to peoples whose cultures are based on oral communication.[3]

Put another way, it may be that cultural transmission through collecting and preserving is particularly Western. All cultures may not value personal acquisition as a sign of power and prestige. In fact, some native cultures power is accrued by giving things away.

We may be at a point when we begin to accept the notion that cultural centers that provide active social support also legitimately transmit culture and may therefore be as authentically classified as museums as those that primarily protect and exhibit objects. In that case, we may grow more comfortable with an enlarged definition of museums. It may become more commonplace and natural to see songs and stories told, language spoken, communal meals served, objects loaned for ceremonial use, and training programs initiated within the normal course of the museum's daily business.

As many urban societies struggle to serve the needs of their disparate communities, we may begin to see the creation of more museums that provide social service and community support as integral parts of their work. I look to members of non-Western cultures to lead us all in the invention and integration of a new, more inclusive definition of museum. I believe we will all be richer for the enterprise.

Notes

1 The initial text of this talk was presented at the ICOM/CECA conference in Jerusalem, Israel, on October 21, 1991, and was published in conference proceedings (Gurian 1991a). I was the deputy director of the United States Holocaust Memorial Museum when this was originally written.

2 From 1989 to 1991 I served first as the deputy assistant secretary at the Smithsonian Institution and then as the deputy director for public program planning for the Smithsonian's National Museum of the American Indian. Among my tasks was the coordination of a series of consultations between selected members of the Native American community and architectural program planners from the firm of Venturi, Scott-Brown, and Associates. The 12 consultations that we held shaped the architectural and program plans for all three sites: The George Gustave Heye Center in the Alexander Hamilton US Custom House in New York City; the Cultural Resources Center in Suitland, Maryland; and the museum on the National Mall. The outcome of the consultations established the importance of continuous direct programmatic relationships with individual tribes and established the "fourth museum," a funded program of continuing dialogue and service to individual community groups.

3 There are many articles written about the changing relationship between nonnative museums reorienting themselves to the descendants of their material holdings. For one view of the role of museums and their relationship with the first people in their countries, see (Anderson 1990), or for the Canadian policy paper on the same subject, see (Hill and Nicks 1992).

Bibliography

Anderson, C. (1990) "Australian Aborigines and Museums, a New Relationship," in *Curator*, 33:3, 165 ff.

Davis, P. (1999) *Ecomuseums: A Sense of Place*, London; New York: Leicester University Press.

Gurian, E.H. (1991a) "The Opportunity for Social Service," in *ICOM-CECA. Annual Conference, The Museum and the Needs of People / Le musée et les besoins du public*, 1991, Jerusalem.

Hill, T. and Nicks, T. (1992) *Turning the Page: Forging New Partnerships between Museums and First Peoples: Task Force Report on Museums and First Peoples*, 2nd edn, Ottawa: Assembly of First Nations and Canadian Museums Association.

Robinson, J. and Quinn, P. (1984) *Playspaces: Creating Family Spaces in Public Spaces*, Boston, MA: Boston Children's Museum.

Taborsky, E. (1982) "The Sociostructural Role of the Museum," in *The International Journal of Museum Management and Curatorship*, 1:4, 339–345.

10

A SAVINGS BANK FOR THE SOUL[1]

About institutions of memory and congregant spaces, 1996

If, disregarding conduct that is entirely private, we consider only that special form of conduct which involves direct relations with other persons; and if under the name government we include all control of such conduct, however arising; then we must say that the earliest kind of government, the most general kind of government, and the government which is ever spontaneously recommencing, is the government of ceremonial observance. More may be said. This kind of government, besides preceding other kinds, and besides having in all places and times approached nearer to universality of influence, has ever had, and continues to have, the largest share in regulating men's lives.

(Herbert Spencer 1897)

Within widely divergent parts of our society a feeling is growing that we must balance individualism with group adherence and independence with compliance. In order for civility to prevail – and it must – we must celebrate diligence and discipline just as we celebrate spontaneity and individual creativity. We must not allow repression, but neither can we condone chaos. We must ascribe to some core orderliness in our families, our cities, and our society.

Excessive individualism is a danger for the society as a whole and for each of us within it. We seem to have upset an important balance that safe society needs, one that celebrates the contribution and creativity of the individual while remaining respectful of the past and the customs that provide necessary anchor and stability. The loss of respect for authority and for adherence to expected norms, within some degree of deviation, leads individuals to act on whim with no attendant responsibility for the consequences of their actions.

In response, many of us are regarding with appreciating value the collective in all its forms – organizations, families, neighborhoods, and even ad hoc groups. While not always benign (such groups can, by repression, coercion, or fear, cause violence and destruction), they nonetheless shape our lives and our society.

Institutions of memory

Some institutions, by their very existence, add to the stability of our society. The ones that store, collect, house, and pass along our past I call "institutions of memory." They include libraries, archives, religious organizations, sacred places, elders (especially in societies that value the passing of information in oral form), schools of all kinds, guilds and societies, courts and systems of law, historic houses, and museums.

Institutions of memory do not necessarily resemble one another in kind, history, structure, or use. What they have in common is that they represent or store the collective holdings of the past. They do so either for select groups or for society as a whole. Neither the method of storage nor the material stored (objects, buildings, words, sounds, music, places, images, and so forth) is their common denominator. What unites these organizations is the responsibility to care for the memories of the past and make them available for present and future use.

Evidence indicates that we do not need to use the organization in question to value its existence and wish for its continuity. We believe, for example, that any church is an important institution even if we are nonbelievers or lapsed attendees. While not blind to their imperfections, we want them around and in good working order so that we can call upon them when we are in need. You might think of institutions of memory as savings banks for our souls.

Disturbing incidents exemplify the importance people ascribe to repositories of history. Why did the Muslims and the Croats, with their limited resources, choose to destroy historic places of their enemies? Surely these sites were not military targets. Why did we force native children to separate from their families and give up their cultural traditions in language, dress, and ceremony in the boarding schools of the early twentieth century?[2]

More positive circumstances also reveal the value we place on these institutions. Why do some native communities use drumming circles in conjunction with alcohol rehabilitation? Why does a majority of US voters approve of funding for the arts and humanities despite being upset by specific examples of artistic excess? Why does a current survey of the Detroit metropolitan community show that the public approves of the Museum of African American History and believes it should receive municipal funding when, at the same time, most respondents say that they are unlikely to visit? Why does a recent survey show that minority tourist travelers in this country chose historic venues as a highly valued destination even when the places visited do not relate specifically to *their* history? (Sharp 1995, Klemm 2002).

These examples tell us, implicitly, that we regard institutions of memory as important to our collective well-being. Accordingly, we must begin to discuss the preservation of these organizations not because they add to the quality of life, or to lifelong learning opportunities, or to informal education venues (though they do all that), but because without them, we come apart.

Congregant behavior

Simply ensuring the continuity of our institutions of memory by strengthening their core functions of preservation and education is not enough to maintain civility or collective safety. These enterprises can also purposefully create safe spaces for congregating and, by encouraging the active use of such spaces, foster the rebuilding of community.

We human beings like to be, and even need to be, in the presence of others. This does not mean we have to know the other people or interact directly with them. Just being in their proximity gives us comfort and something to watch. Further, we will travel to places where other people gather. Being with others is an antidote to loneliness. Human beings get lonely. Many other animals do too. I call this going-to-be-with-others activity congregant behavior.[3]

Consider the group activities we participate in. At some, individual actions are coordinated and synchronous, such as at pep and political rallies, athletic and music events, religious observances, performances, and movies. At others, we expect the people we encounter to be mostly autonomous, peaceable strangers. The actions of these participants are uncoordinated and independent. Occasions like visiting museums, shopping and browsing at shopping malls, markets, carnivals, and fairs fall into this category. In each case, however, the simple expectation that others will be present contributes to the pleasurable anticipation.

While some congregant behavior is mild mannered and peaceable, some can lead to violence. People in crowds can egg each other on. Crowd behavior can be more dramatic and more volatile than the individuals within it might wish. Inherent in group activity is the risk that it might devolve into violence, riots, or stampedes.

Current American society evidences a residual sense of responsibility toward the collective whole and toward individual strangers. Witness how we continue to respond to emergencies and tragedies, where most of the time strangers help each other. Think also of line or queue etiquette in America, where strangers hold each other's place.

Reclaiming community

Encouraging peaceful congregant behavior is one of the essential elements of reestablishing community.[4] Various trends point to a growing public interest in the reestablishment of functioning communities that include opportunities for enhanced congregant behavior:

- Real estate developers are building planned communities that encourage foot traffic and resemble the villages of our memories.
- Front porches are being brought back, and many neighborhoods are adding them to existing homes.
- Shopping malls have (both intentionally and inadvertently) been adding physical amenities such as play spaces, stages, and "outdoor" cafes. Moms go to malls in the winter to let their homebound children run around. Heart patients walk to improve their cardiovascular activity, health and voter organizations set up information booths, and local arts groups perform.

- It is increasingly common for eating establishments to attract customers by putting porch furniture on the sidewalk (even in unlikely and unattractive locations) during good weather.
- Bars have been upgraded from less savory institutions to havens for everyone, drinkers or not. Television series have memorialized them to underscore their neighborliness.
- Coffee bars have appeared in the midst of every social gathering place. They serve as an anchor for new mega-bookstores, transforming the activity of book-buying into a new way to interact with friends, family, and strangers.
- Towns and cities are holding annual invented happenings that take on new public celebratory dimensions. For example, many cities and towns are replicating Boston's First Night — a series of free events in the city's core that provides multigenerational groups a safe and entertaining New Year's Eve.

At the same time that new opportunities for congregant activity are being created, isolation and a feeling of personal danger are increasing:

- The gulf between rich and poor is growing in the United States. The poor are less able to survive unaided, and evidence of their poverty (homelessness and begging) is more apparent for all to see.
- The rise of technological systems (the virtual world) is making it possible for more and more people to work by themselves, connected to others only electronically.
- The population of the country is getting older, and the elderly are becoming more isolated.
- Chain stores are homogenizing most retail experiences, with a loss of local or regional particularity.
- Loyalty to one's employees and employers is eroding, and people are changing jobs more frequently than before.
- Certain areas of our cities are unsafe for everyone, especially their inhabitants.
- News distributors focus on sensational, pessimistic, disillusioning, or tragic matters over which the individual has no personal power. As a result, we feel less in control of our lives than ever.

In revaluing community, we seek environments that we can personally affect. We wish to be known to our neighbors and service providers. We wish to be free from personal danger, and during some of our time we wish to be in the safe company of others.

Many people are choosing to move their offices and homes to smaller communities because, with technological advances, they can do their work anywhere. So many workers are moving that they are affecting secondary markets: the rise of mail order, the decline of the clothing industry, the creation of specialized magazines, and changing real estate values.

The Internet hosts many interest-based bulletin boards that function as a new virtual community with an emphasis on helpfulness. These new communities are created technologically by distant members who sit home alone working.

In 1969, Alistair Cooke said in a radio broadcast:

> Middle-class standards, as they were planted and have grown everywhere in this country, are the ones that have kept America a going concern. It is time to grit the teeth slightly, prepare for a shower of eggs, and say what those standards are: Fair wages for good work. Concern for the family and its good name. A distrust of extremes and often, perhaps, a lazy willingness to compromise. The hope of owning your own house and improving it. The belief that the mother and father are the bosses, however easygoing, of the household and not simply pals. A pride in the whole country, often as canting and unreasonable as such patriotism can be. Vague but stubborn ideas about decency. An equally vague but untroubled belief in God. A natural sense of neighborliness, fed by the assumption that your neighbor is much like you and is willing to share the same laws . . . or lend you a mower, a hammer, or a bottle of milk.
>
> (Cooke 1979)

Cooke may have been talking about middle-class values, or, as I suspect, he may have been speaking about a core set of American values that many aspired to regardless of economic status. In any case, I think the reassertion of these values, with all their imperfections, is emerging nationwide again.

Possible next steps

Now what does all of this have to do with institutions of memory? If we believe that congregant behavior is a human need and also that all civic locations offer opportunities for people to be with and see other people, then why not challenge institutions not previously interested in communal activity to build programs specifically to encourage more civil interaction.

Museums can aspire to become one of the community's few safe and neutral congregant spaces. If we do our work well, all members of society – no matter what ethnic, racial, or economic group they belong to – could be made to feel welcome. In order to create such safe environments we must look at the most subtle aspects of our presentations. Do the building guards think all people are equally welcome? Does the signage use words that require a certain education level or specialized knowledge? Can a non-English speaker decode the message? Are staff members sufficiently representative so the public has a sense that everyone is not only welcome but potentially understood? Are employees sensitized to the many acceptable, though culturally specific, ways of acting when in a public space?

Many churches, museums, schools, and libraries serve as forums for debate that foster balanced conversations on issues of the day. Sometimes the debate takes up physical form on bulletin boards or exhibition; sometimes it is transient and oral.

The programs stem from a belief that "town hall" is an appropriate role for these institutions of memory.

We could, if we wished, offer programs that turn strangers into acquaintances. Robert D. Putnam, in his book *Bowling Alone*, tells us that today more people than ever go to bowling alleys but fewer go as members of bowling teams (Putnam 2000). Putnam cites this example to maintain that people today choose individualism over group camaraderie. Using his analogy, could we redefine the meaning of "group" to include all who go to the bowling alley at any particular time? Then we could begin to program activities for transient and even unintentional aggregations, but groups nevertheless. What if the bowling alley owner encouraged group cohesion by setting up teams for an evening, giving out team clothing, giving all players name tags, and changing playing partners every once in a while? (He might even find his business's bottom line enhanced.)

What if our organizations intentionally enhanced the formation of group cohesion and responsibility? Docent-led groups in historic houses could begin by having individuals introduce themselves to each other. We could locate our cafés in the heart of the functioning institution rather than on the periphery. The Walker Art Center in Minneapolis, for example, embedded a period café within an exhibition and found that strangers began to discuss the exhibition.[5] In all our eating establishments we could set up tables reserved for single strangers to share a meal, as they do in private clubs.

We can make museums one of the few safe and neutral congregant spaces in our communities. If we do our work well, we could help all members of society – no matter what ethnic, racial, or economic group they belong to – feel welcome. To create such safe environments, we must look at all aspects of our presentations and adjust these to enhance interactive opportunities. Is information about neighborhood amenities, like restaurants and other attractions, available in the lobby?[6] Do we invite the museum's neighbors in to see our work and be seen by our visitors? Can we help visitors enter and leave the building without feeling intimidated by the surrounding neighborhood?

Those museums that see themselves as forums for balanced conversations on issues of the day regard their visitors in the transformed role of participants. These museums are also experimenting with programs that invite colloquy. They are using their lecture halls as umbrellas for debate and the airing of ideas.[7] Such programs stem from the belief that serving as a "town square" is an appropriate role for a museum and, conversely, that the museum is a fitting safe place for the discussion of unsafe ideas.[8]

Let us also examine our company culture – the internal climate of our public enterprise – as we build recognizably safer spaces for the public. It is likely that the public can intuit an organization's internal climate. Simplistically, if the staff cares for each other, visitors will feel the staff will be kind to them. If the internal administrative process is arbitrary and biased, if respect for the value of each employee is not the norm, if the internal discourse is allowed to be abusive, then no matter what we do with our programs, I suspect the public will remain cynical and on edge.

The converse is also true. If our program is a little ragged but our spirit is enthusiastic, if we are really happy to see our visitors, they will forgive us our frayed edges and get on with the business at hand, exuding a palpable sense of well-being.

Summary

Most institutions of memory will have to change a great deal in order to be truly welcoming to all. Yet, change or not, they all have a core purpose inherently important to our joint survival: we all need to be rooted in our collective past in order to face our collective future.

In addition, these institutions can significantly enhance their role in the community. They can, if they wish, foster and celebrate congregant behavior within their walls. In so doing, they will encourage civility more generally. Institutions of memory, in making a safe space for all who enter, can add to the safety of the entire community.

Afterword

This paper was originally written prior to the terrorist attacks of September 11, 2001. Thereafter, the preoccupying concern of social conservatives (who held the levers of much of the political power in the United States) moved from excessive individualism to a kind of fearful patriotism that allowed for very little deviation from compliance and conformity. Four years later there is a tentative but uneasy oppositional voice to be heard speaking up for opinions different from the mainstream.

The essay, as written, is a plea for museums to become more civically responsible by encouraging the use of their safe spaces for strangers to congregate. We need such spaces now more than ever but for a different reason than the one that originally motivated this essay. Rereading it reminds me how quickly societies become intolerant of activity outside the norm and how one should not take group acquiescence, or silence through trepidation, for evidence of collective well-being.

When citizens feel threatened by terrorists (real or imagined), it becomes ever more important to find places and activities where groups can cross their own boundaries and recombine with others with some ease. In this context, all sides must see museums as fair and balanced venues. Museums have many assets to work from. Most people perceive them as trustworthy and educative. They fall in the category of important civic venues, yet, I would contend, they have far to go to realize their civic potential.

They are not universally seen as welcoming or useful in the ordinary sense. Many, most especially art museums, are seen as elitist. Many are difficult to navigate for the novice. A study to determine what minority visitors thought of museums was commissioned by the Museum and Galleries Commission of the United Kingdom in 1997. The groups interviewed were half nonvisitors and half museum users.

Their opinions were similar, irrespective of ethnicity:

> "The Museum" is still the way that museums are perceived; an old building with an imposing appearance, like the British Museum. Typical contents include "Kings and Queens, crowns, suits of armour, weapons, and 'broken pots and rocks'." The atmosphere was described as quiet, reverential and un-welcoming to children. Not surprisingly, this rather unpleasant place was felt to be for intellectuals, and posh people. Art galleries were perceived as even more distant and elitist. There was a real fear that the displays would be too difficult to understand.
>
> (Hooper-Greenhill 1998)

Yet when the program appeals diversely to the visitor, when outside leadership declares the museum to be welcoming, when one finds the outing supportive and enlightening to one's family, when museums raise to accept the challenge of sustaining the community through unexpected catastrophes, the museum can, if it wants to, fulfill its broadest mission as a useful and engaging savings bank for the soul.

Notes

1 This chapter was originally prepared as a keynote speech at the Museums Australia 1996 Conference, Thursday, October 30, 1996. It was subsequently published in two different versions (Gurian 1995c, 1996). This chapter is a mixture of both those published papers with an afterword to comment on the issues from a more current perspective.

2 For further discussion on objects as important to the "soul" of a people see (Gurian 1999b).

3 I understand that "congregant space" or "congregant behavior" is an unorthodox use of the term congregant, which has a dictionary meaning of "one who congregates, especially a member of a group of people gathered for religious worship." I use it as a form of congregating which means "to bring or come together in a group, crowd, or assembly" without the religious connotations. I continue to use the term throughout many of my papers.

4 For further explication of the many spaces that fit within the category of "congregant space" see (Gurian 2005).

5 There have been a number of successful experiments with placing food venues within visual sight of exhibition material. One such venue is the new Walker Art Center building and program whose slogan is "where art meets life." Another is to be found on the mezzanine of Te Papa, the National Museum of New Zealand in Wellington. And increasingly, museums are displaying objects in sealed cases used within food service venues. While they might serve merely as decoration, they might also prompt conversation.

6 The Mexican Fine Arts Center Museum in Chicago has intentionally decided not to have in-house food service so that people will patronize local eateries. Visitors find out where to go by speaking to someone at the front desk. While this practice reduces potential income (the museum has no admission fee), it makes the museum a very good neighbor and prized by local establishments, since it is an attraction that brings people to the neighborhood for the first time (Tortolero, personal communication).

7 The Newseum in Washington, DC has regularly scheduled programs that are broadcast throughout the country. The audience is invited to participate. Similarly, the National

Museum of Australia, in Canberra has a professional broadcast studio where students question important officials on the air.

8 For example, the mission of the Association of Children's Museums (ACM) is: The Association of Children's Museums builds the capacity of children's museums to serve as town squares for children and families where play inspires creativity and lifelong learning.

Bibliography

Cooke, A. (1979) "Eternal Vigilance by Whom?" in Cooke, A. (ed.) *The Americans*, New York: Berkeley Books.

Gurian, E.H. (1995c) "Offering Safer Public Spaces," in *Journal of Museum Education*, 20:3, 14–16.

Gurian, E.H. (1996) "A Savings Bank for the Soul," in *Grantmakers in the Arts Reader*, Seattle, WA, 7:2, 6–9.

Gurian, E.H. (1999b) "What Is the Object of This Exercise? A Meandering Exploration of the Many Meanings of Objects in Museums," in *Daedalus*, Cambridge, MA, 128:3, 163–183.

Gurian, E.H. (2005) "Threshold Fear," in Macleod, S. (ed.) *Reshaping Museum Space: Architecture, Design, Exhibitions*, London: Routledge.

Hooper-Greenhill, E. (1998) "Cultural Diversity, Attitudes of Ethnic Minority Populations Towards Museums and Galleries," in *GEM News*, London, 69 (Spring): 10–11.

Klemm, M.S. (2002) "Tourism and Ethnic Minorities in Bradford: The Invisible Segment," in *Journal of Travel Research*, 41:1, 85–91.

Putnam, R.D. (2000) *Bowling Alone: The Collapse and Revival of American Community*, New York: Simon & Schuster.

Sharp, D. (1995) "Welcoming Minorities in Cities Coast to Coast," *USA Today*, September 19, 1995, p. 8D.

Spencer, H. (1897) "The Principles of Sociology," in Goffman, E. (ed.) *Relations in Public*, 1971, New York: Basic Books, Inc.

Tortolero, C. (2004) Executive director, the Mexican Fine Arts Center Museum, personal communication.

Part III

SPACE, THE FINAL FRONTIER
Museums, construction, architecture, and space planning

When museums want to diversify their audiences, they tend to concentrate on developing programs that they consider inclusionary. But program expansion, while interesting to many, is not enough. At the same time, museums have devoted much attention and money to the physical expansion of their facilities and the architectural statement these buildings make. Museums have rarely understood – and even more rarely exploited – the connection between the creation of new spaces and the rhetoric of inclusion. This section suggests important relationships between the desire to broaden the audience and decisions concerning design and use of the building.

11

FUNCTION FOLLOWS FORM

How mixed-used spaces in museums build community,[1] 2001

Civic life is what goes on in the public realm. Civic life refers to our relations with our fellow human beings – in short, our roles as citizens.
(James Howard Kunstler 1996)

Introduction

Many subtle, interrelated, and essentially unexamined ingredients allow museums to play an enhanced role in the building of community and our collective civic life. Museum professionals generally acknowledge that the traditional mission of museums involves housing and caring for the tangible story of the past, materially illuminating contemporary issues, and creating a physical public consideration of the future. Increasingly, museum leaders are also asserting that museums can become safe places for unsafe ideas, meeting grounds for diverse peoples, and neutral forums for discussing issues of our day. Of course, museums vary in their stated purpose, and not all museums' leadership believes community building to be central to their work. Nevertheless, this essay will consider some ways that museums can enhance their role in building community. Underlying the discussion that follows is the notion that all museums are an important part of civic life; that whatever their overt mission may be, museums have become an important agent in the creation of a more cohesive society.

Interestingly, it is the economic and social theorists (and pragmatic practitioners – property developers and civic leaders) who are asserting (often in stronger terms than museums use themselves) that the not-for-profit sector plays an unparalleled role in community building. For instance, Peter Drucker, the management pundit, writes:

Only the institutions of the social sector, that is the non-government, nonbusiness, nonprofit organization, can create what we now need, communities for citizens and especially for the highly educated knowledge workers who, increasingly dominate developed societies. One reason for this is that only nonprofit organizations can provide the enormous diversity of communities we need .... The nonprofit organizations also are the only ones that can satisfy the second need of the city, the need for effective

99

citizenship for its members. . . . Only the nonprofit social sector institution can provide opportunities to be a volunteer and thus can enable individuals to have both: a sphere in which they are in control and a sphere in which they make a difference. . . . What the dawning twenty-first century needs above all is equally explosive growth of the nonprofit social sector organizations in building communities in the newly dominant social environment, the city.

(1998)

Considering museums and community, writers within our profession have focused on broadening audiences, public programs, collections, and exhibitions. Physical spaces have been regarded as necessary armature but not as catalysts themselves. And the element that authors outside our profession refer to as "informal public life" – which arises spontaneously within these spaces – has been largely ignored in museum writings.

Redressing this oversight, this paper concentrates on three elements largely overlooked by our field – space, space mix, and unexpected use – and attempts to show that if museum planners were to pay overt attention to these, they could greatly enhance the community-building role our institutions increasingly play.

Museums are behind the times in considering these concepts. The proposition that space and space mix are important ingredients in humanizing an urban setting has been explored since the 1960s. An Internet search using a common space-planning buzzword, "mixed use space," was completed in 0.73 seconds and revealed 628,000 Web pages. Even refining the search by adding the word "museum" resulted in a list of 57,400 pages.

Like many of these websites, museums and community-building ideas benefit from the planning theories of Jane Jacobs (1961). Many consider Jacobs to be the founder of city-planning ideas and practices now known as the livable cities movement or as new urbanism (Katz 1994, Fulton 1996). Proponents hold that to build a functional sense of community and civility, planners should fashion spaces (streets) that foster a sense of place, are ecologically sensitive, put reliance on foot rather than auto traffic, are utilized over many hours each day, and offer a mix of activities that appeal to many. They maintain that the juxtaposition of spaces as mixed-use environments must be present if community building is to succeed.

Jacobs describes another necessary component: the ad hoc, seemingly unprogrammed social activity that arises within public space.

Formal types of local city organizations are frequently assumed by planners and even by some social workers to grow in direct, commonsense fashion out of announcements of meetings, the presence of meeting rooms, and the existence of problems of obvious public concern. Perhaps they grow so in suburbs and towns. They do not grow so in cities. Formal public organizations in cities require an informal public life underlying them, mediating between them and the privacy of the people of the city.

(1961)

An example of public mixed-use space

I first began to encounter the subtle interrelationship of space, its use, and emergent civility in the shopping strip in Barcroft, my multiethnic, multieconomic neighborhood close to Washington, DC. The shopping center used to be failing but is now very active, day and night. Its metamorphosis has been fascinating and instructive to watch. A shop will open with a sign that announces a needed and straightforward function. Thus we have, for example, signs for a laundromat, a dry cleaner, and separate Asian, Latino, and Halal food markets.

Upon closer observation and through experience, one sees that the laundromat has pool tables, a child's play area, and a barbershop. It had a money order and check-cashing booth, but that moved to its own shop next door and combined with the utility bill-paying function that used to operate out of the Asian food market. The Asian owners speak Spanish and sell Asian and Latino food as well as beer and liquor. Not to be outdone, the Latino food market sells lottery tickets, phone cards, and is the French pastry outlet. The Halal food store rents videotapes and sells clothes. The hours of use are nearly around the clock.

I have watched these entrepreneurs expand their businesses without regard for their announced and original niche functions. Their motivation has been to follow the money. Without plan or foreknowledge, they are reinventing the general store, combining the outdoor market of their native countries with a more rural American corner store of former years. (And if you look closely at supermarkets, chain bookstores, and pharmacies, they are following the same trend.)

Arising out of these multifunction spaces has come an interesting array of more subtle mutual supports within the community. There is tolerance for the presence of mostly male hangers-on who stand around (varying from sober to intoxicated) and who watch out for, and comment benignly on, the ensuing foot traffic. The other day, I saw the community police hanging out with the hip-hop Latino teenagers in the parking lot, the babies in the laundromat playing with each other and learning English, the community bulletin board offering baby-sitting services at the pizza parlor, and the Asian food store proprietors refusing to sell alcohol to an already drunk adult, sending him home to his family.

Barcroft is safe, friendly, and welcoming most of the time. It is not always entirely tranquil. It is above all an active, useful mixed-use space that has the effect of building civil community.

Jane Jacobs and the components of a livable city

Jacobs wrote in response to the postwar central-city revitalization efforts (after the middle class had fled to the suburbs) amid predictions of the impending death of most downtowns. Planners in the 1960s were offering models of city reinvigoration that focused on tearing down inner cities and rebuilding them along theoretical precepts that Jacobs found sterile and alarming. She believed plans like these would destroy the essential social order to be found within old neighborhoods.

Jacobs wrote,

> This ubiquitous principle is the need of cities for a most intricate and close-grained diversity of uses that give each other constant mutual support, both economically and socially. The components of this diversity can differ enormously, but they must supplement each other in certain concrete ways.
>
> (1961)

Jacobs and others prescribed a list of attributes needed for making streets vibrant and the people using them civil and safe.

The space components should allow:

- The mingling of buildings that vary in age and condition, including a good proportion of old ones so that they vary in the economic yield they must produce.
- Priority for pedestrians rather than cars.
- Wide and pleasant sidewalks.
- Short streets and frequent opportunities to turn corners.
- A clear demarcation between what is public space and what is private space; they cannot ooze into each other.
- Sufficiently dense concentrations of people, including those who live there.
- A disparate mix of useful services.
- Use of services as many hours as possible, especially at night.
- Opportunities for loitering and the encouragement of people-watching (e.g. benches and small parks).
- Windows overlooking the street to encourage unofficial surveillance.

If the space has these attributes, then users will:

- Represent as broad a social and age mix as possible.
- Feel personally safe and secure among strangers.
- Exhibit a range of acceptable, though not uniform, behaviors and intercede with those who violate the norms.
- Have varied motivations for using the street, including intentional and targeted shopping, passing through on the way to somewhere else, and going to and from their homes.
- Walk, thereby encouraging unplanned interaction.
- Allow children's use of the space in unplanned and seemingly unsupervised ways.
- Share responsibility for the safety of all users, including children.
- Set up unspoken standards for cleanliness and repair accepted by all.
- Use the street on a regular basis and thus develop a cadre of "regulars."
- Tolerate and even encourage "hangers-on."

The creation of such a space would then encourage an overlay of social activities, which would include:

- Formal and informal (voluntary) surveillance: "There must be eyes upon the street, eyes belonging to those we might call the natural proprietors of the street" (Jacobs 1961).
- Intercession when danger threatens.
- Casual social interchange, which does not invade privacy or cultural norms for acknowledging strangers and acquaintances rather than friends.
- Loitering developed to a social art that promotes interactivity.
- Ad hoc additional services (leaving a note with a grocer, using the telephone of the pharmacist, picking up supplies for neighbors).
- The establishment of occasional formulized rituals (parades, celebrations) and informal ones (neighborhood cleanup, cook-outs).

If all these characteristics are present, the result will be "the trust of a city street... formed over time from many, many little public sidewalk contacts. ... Most of it is ostensibly utterly trivial but the sum is not trivial at all" (Jacobs 1961).

In *The Great Good Place* (Oldenburg 1989), Ray Oldenburg writes about the importance of overt neighborhood gathering places (such as bars and cafés) and describes a few additional ingredients for making such places successful. Gathering places should be:

- On neutral ground, not seen to be owned by any clique or faction.
- Seen as a social leveler in which social status is not the currency of interchange.
- Conducive to conversation.
- Physically plain or modest in its internal space to reduce self-consciousness.
- Welcoming or even playful in mood.

How museums came to have mixed-use space

Without necessarily intending to, museums have become mixed-use environments. Starting in the 1960s, US museums found that financial viability required new revenue sources to augment their traditional financial base of endowment revenue and private donations.

The need for additional income led to two seemingly unrelated developments. The first was a new emphasis on financial business models, which included expanding sources of earned income. The second was increased budgetary reliance on government allocations, and competitive grants from foundation and government sources.

Museums adopted commercial management models, appointed more business-trained leadership to their boards and staffs, explored revenue opportunities (not just shops and cafeterias) from as broad a menu as possible, professionalized and expanded their fund-raising apparatus, explored corporate sponsorship, and imposed or increased entrance fees. Within the profession, there was much discussion that museums were subverting their core mission. Nevertheless, economic imperatives caused museums to become more professionally managed and more money conscious.

As museums increasingly turned to government and private foundations for economic survival, they discovered that most foundations and granting agencies focused on social needs. Aligning with the guidelines set out by these funders, museums increased their service to underserved communities and elevated education programs for schools and the general public to a higher priority. This, too, caused much internal discussion about the core functions of museums (Newsome and Silver 1978), and some suggested that social and educational agendas, while worthy, were not central to museum activity.

These two financial streams – business revenue (money in) and social and educational service (money out) – led to a broader mix of programming and, as a consequence, an altered set of space requirements. As a result, the ratio of permanent gallery space to other spaces often decreased. Food service and shops were created, revamped, or enlarged. After-hours fee-based activities were superimposed on spaces formerly used exclusively as galleries. Classrooms and auditoriums grew in number and often in size.

During the same period, cities were changing their shape. There was flight from the central cities to suburbia, an increased reliance on cars, and the beginnings of urban sprawl. As one response, city rehabilitation advocates and commercial developers, interested in tourist dollars and the rejuvenation of neglected cities, included museums, historic houses, performing arts centers, and other educational attractions in their city-planning mix. Like the Barcroft shopkeepers, the revitalizers were following the money. Studies of tourist spending, often urged by arts organizations, showed that cultural attractions enhance income for local hotels, retail, and food service. Government-sponsored cultural revitalization came in two forms: cultural centers such as New York's Lincoln Center, with a surround of related amenities; or a mix of functions within a larger building, like the Centre Pompidou (Beaubourg) in Paris, where galleries, a public library, restaurants, and a museum occupy the same building.

Mayors of US cities budgeted for the construction of museums in the heart of their decaying core cities (Detroit, Richmond, Virginia, and Baltimore for example). These local mayors persisted despite federal policy makers' attempts to reduce funding for the arts and cultural programming. On the international scene, the Guggenheim Museum Bilbao comes to mind as a similar example of a museum initiated by local government to leverage community revitalization.

Guided by the social planning insights of people like Jacobs, government initiatives often included dollars allocated exclusively to cultural amenities. Percentage for art programs were part of government-funded revitalization schemes. Similarly, vest-pocket parks and green-space setbacks were included in the planning guidelines. This encouraged museums to include such outside spaces, if they were part of larger redevelopment plans.

New York City Partnership and Chamber of Commerce Business Partnership considered redevelopment for Lower Manhattan:

> The plan that emerges should enable Lower Manhattan to become a world class, high tech community – a twenty-four hour, mixed use neighborhood. It should be full of high-performance buildings, nodes of housing and retail stores, commercial space for industries such as biotech, enterprise software and international business. Lower Manhattan should be made more attractive than ever, with cultural amenities and, of course, a memorial to those who lost their lives on September 11. This region of New York should become the envy of its global competitors.
>
> (November 2001)

Examples of outdoor mixed-use spaces

The physical placement of museums within their immediate neighborhoods can make them more or less "owned" by the surrounding community. For years, the Museum of Fine Arts (MFA) in Boston shut its entrance on the more populous neighborhood side (which also had a trolley stop), and opened itself instead to the parking lot – making it clear that those driving from outside the neighborhood were more welcome than those who lived nearby or came by public transport. Now the MFA has reopened the neighborhood door, and there is, I am told, a decidedly positive attitude change in the community about the museum.

But in museums that are not yet naturally "owned" by residents, neighbors sometimes create unexpected activity that can be encouraged or enhanced. The outer courtyard of the Centre Pompidou is always filled with buskers who enhance the activity in the whole surrounding area. The new National Museum of Australia's (NMA) campus includes contoured outdoor performance amphitheatres, used for planned and spontaneous activities external to the museum building.

The director of the Brooklyn Museum of Art, Arnold Lehman, tells this story. Many dark winter evenings as he was walking to the subway, he noticed that the forecourt leading to the building's entrance was bright with floodlights placed there for security reasons. Capitalizing on the lighting, that space had become a nightly spontaneous community gathering place for recreation and performance, with different groups using the lighted space for different needs. His current capital campaign to renovate the front of the building recognizes, encourages, and augments that function. He hopes that the formalization of the space will not end the activity.

The inside as outside

Thinking about museums' internal spaces as neighborhoods within themselves opens up additional possibilities for planning. Reading Jacobs' list of required city attributes makes clear that today's museums already include many of the aspects of an effective village: strolling opportunities, frequent corners to turn, demarcations between public and private space, comfortable opportunities for hanging out, and a mix of services provided over an ever-lengthening number of hours and for broader segments of the populace. Museums' internal spaces are like streetscapes and as such are an important part of the public realm.

> The public realm is the connective tissue of our everyday world. ... The public realm exists mainly outdoors because most buildings belong to private individuals or corporations. Exceptions to this are public institutions such as libraries, museums, zoos, and town halls, which are closed some hours of the day, and airports and train stations, which may be open around the clock. The true public realm then ... is that portion of our everyday world which belongs to everybody and to which everybody ought to have equal access most of the time.
>
> (Kunstler 1996)

Accepting their responsibility for being part of public amenities, many museums are now planning new facilities with spaces explicitly for use by other constituents. Nancy Matthews, curator of education at the Kenosha Public Museum, reflected on this trend:

> The concept of the new Kenosha Public Museum (Kenosha, WI) being a community center with flexible spaces that could be used for a variety of meetings, functions, receptions, parties, etc. by outside groups definitely has steered the design of many spaces. ... Many community groups are already asking about using the space. We will have rentals but we will also have regular outside groups who will use the museum as meeting space as long as their group is within the scope of our mission.
>
> (Matthews, personal communication)

The arrivals hall as an inside street

Perhaps more interestingly, one might consider the uses of traditionally nonprogrammed museum spaces. The entrance hall of museums is the one location where the most concentrated and differentiated activity happens, with hours often longer and more varied than the museum itself. Like malls and even new office buildings, these indoor spaces are often multistoried, lead directly to many different venues (including the shop and the café), and often benefit from natural light. These spaces encourage strolling and resting regardless of the outside climate.

Entryways can have an overlay of programs, both intentional and unexpected. Those with icons in their atriums – like the dinosaur at the Field Museum or the elephant at the Smithsonian Institution's National Museum of Natural History – become meeting-place destinations. This is true of I. M. Pei's addition to the Louvre in Paris, which is beautiful, free, handicapped accessible, and a gateway to shops, archaeological excavations, and cafés, as well as to the museum itself.

Some museums have begun to program these spaces intentionally. Jay Heuman of the Joslyn Art Museum says that, in addition to its regular functions and rentals,

> The museum uses the atrium for...a monthly concert,...our Holiday Fair, when our atrium is transformed into a "sidewalk sale" for Christmas shopping,...Family Fun Days, in conjunction with many exhibitions, events that use up much of our atrium space.... [And]...every day we have "Exploration Station" on the bridge in our atrium – intended to be used by parents with their children as a hands-on educational activity.
>
> (Heuman, personal communication)

The new Charles H. Wright Museum of African American History in Detroit was designed with an outsized central social space to deal with the large crowds it drew annually for Martin Luther King Day and other important holidays. The museum discovered that the space was highly desirable for after-hours functions, which contributed a great deal of revenue to the museum. But on the occasion of the death of Coleman Young, the long-time mayor of Detroit, city officials felt that the museum atrium was the appropriate location to host his public laying-in-state. The museum remained open around the clock for a week as people lined up around the block during all hours of the day and night. That unexpected function under-scored the museum's status as an institution of contemporary importance, central to the community.

The public's decision to enter the museum building can be based on reasons as diverse as the offerings within it. Not everyone is going to museums to view the exhibitions. It makes sense that the more varied the internal spaces, the more diverse the audience. Fast food restaurants bring in lunchtime workers from nearby businesses. Port Discovery in Baltimore has a free public library embedded within it, and Henry Ford Museum and Greenfield Village has a charter school, just to name a few examples.

Not surprisingly, it is in the museums, without entrance fees where one sees the most street-like mix of people. The Smithsonian's National Museum of American History has day care centers, galleries, libraries, hands-on children's areas, multiple food venues, and different shops located on different levels. Parents drop off their pre-school children, workers meet for lunch, and some come to use the shop or the resource centers. Some of these users change their minds unexpectedly and sample what they have passed; others don't. In each case the mix of activities allows visitors to partake of gallery offerings if they choose and feel welcome even if they don't.

Recently on a Sunday, I witnessed hundreds of people streaming out of the Museo National de Bellas Artes in Santiago, Chile, on its free day. I discovered they were mostly Peruvian immigrants on their day off. They are working in low-paying unskilled and domestic jobs and are not experienced at visiting art museums. They come every Sunday from all over the city to the square in downtown Santiago to see each other and get news from home. During good weather, they promenade down the avenue, eating food they buy from vendors and taking in the art museum, which is on their route to the playground where their children work off excess energy. How lucky for the museum, I thought, to be in the path of this ritual promenade. The director, however, was not altogether happy with this uninitiated audience. Other art museums, like the Denver Art Museum, the Minneapolis Institute of Arts, and the Walker Art Center, which are overtly interested in building community, might have been thrilled.

People watching

Walking is certainly the transport mode within museums, and increasingly museums have focused on building strolling perimeters that include seats and other amenities to aid visitors in people-watching and to encourage conversation between strangers and within families – another ingredient in the creation of the civil street. While once considered extraneous, social interaction within museums is now understood to be part of the experience. Research into museum visitor behavior has pointed out that, on average, visitors spend fully half their time doing something other than attending to the exhibitions and about one-third of their time interacting with other people (Falk *et al.* 1985). This finding initially made some museum administrators feel that they were failing in their work since they felt the public should be focusing attention to exhibition content. But Jacobs points out that people-watching aids in safety, comfort, and familiarity for all. And Falk and his colleagues posit that learning is enhanced through social interaction. These observations suggest that perhaps museums should allow for even more people-watching by designing spaces, especially within the galleries, that encourage social interaction. Te Papa, the National Museum of New Zealand, has added a coffee bar within its exhibition thoroughfare, to very good effect.

Among other things, people-watching can teach the uninitiated visitor about museum behavior. Jacobs indicates that streets must have an overlay of acceptable behavior (albeit not excessively restrictive) in order to remain safe.

Foucault and others have pointed out that museum behavior is not intuitive, and museum novices fear to go to museums because they worry that they may not behave correctly (Foucault 1970). In situations where passive observation can happen easily, this worry might diminish. The creation of mixed-use space and easy access to it creates an audience of regulars that probably has a broader profile than when museum use is exclusive to traditional museum patrons and so brings with it a secondary benefit of behavior that is acceptable but of a broader range.

Casual surveillance

Jacobs is much concerned with casual surveillance as a way to keep shared social spaces safe and behavior within acceptable bounds. Sometimes the museum visitor aids in that role. In the United States Holocaust Memorial Museum, it is common for visitors to remind teenage strangers of appropriate behavior when they are inappropriately rowdy. Similarly, it is usually the visitors who make sure that the handicapped or elderly are moved to the front in order to see better.

Museums' visitor-services staffs also serve in the capacity Jacobs would describe as "public sidewalk characters are steadily stationed in public places" (Jacobs 1961). These "regulars" permit a reduction in the number of uniformed guards. And visitor-friendly "hangers-out" create an ambiance different from the tension inherent in having uniformed security staff present. So having customer-focused front-of-house personnel creates an ambiance more akin to the civil street.

Visitor services personnel are not the only regulars in the museum; repeat visitors are, as well. In a new facility, staff will notice that the museum is much easier to operate after the first year. They assume it is because they know how to run the building better, and so they do. But they also need to take into account the growing number of visitors who have been there before, regulars who have begun to regulate the flow of traffic. When a stranger needs information, someone who looks like they know what they're doing becomes a reliable guide, and the number of staff-mediated questions goes down. In effect, the repeat visitors are helping to change the museum into a functioning neighborhood by providing the casual social interchange that civil streets engender.

Unanticipated use

In another Brooklyn Museum of Art story, Arnold Lehman says that having opened the museum in the evening one night a week, the Hasidic Jewish community has declared the museum as a permissible dating venue. At the Cranbrook Institute of Science, the observatory's evening hours encourage visitation by young adolescents by providing a safe location for unescorted entertainment. And the Arts and Industries Building of the Smithsonian once had singles socials organized by Smithsonian Associates, the institution-wide membership organization.

Parents of home-schoolers gravitate toward educational public spaces so that their solitary children can find increased social interaction. These parents also need examples of the material they teach but lack in their homes. Without informing the museum, and without programs specifically established for their use, some home-schooled youngsters and their parents regularly come to museums during the afternoons when attendance normally is low. They make friends with each other, use space organized for drop-in visitors, and socialize weekly in the café. (Kirsten Ellenbogen, personal communication). Museums observing this unexpected new audience, especially science museums, have begun catering overtly to their needs.

These examples illustrate the serendipitous uses that occur when a confluence of space, program, and social interaction arises. The Hassidim decided to use the museum as a dating program, the home-schoolers came unbidden, the Peruvians were unexpected on a Sunday in Chile. Museums should stay attuned to and then encourage such broader social uses of their spaces as important opportunities to enhance community building.

In the late 1970s, the Children's Museum in Boston desired to become the home base for an annual native pow wow. To be a successful host, the museum needed a round, flat dancing space, booths on the perimeter to allow vendors to sell native goods (not controlled by the museum shop), and an area to serve food for dancers and spectators within the exhibition space. The museum agreed, even though, at the time, there was no obvious dance floor, eating was not permitted within the museum, nor was anything allowed to be sold outside the shop's control. Now the Smithsonian Institution's National Museum of the American Indian (NMAI), having listened to the community and to their museum colleagues, has created a mix of these spaces and attendant programs in its new museum on the National Mall in Washington, DC.

Children in museums

Jacobs and others speak eloquently about the need for children to have safe but seemingly unstructured and unsupervised space in which to grow up successfully. "Children cannot acquire social skills unless they circulate in a real community among a variety of honorably occupied adults, not necessarily their parents, and are subject to the teachings and restrains of all such adults," suggests Kunstler (1996). During any of the annual meetings of the Association of Children's Museums, leaders talk about the entirely too regimented life of children today and the hope that children's museums would aid in bringing back the go-out-and-play exploration opportunity of our past. Taking that responsibility seriously, some children's museums are creating outdoor and indoor unprogrammed discovery spaces, inviting children's exploration with supervising adults seated unobtrusively nearby.

For a long time, most adult museums have found themselves filled with mothers and toddlers during the morning of the work week and with strollers during the weekend. Where once museum staff felt this to be an inappropriate audience, there are now toddler play spaces in museums such as the Smithsonian Institution's National Museum of Natural History and the Field Museum. Responding to this unexpected use, the museums now encourage families to sit and let their children unwind and run around.

Parents sometimes drop their unsupervised kids off in museums, and children, especially kids of working parents, can be found trying to use museums unattended. Most museums still reject this practice quite adamantly. Yet others amend their policy to assist in this social need. As a youngster, Michael Spock, the famed former director of the Children's Museum in Boston, used to hang around the Museum of Modern Art in his New York City neighborhood. He was there so often that the museum invented the category of child member for him, and then offered it to others. There are many stories of museums discovering the same groups of neighborhood children hanging out in the building and setting about to build programs to serve them, the Brooklyn Children's Museum's Kids Crew being a shining example. And funders, having noticed this need, have become very interested in museums expanding their work with the after-school latchkey crowd, thereby formalizing this serendipity.

Overnights, programs where youngsters sleep in the museum – often in galleries – would have been unthinkable 20 years ago. (Though the idea was immortalized as fantasy for youngsters of that era in the beloved children's book, *From the Mixed-Up Files of Mrs. Basil E. Frankweiler* (Konigsburg 1972).) Now museums routinely host groups to learn, play, and sleep in there.

In all these cases – after-school, overnights, babies in strollers, home-schoolers, over-programmed or unsupervised youngsters – spaces are being built or adapted within museums to cater to the unexpected use that members of the community have brought there. Overtly or not, museums are accepting their role in the rearing of all our children.

Options to consider

These examples demonstrate that museums are already doing a lot to use space in ways that encourage community building. Yet, by and large, museum leadership has not capitalized upon the interplay between space planning, programming, and the emergence of unplanned social activities. The cost of building and maintaining space discourages planning seemingly unprogrammed areas that do not demonstrate immediate financial returns. Without demonstrated overt usefulness, these spaces inevitably get cut in a value-engineering exercise. Therefore, the justification for creating such spaces needs to be given priority when creating an architectural program plan. Yet in this one finds an unexpected ally: the architect who is interested in and fighting for the creation of signature spaces. These spaces typically are based on aesthetics rather than functionality and are often included in the final design (sometimes over the objection of program planners). We should be alert to opportunities to make such grand statements work in ways that help.

While many museums may voice support for community needs, rarely are programs of community building included in the general operating budgets (with the exception of something vaguely termed outreach, whose function is often ill defined, however well intentioned). Some successful programs have been covert "guerrilla" activities (staff initiatives tolerated by museum leadership without formal acknowledgment), often the result of short-term funding from social-service agencies. When the funding is gone, the programs shrink or cease.

Museums often use the terms meeting ground and forum without having thought through the attendant prerequisites or consequences. And some staffs maintain that programs like outreach or ethnically specific special events will, by themselves, encourage broader user mix – and then wonder why it is not sustained. The evidence presented here suggests that program offerings alone are not enough.

Some may not want our museums to become informal social hubs like the complex older streets described by Jacobs, or the "third places" like cafes, coffee shops, community centers, beauty parlors, and general stores described by Oldenburg (1989). Yet both of these writers have demonstrated that it is these third places, the "informal meeting place where citizens can gather" (in addition to work and home, the other two paramount places used by individuals) that help create community.

111

Taking informal meeting places seriously, museums should consider "gathering" as an activity they should enhance. Museums could offer their public spaces not only to outside community organizations but also to the individual piano and dance teacher and to hobby clubs meeting informally. They could provide more free seating and access to resource centers outside the admissions barrier. They could set up more systems for latchkey kids, places for elders to play checkers or dominos, and even group lunch among strangers. In doing so, and depending on our definition of social responsibility, we should not be surprised if we are confronted with and forced to accommodate the undesirables who also use the airports and train stations of our cities.

Jacobs insists that one must provide for ranges of economic choices and consequently a range of rental income within the complex of each street. It may be interesting for museums to consider the mix of price points rather than trying only to maximize income per square foot. Such thinking could, for example, lead children's museums to house consignment shops of used children's merchandise in addition to selling new things.

Museums could participate in activities like voter registration and blood drives, as some shopping malls and libraries already do, and directly acknowledge their role in social service. And even more critically, museums could enhance their quick responsiveness to contemporary issues so that, for example, the immense spontaneous public mourning of Princess Diana's death would have been naturally accommodated within museums rather than relegated to unrelated outdoor monuments. It is interesting to note that following the September 11, 2001, terrorist attacks in the United States, many museums responded with free admission and special programs for parents to work with their children about the tragedy.

Putnam (1995, 2000) writes about the collapse and revival of American community, suggesting that as people join organized groups less and less frequently, they have less community affiliation as a consequence. He also alludes to the power of casual, but nonetheless satisfying, affiliation between strangers – in cafés, bookstores, and museums or online. "Like pennies dropped in a cookie jar, each of these encounters is a tiny investment in social capital" (Putnam 2000). Putnam sees safe interaction among strangers as a necessary prerequisite toward building a more harmonious society.

Museums could facilitate interactions between strangers. Talk-back boards and visitor comment books are exhibition strategies that already allow strangers to talk to each other. These could be made more central, more customary, and could elevate the stranger as co-leader. In that regard, docents could share leadership of group tours by allowing knowledgeable strangers to interject. Informal areas for public debate could be encouraged more often.

There are many examples worldwide of museums facilitating safe interaction between strangers. The ubiquitous preschool spaces, piloted by the Children's Museum in Boston in the 1970s, were overtly designed to encourage the exchange of parenting information between strangers while watching their children at play. Different community clubs meet on the same night every week at the Cranbrook Institute of Science; the museum provides coffee and cookies in a neutral space after the meeting so that the members of the disparate groups can meet each other and socialize. The Walker Art Center set up chess tables within an exhibition, and community members came inside to play chess and meet each other. Putnam points out that it is not the organization that builds community but the interaction and ensuing occasional civic conversations that build social capital.

Museums' most useful community enhancement might be the elimination of admission charges. Before the 1960s many museums were free. In the 1980s, the Minneapolis Institute of Arts dropped admission charges and increased the space devoted to its café and fee-based programs. In so doing it built community trust. Director Evan Maurer has demonstrated that an institution of fine arts with an aura of exclusivity can become, at the same time, a treasure widely used by the surrounding neighborhood. By contrast, when government museums in England instituted admission fees, the demographics of users narrowed and their numbers declined dramatically. Many British museums, having suffered the consequences of instituting charges, have announced their abolition. If museums are to become institutions that intentionally facilitate community development, then we should consider eliminating our entrance fees and recapturing the lost income from alternate sources.

Oldenburg has postulated that for civility to be enhanced, humans need three kinds of spaces – our homes (intimate private space), our work space (set aside for our vocations with our work mates), and, perhaps no less essentially – informal public space where strangers can mingle on a regular basis. Among public places, institutions like museums that store our collective memories and allow for the broadening of our collective experience are especially precious. The work of Jacobs, Oldenburg, and others has great value to the museum profession if our institutions are to be effective public forums and catalysts in the creation of a truly civil society. In Putnam's words,

> To build bridging social capital requires that we transcend our social and political and professional identities to connect with people unlike ourselves. This is why team sports provide good venues for social-capital creation. Equally important and less exploited in this connection are the arts and cultural activities.

(2000)

Note

1 A version of this essay was first published in *Curator* in 2001 (Gurian 2001).

Bibliography

Drucker, P.F. (1998) "Introduction: Civilizing the City," in Hesselbein, F. (ed.) *The Community of the Future*, San Francisco, CA: Jossey-Bass.

Ellenbogen, K. (2000) "Home-schooling Thesis," personal e-mail, October 12, 2000.

Falk, J.H., Koran, J.J., Dierking, L.D., and Dreblow, L. (1985) "Predicting Visitor Behavior," in *Curator*, 28:4, 326–332.

Foucault, M. (1970) *The Order of Things: An Archeology of the Human Sciences*, London: Tavistock.

Fulton, W. (1996) *New Urbanism: Hope or Hype for American Communities?* Lincoln, MA: Lincoln Institute of Land Policy.

Gurian, E.H. (2001) "Function Follows Form: How Mixed-Used Spaces in Museums Build Community," in *Curator*, 44:1, 87–113.

Heuman, J. (2000) "Joslyn Art Museum," personal e-mail, October 10, 2000.

Jacobs, J. (1961) *The Death and Life of Great American Cities*, New York: Random House.

Katz, P. (1994) *The New Urbanism: Toward an Architecture of Community*, New York: McGraw-Hill.

Konigsburg, E.L. (1972) *From the Mixed-up Files of Mrs. Basil E. Frankweiler*, New York: Simon & Schuster.

Kunstler, J.H. (1996) *Home from Nowhere: Remaking Our Everyday World for the Twenty-First Century*, New York: Simon & Schuster.

Matthews, N. (2000) "Kenosha Public Museum," personal e-mail, October 15, 2000.

Newsome, B.Y. and Silver, A.Z. (eds) (1978) *The Art Museum as Educator*, Berkeley, CA: University of California Press.

New York City Partnership and Chamber of Commerce Business Partnership (November 2001) *Working Together to Accelerate New York's Recovery. Economic Impact Analysis of the September 11 Attack on New York.*

Oldenburg, R. (1989) *The Great Good Place*, New York: Paragon House.

Putnam, R.D. (1995) "Bowling Alone: America's Declining Social Capital," in *Journal of Democracy*, 6:1, 65–78.

Putnam, R.D. (2000) *Bowling Alone: The Collapse and Revival of American Community*, New York: Simon & Schuster.

12

THRESHOLD FEAR[1]

Architecture program planning, 2005

The nature of our buildings and streets affects our behavior, affects the way we feel about ourselves and, importantly, how we get along with others.

> (MacDonald Becket in *Designing Places for People, a Handbook for Architects, Designers, and Facility Managers* (1985))

At the small museum, there are no inflated expectations, no pretensions, and no awful waits. The exhibitions may be small and somewhat idiosyncratic, but they mirror the small, somewhat idiosyncratic world we know, close to home.

> (Ron Chew 2002)

Members of our museum community write often about inclusion and of the "new town square," that they wish museums to become. In this paper, I take the position that for museums to become fully inclusive, they will have to make many and multivaried changes because there are both physical and programmatic barriers that make it difficult for the uninitiated to experience the museum. The term "threshold fear" was once relegated to the field of psychology but is now used in a broader context to mean the constraints people feel that prevent them from participating in activities meant for them.[2] To lower these perceived impediments, the fear-inducing stimulus must be reduced or dissolved. There has been little discussion within the museum field about the aspects of museum spaces that are intentionally welcoming and help to build community. There has been, in fact, a disjuncture between museums' programmatic interest in inclusion and the architectural program of space development – a gap that this essay tries to redress.

Museums clearly have thresholds that rise to the level of impediments, real and imagined, for the sectors of our population who remain infrequent visitors. The thresholds in question may be actual physical barriers – design ingredients that add to resistance – and other more subtle elements such as architectural style and its meaning to the potential visitor, wayfinding language, and complicated and unfamiliar entrance sequences. Further hindrances include the community's attitude toward the institution, the kind and amount of available public transportation, the admission charges and how they are applied, the organization of the front desk, insufficient sensitivity to many different handicapping conditions, the security system upon entering, and staff behavior toward unfamiliar folk. My thesis is that when museum management becomes interested in the identification, isolation, and reduction of each of these thresholds, they will be rewarded over time by an increased and broadened pattern of use, though the reduction of these thresholds is not sufficient by itself.

I started with the assumption that most museums wanted to broaden their audiences, that is, they wanted the profile of visitors to include more people from minority, immigrant, school drop-out, and working-class groups than was currently the case. I further believed that in order to achieve that aim, they would need a multilayered approach that would include less well-known and often untried elements, because many museums had experimented with choice of subject matter alone and had been largely unsuccessful in changing their visitation patterns over the long term. I postulated that if we worked with city planning theories and paid better attention to the aspects of space creation and planning that helped build community, museums might be more successful in their goal of inclusion, especially when they combined this work with the elements they were already using: expanded programming, community liaisons, and targeted free or reduced admissions. Trying all these options together, museums might finally solve the difficult long-standing problem of the narrow demographics of current museum users.

I sought to look at other institutions I believed served a broader audience and, while not in exactly the same business as museums, had sufficient similarities to serve as useful examples: zoos, libraries, for-profit attractions, and shopping malls.

Now, after researching the topic, I am less certain that broadening the audience for museums is achievable in general. Museums of real inclusion may be possible only if the competing traditional object-focused aspirations are reduced or even discarded. On a continuum, individual museums can be positioned from cultural icon to hometown clubhouse, with many stops in between. Cultural icons serve very important purposes, but these, I have reluctantly begun to realize, may be quite different from, and perhaps even mutually exclusive with, museums focused on community well-being. Sadder but wiser, I will argue that there are certain subtle things we can do related to space and city planning that will help museums that are really interested in broadening their visitation. Decisions about space do have a correspondence with mission. That thesis remains intact. However, it is my view that the mission aspired to by many art museums to create a temple of the contemplative, for example, has an easier correlation with both traditional and contemporary architecture than does the mission to create a welcoming, inclusionary museum.

That many museums do not really wish to become more inclusionary institutions is the subject for a different paper. Let me preview that elusive paper as follows. We know a lot about the amalgamated profile of current museum users. The typical visitor is well educated, relatively affluent, and generally has a wage earner who is white collar or professional within the family unit. Many museums, like good commercial product marketers, are programmed to satisfy this niche market – their current users.[3] Many museums, especially the more notable ones, are important elements of the tourism infrastructure in their metropolis, and tourism is primarily a middle- and upper-class activity. These same institutions are often described in the "quality of life" rhetoric that is intended to elicit more managerial-level business relocation, an aspiration intended to enlarge the overall financial base. Finally, and maybe not surprisingly, visitors and nonvisitors alike may not wish museums to change because many citizens separate their belief in the value of museums from their actual use of them.

I have come to believe that to become truly inclusionary, a museum must provide services that the user sees as essential, available on demand, timely, and personally driven. The definition of essential has to do with the personal impulse to transform an internal inquiry into action. Thus going to the library to get a book on how to fix the leaking sink at home makes the library an essential place. To change an institution from "nice to have" to "essential" is difficult. For most museums, concentrating on being the storehouse of the treasures of humanity may seem like virtue enough, regardless of the use visitors make of them. While useful for the overall needs of society, this focus does not make for essentiality.

This essay focuses on some of the space elements that can either help or hinder the mission of the museum, focusing on the elements that foster inclusion – should the museum wish to add space to its programmatic arsenal for just that purpose, understanding now that many may not.

For architects, designing a museum is among the most coveted commissions of the day, and iconic architecture frequently turns out to stimulate increased attendance. The typical affluent educated museum-goer is much impressed with the current architectural emphasis of museum buildings. Thus the creation of new architecture will increase, at least for a limited time, the quantity of users without necessarily changing the demographics.

But when architects do not care about the needs of the visitor (as happens more often than I care to report), especially if visitor needs are seen to interfere with artistic vision, architects create museums that are difficult to use. These inhospitalities reinforce the nonwelcoming nature of museums overall and add to the discouragement of the tentative user. That is a problem both of new buildings and of the augustly overwhelming museums of the past.

If the architect wants to combine a really interesting building with one that is welcoming to the novice user, then, I would contend, he or she must be interested in hospitable and less intimidating spaces, a plethora of easily locatable human amenities, and understandable wayfinding. The grand museums assert monumentality and present themselves as revered but not necessarily comfortable icons. Very few new buildings of note can be seen as friendly and comfortable. There are exceptions of course: the Picasso Museum in a historic building refurbishment in the Marais in Paris and the building I.M. Pei designed for the Herbert F. Johnson Museum of Art at Cornell University are two of them.

With these thoughts in mind, in the following sections I will draw upon a number of architectural planning theories in order to consider some of the spatial and related organizational problems of the museum. Then I will suggest some changes museums might make to become more inclusionary.

Congregant spaces

The populace needs congregant public spaces and has many at its disposal. Some theorists believe that in order to maintain a peaceful society, people need access to three kinds of spaces: places for family and friends (our most intimate relationships), places for work, and places where it is safe to interact with strangers (Oldenburg 1989). The last category has important meaning beyond the functions these places overtly serve. That they exist and are available to strangers reassures the public that there is order and well-being to be found in populated centers. Whenever these places are considered unsafe for any reason, they are abandoned, sometimes permanently, and society becomes more balkanized.

The congregant places organized for strangers fall into a surprisingly long list. They include (but are not limited to):

- Transportation hubs such as railway stations and airports, and the transportation vehicles themselves.
- Religious gathering places like churches, mosques, and synagogues.
- Places of large and small commercial transactions, such as shopping malls, markets, public streets lined with shops, and the shops themselves.
- Places organized for eating and socializing, such as restaurants, pubs, and cafés.
- Places used for recreation, such as bathing beaches and parks.
- Civic buildings, such as judicial courts and town halls.
- Places that hold access to information and/or present experiences, such as libraries and archives, theaters and concert halls, athletic arenas, schools, and public spaces used for celebrations like parades and pageants.

Museums, historic houses, zoos, botanic gardens, and historic sites belong to this last segment: sites that hold access to information and experiences.

All civic spaces used by strangers have some commonalities, and many kinds of civic spaces have more in common with certain museums than with others. Certain elements of libraries, zoos, shopping malls, attractions, stadiums, and train stations can become models for museums. It is unfortunate that museum personnel have often felt that associating themselves with the kinds of congregant spaces on this list is a disservice to their own uniqueness and status. I would suggest the contrary.

The city planning theory of Jane Jacobs and her followers

Architectural theorists and city planners refer to physical spaces offering a variety of services often co-located in residential areas as mixed-use space. Mixed-use spaces can be small, found within one strip mall, one city street, and one building, or so large so that they encompass whole sections of cities. These mixed-used spaces particularly interest such theorists as Jane Jacobs (Jacobs 1961). Studies of these spaces have had a profound effect on the development of planned communities and the refurbishment of downtown cities. Theorists have postulated that the broadest array of users inhabit locations that house a multitude of offerings: products selling for a wide range of prices, a combination of useful services (shoe repair, pharmacy, etc.) mixed with more exotic specialties, open hours that are as close to around-the-clock as possible, residential units, public amenities such as seating, and, most important, foot traffic.

They go on to postulate that these mixed-use spaces are perceived as safe to use because they are busy, lighted, and have many people present all the time, including "regulars" and "lurkers" who are vigilant and proprietary but also welcoming, exemplifying a peaceful and even friendly code of behavior that strangers can easily perceive (Gurian 2001).

Since the 1970s, in addition to an explosion of new museum buildings and commissions for high-profile architects, museums have also become keystones to economic revival plans in urban settings recognized as having positive fiscal impacts for the city. A change in the economic base of museums – from philanthropic and governmental support to an emphasis on earned income from retail activities within the building – has profoundly revised the architectural program that museums need and has changed museums (inadvertently) into mixed-use spaces (Gurian 2001).

Museums now offer spaces that provide exhibitions, programs, restaurants and cafés, shopping, and party spaces under one roof. Museums often either incorporate or are adjacent to public transport and to other services (child care, schools, performance spaces, parks, and additional food and shopping opportunities). As they incorporate or align themselves with such services, they become a thoroughfare for a broader population who may have different motivations for entering and different stay-lengths and who use the facility during different times of the day. This quality of mixed use can also be seen in zoos, libraries, and shopping malls.

Architectural program planning

There is little understanding within the museum community that creating these varied spaces within one building has yielded a more inclusionary whole. There has been little overt discussion about the spatial considerations that might help provide increased service to a wider community, and there is often a disjuncture between the museums' professed programmatic interest in inclusion and the resulting architectural program of space development. I have often found that prior to embarking on construction of a new expansion or building, senior museum personnel do not understand the architectural process sufficiently, so they do not grasp the relationship between programmatic intention and physical planning. As a result, the museum's strategic direction and its architectural development diverge.

"Architectural writing beginning in the 1960s is full of humanistic philosophy, behavioral design, and a keen interest in the creation and sustainability of livable cities" (Alexander 1964, 1987). Finding this disjuncture between many contemporary museum buildings and the philosophy espoused, conclude that the people involved (both on the architectural and the museum teams) either did not realize that the new architectural literature could positively affect building plans or were not sympathetic to that nation.

My experience working with architects and museums on architectural program planning is illuminating. First, most museum staff do not know that a process called architectural program planning exists; they think in terms of blueprints and do not know that there is a prerequisite step that focuses on volumes and adjacencies, which is driven by the museum's articulated programmatic needs. They often are not coached by the architect about the process and do not do a thorough job of stating their philosophy, their specific programmatic needs, or their future aspirations. One cannot hope to have a building that corresponds to the philosophic aspirations of the museum leadership without first divining the strategy directions of the museum and translating those into binding architectural terms. Second, some, though certainly not all, architects are happier to gloss over this planning stage because without it the architect is left to design without constraints. Finally, boards of directors, government officials, and directors often wish to build a museum that will enter the world stage by virtue of architectural excellence and novelty. So they come to believe that putting programmatic or even budget restrictions on the architect will only point out their own philistine-like nature. And some architects are happy to capitalize on that fear.

The situations described work against having an architectural program plan of any specificity or rigor. When a museum lacks a specific guiding programmatic document, evaluating the subsequent designs against established criteria becomes difficult. In this regard, it does not matter if we are talking about new buildings, refurbishment of existing structures, or even just rearrangement of the current fit-out. My advice to my clients is that the architectural program plan is the most critical element in the building process.

Location on neutral ground

City planners, imbued with the theories of Jane Jacobs and her successors in the livable cities movement, are increasingly interested in enriching the services and liveliness of neighborhoods by enhancing foot traffic, expanding public transport, and creating easily accessible parking in an off-site location. Some institutions are seen to be on neutral ground, equally available to all people, and others seem intentionally isolated and relatively unavailable. Location and placement often create, overtly or inadvertently, turf boundaries where citizens believe that the spaces in question are reserved predominantly for a small segment of society. I am old enough to remember the protests and legal action over the then-legal segregation of swimming pools and playgrounds in my country. Ending legal segregation did not necessarily end *de facto* segregation. Some of these very same swimming pools are still almost exclusively used by either blacks or whites because the area surrounding the pool, while no longer legally segregated, is virtually so.

The creation of such nonneutral space can be unintentionally alienating or intentionally off-putting.

Museums must look at their own locations with care. It seems axiomatic that the more accessible its location, the more likely a museum will have a heterogeneous group of users. What constitutes site "ownership" is not always apparent. The regular clientele of one local pub may be a clique established by custom even though there may be many pubs to choose from within a close proximity.

Museums on once-neutral ground can become segregated by changes in resident patterns in the surrounding neighborhood. Similarly, non-neutral space can be turned into more inclusive space by the acceptance and even encouragement of public activities taking place inside and outside the facility that change the perception of use. The Brooklyn Museum of Art, finding its forecourt used by skateboarders, invited them to continue (most building administrators would oust them). Turf ownership, while seemingly entrenched, turns out to be mutable.

Potential visitors' common understanding of how safe or dangerous the surrounding neighborhood will be becomes an important factor in deciding to visit. New Yorkers' perception of the safety of any borough other than middle and lower Manhattan makes visiting museums in the other boroughs adventurous and seemingly fraught with danger for Manhattanites. It was interesting to watch the visitor's hesitation when getting off the subway and trying to locate the Museum of Modern Art in its temporary location in Long Island City, Queens. The reverse is true when a Queens resident decides to visit the Metropolitan Museum of Art. That is also an activity of some adventure. I know; I grew up in Queens.

Learning the resources before visiting

Civic sophistication can sometimes be measured by citizens' ease in using unfamiliar available resources. In effect, research management occupies part of everyone's daily transactions. "Which shop will have the specific material we might need?" and "Is the owner reliable?" Much of the most readily available information comes from talking to trusted intimates. Thus word of mouth and street credibility has much to do with use.

In the museum world, we are more reliant on previous satisfied users than we understand. Most new users are people who know and trust someone who has already been there. Spending more time cultivating adventurous pioneers by giving them reliable sources of information, and developing positive street credibility, is an essential task for institutions that want wider attendance. Further, when we diversify our staff, we begin to gain the kind of credibility that pierces many neighborhoods. It is one of the positive outcomes of internalized diversity.

Getting there

In Britain (as in many countries), there is an increased reliance on automobile transportation. A study reports that more than 50 percent of all children's trips involve riding in a car, and there is a much-decreased use of the bicycle.[4] This means that children can go fewer places on their own. For parents it means that things that can be done within walking distance of one parking stop are easier to contemplate than several errands, each needing its own exclusive parking. Hence the growth of the shopping mall and the increase of pedestrian traffic associated with convenient parking.

Here again, museums embedded within public walking thoroughfares can more easily become casual visits and even multiple visits – an ingredient often seen in the more "essential" institutions, such as libraries, which accommodate short, focused, and efficient visitation. The monumentality of the large museum set off by itself, with its need to accommodate patrons' parking or the added cost of a parking garage, militates against casual use.

In the United Kingdom, there are a series of fascinating Web sites that look at social exclusion and its relation to public transportation. One study looks the interconnectedness of public transport availability and the knowledge required for using transport to unfamiliar sites.[5] It seems all too evident that lack of available public transport coupled with inexperience makes it less likely for the nonuser population to visit. However if the motivation is high enough, such as "seeing the doctor" or "going for a job interview," the person will brave the trip if possible.

Visitation becomes a less fearful activity when public transport is in place, experienced users ride along with the inexperienced, and drivers are especially helpful. There is only occasional interest in the museum sector to view public transport as an essential ingredient toward enlarged public use. And rarely are museum personnel involved in lobbying efforts toward improved public transport.

Entering

Once potential visitors have gotten themselves to the front door, it seems easy, on the surface, to enter a museum without the potentially uncomfortable task of revealing too much personal information. Actually, visitors need to reveal quite a lot during the entrance process. They need to show that they can afford the price of admission by paying. If they visit during weekday hours, assumptions will be made that they are on holiday, unemployed, retired, a student, or somehow not in the workforce. Visitors must dress and behave superficially "normal" in order to be allowed to remain in the building. Most of these assessments, and any anxieties they may engender, rest within the potential visitors' minds, of course. But this mental projection is very real to the novice user and impossible to ameliorate except by training museum personnel to become sincere but not effusive welcomers and, most important, to review the entrance sequence to reduce the level of mandatory interaction required.

Much of the initial person-to-person engagement begins at the admissions desk. Since this transaction is directly interpersonal, the collection of charges, I believe, is the single biggest disincentive for entering. Charges make visits to the museum an "outing" rather than a useful casual drop-in errand. A look at the free museums located on pedestrian ways often shows a steady stream of users who are pursuing short-time or casual activities. By eliminating charges, the museum eliminates this scrutiny from the encounter. I contend this change will go a long way toward the reduction of threshold fear.

Unfortunately, eliminating charges itself does not seem to change the demographic make-up of visitors. Many museums in the United Kingdom have gone from free to admission charges and back to free again. In the process, they learned that the total number of visitors falls precipitately when charges are instituted and rise again when they are reversed, but the demographics of their users do not change appreciably.[6]

I would contend that the entrance sequence itself must be rethought so that the novice visitor can become a "lurker," figuring out the process of entering by passive watching from an anonymous location. It helps to have a large lobby available before the entrance sequence or a transparent front wall visible from the outdoors. Large railroad stations allow for such decoding.

More recently, because of perceived security needs in many countries, the encounter that precedes admissions is the most threatening of all: security checking, requiring surveillance by a policelike person. I look forward to the day when museums will eliminate security from their entries. Passing a security checkpoint is a very high threshold for anyone. That is why few libraries and fewer shopping malls use overt security screeners in their entrances. I am convinced that they are just as vulnerable as museums but remain more anxious to serve their public.

Malls and other animals

A review of the organization of shopping malls in most countries gives credence to the rightness of Jane Jacobs' philosophy. Shopping mall design intentionally includes the ability to enter anonymously, the possibility of sitting and strolling without committing to organized activity. These amenities allow unfamiliar users to figure out the services and customs required without drawing attention to themselves. Malls offer simple access to easily understood facilities such as toilets, and there are plenty of opportunities to socialize while eating. Finally, they welcome multigenerational groups and increasingly try to understand packs of adolescents who find strolling and meeting in the mall their main avenue of socializing. Museums, though they currently don't think so, might be lucky if they found themselves with this problem (Kelly *et al.* 2002). While museums have many of the same amenities as the mall, using them requires passing an entrance sequence.

A museum lobby, like the strolling spaces in malls, can become a meeting place for people who may not intend to visit the exhibitions. What mall designers understand is the notion of impulse buying (Kelly *et al.* 2002) (if you are there anyway, you might discover you need something). I believe museums must begin to value impulse visiting – that is, savoring a small segment of the museum for a short fragment of time – which will require museums to think of themselves differently.

It is sometimes surprising to find out why some civic spaces are more popular than others. Most zoos provide venues for picnicking with food brought from home. They allow groups (those that have dietary restrictions or do not trust food prepared by strangers) to come to a public place and inadvertently socialize with others. In a community meeting I held in Israel, I learned that being able to picnic using one's own food made the zoo the last remaining neutral public space in Jerusalem used by both Palestinian and Israeli and by both orthodox and nonorthodox Jewish family groups who were otherwise fearful of each other. Upon hearing this, Jerusalem's Bloomfield Science Museum decided that it, too, could arrange for picnic tables and refrigerators, so that in the hopeful future when a more tentative peace might emerge, they could be a location for social interaction among strangers.

Museums have overtly learned from the attractions industry about the importance of customer service. There are now customer-friendly hosts in many museums. These hosts, if they represent the diversity found in the community and are sensitively trained, make the experience more understandable and less alien for the novice. In Jacobs' terms, visitor service personnel act as "regulars" offering reassurance and knowledge on the one hand and demonstrating the behavior norms required on the other.

Malls, zoos, attractions, and libraries suggest other considerations that might increase use by a wider population:

- Create spaces both for small-group interaction and for private contemplation. See that they don't interfere with each other.
- Have help staff available in a physical location that can be easily seen, but do not require interaction from the visitor.
- Train visitor services staff not to be intrusive but still welcoming.
- Hire staff from many different cultural groups and include nonnative speakers. Reorient the building toward public transportation and foot traffic.
- Introduce more easily accessible visitor amenities, such as seating, toilets, cafés, and baby spaces.
- Watch for the ways the public actually uses the building, and then formalize these unexpected and even serendipitous uses.
- Revamp systems to focus on avenues of self-directed learning like browsing in the library. This probably means providing visible access to the collections, or at least access to collections information without staff intercession.
- Set the hours of operation to suit the neighborhood rather than the staff.
- Accept behavior, clothing choice, sound level, and interaction styles that are consistent with norms of courtesy of the individuals' community.
- Trust the visitor so that intrusive security can be minimized. Organizing for the best in people is a risk worth taking.
- Last and most important, understand the significance visitors place on seeing the evidence and so encourage interaction with three-dimensional experiences. Museums' special legitimacy remains visual and even tactile access to physical things.

The repair of the dead mall and other conclusions

When a mall begins to lose income or even "dies," there is an economic imperative to fix it, tear it down, or repurpose it. A Web site run by Los Angeles Forum held a competition to fix "dead malls."[7] The winning entries offer fascinating glimpses of what architects and merchants think is needed to enhance the usage of moribund shopping centers.

One entrant used the following four categories when contemplating useful spaces: big box cathedral – gathering; global vortex – raving; elastic bazaar – wandering; and smart mobs – swarming. Even the words chosen for the categories intrigue me. Imagine if there were museums that wished for raving and swarming. I think these word choices (and the rest of the Web site) foretell the kinds of spaces needed for increased museum use.

Museums remain one of the important congregant spaces in any community. To encourage use by all citizens we need to be more sensitive to the space requirements that make it clear that the visitor, regardless of previous experience, is welcome. It is my hope that as we readjust the way we build, repair, and reinstall museums we will invite more citizens to join us. I once said I wished museum audiences to be as diverse as those to be found at any given moment in Grand Central Station. Mindful that some do not share my vision, I hope for that more today than ever.

Notes

1 This text was originally delivered as a keynote at the Creative Space conference April 5–7, 2004 at the University of Leicester Department of Museum Studies in Leicester, United Kingdom. A version of this paper was published (Gurian 2005).

2 See for example, *Gypsies and Travelers in Belgium – an Online Interview*. Available http://home2.pi.be/tmachiel/educati2.htm (accessed August 14, 2004).

3 "Our visitor profile and demographics demonstrate why Museum sponsorship is an ideal way to magnify your company's image." Museum of Science, Boston, Web site enticing corporate sponsorship by pointing out that 74 percent of visitors have a college degree or higher and a median annual income of $82,000 (Museum of Science 2005).

4 National statistics of Great Britain. Available http://www.statistics.gov.uk/STATBASE/ssdataset.asp?vlnk=3661 (accessed February 25, 2005).

5 Households without a car, in a society in which household car ownership is the norm, are socially excluded within our definition of the term, since they cannot fully participate, that is, behave as the vast majority of society behaves. See "Social exclusion and the provision of public transport, summary report." Available http://www.dft.gov.uk/stellent/groups/dft_mobility/documents/page/dft_mobility_506794-05.hcsp#TopOfPage   (accessed February 23, 2005).

6 "Research conducted to determine the impact of free entry to museums and galleries throughout London shows that increase in visitation has been greater among the AB social group. Although free entry was introduced to encourage visitation from all social backgrounds, this has not been reflected in the visitor profile." Maritime Museum UK report, Comparative Visitor Profile 1999–2001. Available http://www.nmm.ac.uk/uploads/pdf/Comparative_visitor_profile.pdf (accessed January 29, 2005).

7 *The Dead Mall Competition Web Page.* Available http://www.laforum.org/deadmalls/index.html (accessed December 14, 2004).

Bibliography

Alexander, C. (1964) *Notes on the Synthesis of Form*, Cambridge, MA: Harvard University Press.

Alexander, C. (1987) *A New Theory of Urban Design*, New York: Oxford University Press.

Chew, R. (2002) "In Praise of the Small Museum," in *Museum News*, March/April, 36–41.

The Dead Mall Competition Web Page. Available http://www.laforum.org/deadmalls/index.html (accessed December 14, 2004).

Deasy, C.M. (ed.) (1985) *Designing Places for People, a Handbook for Architects, Designers, and Facility Managers*, New York: Whitney Library of Design.

Gurian, E.H. (2001) "Function Follows Form: How Mixed-Used Spaces in Museums Build Community," in *Curator*, 44:1, 87–113.

Gurian, E.H. (2005) "Threshold Fear," in Macleod, S. (ed.) *Reshaping Museum Space: Architecture, Design, Exhibitions*, London: Routledge.

Gypsies and Travelers in Belgium – an Online Interview. Available http://home2.pi.be/tmachiel/educati2.htm (accessed August 14, 2004).

Jacobs, J. (1961) *The Death and Life of Great American Cities*, New York: Random House.

Kelly, L., Bartlett, A., and Gordon, P. (2002) *Indigenous Youth and Museums: A Report on the Indigenous Youth Access Project*, Australian Museum, Sydney.

Museum of Science (2005) *Corporate Sponsorship*. Available http://www.mos.org/doc/1026 (accessed March 1, 2005).

Oldenburg, R. (1989) *The Great Good Place*, New York: Paragon House.

13

FREE AT LAST[1]

A case for the elimination of admission charges in museums, 2005

> Point of entry charging is a relatively straightforward way to generate
> revenue, and it offers visitors a simple purchasing choice. But it also
> raises practical problems, as well as philosophical, ethical and
> community concerns, which may outweigh its commercial advantages.
> (Mark Lindsay 1994)

I have reluctantly, but unequivocally, come to the conclusion that general admission charges are the single greatest impediment to making our museums fully accessible.

It is time for a study on the budgetary and social impacts that removal of charges would have on our various institutions. I am not talking about straight-line review of the loss of income represented by the elimination of charges. This is an obvious mathematical exercise, and I know that the aggregate reduction of revenue would be a whopping big number. Rather, I suggest a search for additional compensatory income streams that would need to be generated to counteract the loss and ways to help individual organizations develop them. This study would need to deal with probability and percentages of income mixes, and factor in the reduction in operating costs and the increased "spend per head" that unfettered visitation would represent. The mix might also include (in addition to the case needed to be made to governments large and small for increased support) multi-institutional pass systems, charges for special services, the selling of air rights and increased ownership of for-profit property and business, and suggestions generated by others but unknown at this time to the author.

I ask for such a study reluctantly because I know that since the 1960s, private not-for-profit museums have increasingly become dependent on admission fees as their largest source of earned income. I am acutely aware that even with the increased ancillary revenue engendered by increased visitorship, administrators would be forced to find substantial alternate subventions to offset the loss of admissions income. Worse, since they have already been entrepreneurial in developing additional sources of income, there is no easy untapped additional source. And to be clear, I am not calling for the removal of all charges to all activities. Quite to the contrary, I believe that in order to maintain fiscal solvency, museums will have to look for additional fee-for-service opportunities to increase their "per capita" income. I am, however, suggesting that free admittance cover the "core" functions of the museum including permanent installations, and access to ancillary services like reference centers, libraries, and study storage.

The complete replenishment of revenue loss is unlikely to happen without some level of government intervention. This proposal rests on the notion that governments, even in these hard times, can be persuaded to contribute to the running of museums as a matter of civic responsibility – even though we have not universally persuaded them to do so in the past. However, I believe the case for government assistance cannot be effectively made with general admission charges in place.

I am hopeful that this call for the removal of general admission is neither "pie in the sky" nor "dead on arrival." Witness some recent developments – the labor government of the United Kingdom has reinstated free admissions for their largest museums after having imposed charges for some years. The Swedish government has taken away all charges from their major museums in Stockholm as of the first of the year, 2005. The National Museums of the United States, Canada, Australia, and New Zealand have convinced their governments that they should be free (having made the case, often with position papers, about the benefits and consequences). Like private museums, all these national museums generate a variety of earned income to augment the government infusion.

Although the aforementioned examples are all national museums, the proposition is not meant to pertain to national or government museums exclusively. I am especially interested in private museums. There are numerous examples of municipal government allocating revenues earmarked as operating offsets for cultural organizations. As an example, the Minneapolis Institute of Arts, a recipient of local tax revenue, removed its admission fee in the 1990s. It succeeded in involving the community, reoriented its attention and services accordingly, and generated an increased "spend per head" that offset the lost revenue. The Minneapolis Institute of Arts could not have attempted that, however, without partial underwriting from the city.[2]

The arguments for free admission

The reasons for reorganization of museum finances are not primarily monetary but philosophical. I am convinced that charging admissions fundamentally alters the nature of museums and categorically changes their functions and orientation. Museums cannot argue that they hold the patrimony of all if only some can afford to see it. They cannot argue that they are the meeting ground, town square, forum, and safe civic space for strangers if only some strangers (those that pay) can take part. And they cannot argue that they are a resource for those impelled to learn something if the learner must first determine if they can afford to learn. There is a fundamental disconnect between the mission statements we write and the act of imposing an entry fee.

The operational arguments for establishing free admission are many:

- The admission process as the first experience is off-putting and adds to resistance by non-users.
- The ways that individuals make use of free venues is entirely different from the ways they visit venues that charge. The imposition of charges makes the museum experience a special and occasional one rather than an easily repeatable one. It is the ease of entry and potential of repeated use, I would contend, that converts institutions from "nice to have" to "essential" on the civic menu.
- Some have said that the charges imposed by many museums are now exorbitant.[3] The aggregate cost for a young family of four is sufficiently daunting that even traditional museum goers with modest incomes (some of our most motivated visitors) cannot come as often as they might wish.
- A need to offer reduced admission costs is recognized by museums who promote various free or reduced admission schemes. However taking advantage of this requires forethought and planning and so tends to be used primarily by more experienced and organized visitors.
- The argument is offered by some cognoscenti that charges help keep attendance down, which they prefer. This is antithetical to our professed desire to have all who wish attend.

I am not maintaining that the removal of admission charges will, in and of itself, change the profile of museum users. Recent demographic studies of British museum users, following the transition back to free admission, suggest otherwise.[4] The number of overall visitors rose in all categories, though the percentage of non-museum users did not appreciably change. This potential audience continues to feel that the museum is not their place and so additional work, even with the absence of admission, would have to be done. However a study in Germany revealed "entrance fees to be the only significant subjective barrier" to attendance.[5] Thus free admission while not the entire answer remains an essential ingredient toward our goal of inclusion.

Entering

I am arguing that the very sequence of entering a museum (including the payment of fees) changes the museum experience from a casual repeatable occurrence to an occasion. It is not only the money expended but also the process itself which effectively works as an emotional means test. One cannot enter a museum unobtrusively. I think that potential, but ambivalent, attendees are made decidedly uncomfortable by the prospect of the first encounter, and thus eschew it.

Getting "the lay of the land" visually before commitment works best for the tenuous. Jane Jacobs in her book, *The Death and Life of Great American Cities* (Jacobs 1961), extols the virtue of "lurking" as orientation. I am not surprised to see that those institutions that are dependent on the process of "dropping in" and browsing have not imposed charges (nor in most cases visible security screening) at the entry. These places include most libraries, shopping malls, and even airports prior to boarding areas (even though moving security to inside the building increases the vulnerability of the building).

Libraries often have screening at the end of the visit so that leaving with unchecked books is made difficult but entry and browsing are not. The fact that most libraries are seen by all as a civic service worthy of government support may be related to their entrance policy. In any event, it is clear that American politicians are much clearer about their public responsibility to libraries than they are to museums.

Because libraries are free and organized for browsing, the public uses them differently than they use museums. People often go to libraries on a focused self-motivated pursuit. The librarian makes no judgment about the nature of their quest and offers help (only if asked) to solve the questions at hand. Library patrons don't feel obliged to ration their visits; indeed it is perfectly acceptable to have multiple visits for multiple reasons. The library stay length can be short and focused or leisurely and random. The tempo for museum visits, however, tends to be different. Having paid one's money, visitors stay as long as they can manage within their social calendar and urgently cover as much ground as possible. They know they will not come back soon.

There is an important exception to this pattern. The museum visitor who functions like the library visitor in an admissions-based museum is the "member." Members typically pay a one-time fee which allows for free (and arguably more cost-effective) access for a year afterward. Once paid, they feel they are entitled to come "free" as often as they like and for as long as they wish. However, only those who forecast they will want to come multiple times (and who have ready access to a large one-time payment), buy memberships. Members are a more exclusive community than are library users.

There is a system that most closely matches my museum hopes. Libraries (often in poorer neighborhoods) pay museums an annual negotiated fee. Libraries then offer membership passes on a check-out basis, and the visitor, on presenting such a pass to the museum, is accorded all the rights of a regular member. However this membership pass requires a two-stage process – going first to the library and then the museum which requires much forethought. The emotional credit for this pass is given the library, rather than the museum, enhancing the citizen's sense that the library is a civic amenity while the museum is a restricted location.

Some countries and US cities offer another alternative: the purchase of multiple site passes to a range of cultural institutions, with the income received divided among the participating institutions. This system, a variant on membership, is worth further investigation.[6,7]

Volume of visitors

The British museum situation is both instructive and controversial. Historically the museums charged no admissions and were well used. Taking note of the private not-for-profit American museum experience, where charges were begun during the 1960s and onward, the Thatcher government encouraged the imposition of admission fees. Charges, sometimes voluntary, were instated, whereafter the attendance dropped precipitously. The current Labor government has now removed charges from many of the major museums replacing them with an annual operating cash infusion. The attendance has increased in large numbers.[8]

Some of the British museum community has argued that this is not an entirely good thing. They point out that the subvention does not fully cover the higher costs of operating and should therefore be increased. They further note that while visitation has increased, the demographic profile of visitors has not changed (Martin 2003). And they argue that the free museums get unfair advantage over those that still charge.

Limited free admission schemes

It is clear that museums see sufficient benefit to free admissions that they provide all manner of schemes to offer it. The most prominent are free days. Sometimes these are just once a year, sometimes once a month, or once a week. For visitors to participate, they need to be informed, read the paper, plan ahead, and lead an organized life.

The other free situations occur as a marketing effort using coupons, a library card, a free pass, something that you have in your hand. Again you must be organized and prepared to bring the appropriate material with you.

A third way is organized free events, on special holidays or because a special historic event has happened. Some cities have organized widespread free nights – for example, the third Thursday in the month. Because these are consistent and cover more than one institution they tend to be well attended but not on the casual basis that libraries are used.

The users of these free times tend to be the less well-to-do segments of the already-museum-going society, who know how to take advantage of such events, appreciate museums, and know how to use them.

Where is the admissions desk located?

Along with the question of whether museums should charge admission is the issue of where visitors should be asked to pay. Even those museums that believe they must charge could probably position their admission desks farther back in the visitors' experience, encouraging "lurking" by placing a wider variety of public experiences in front of the admissions desk. Many newer museums have restaurants and shops located near their front doors but precious few offer any other experiences without payment. If orientation theaters and interactive experiences – high and/or low tech – along with comfortable seating and public restrooms were available to anyone who ventured in, these amenities could encourage potential visitors to test the waters. They could also encourage repeat visitation, which might eventually lead to purchasing a ticket for admission to the galleries. I'm reminded of Sherman Lee's description of the museum as a "wilderness," which is something that must be approached in small steps.

(Fischer, personal communication)

Things I never knew

There are, it turns out, many academicians in economics, sociology, and technology, who take the issue of charges in museums and heritage sites very seriously. They are interested in models and variables. They use terms museum people are not necessarily familiar with. Technology terms like "endpoint admissions control" and "flow set-up latency" (Choi and Beettati 2001) and economic terms like "managerial incentives," "public and private good," "market failure," "travel cost method," etc. (Bailey and Falconer 1998, Rodríguez and Blanco 2003). They conclude that admission charges are an impediment to visitation. Since the case for replacement revenue from government has not been convincingly made, in part because the variables are so interdependent, there will have to be a blend of possible solutions. Nevertheless, these academicians see museums as a public good which cannot be sustained through purely market forces. They are joined by politicians who place the value of museums, historic sites, and natural sites in a mix of rhetoric that includes economic development, a definite but unquantifiable "quality of life" for their citizens, and some notion of long-term responsibility to future generations. A majority of the public seems to agree, maintaining that public funding for cultural institutions in their cities and states is appropriate (DiMaggio and Pettit 1998).

Conclusion

With social scientists concluding that variables are many and the economic models not yet perfected, a decision to contemplate free admission, from whence most museums came, will arise, only in the first instance, from mission, philosophy, experimentation, faith, and gut feeling. Of course, careful economic analysis will have to follow shortly thereafter, understanding that without government subvention and some, as yet unexplored revenue enhancement, there is no evident solution on the horizon. Nothing is simple in life.

If everyone gets free entrance into the building and free access to its basic services, then payment for such things as classes, lectures, special exhibitions, and special events seems reasonable. Further, if we are hungry we can all pay for food and feeling acquisitive, buy something in the shop. I can live with that.

Museums, if they remain oriented toward their paying customers, will not, I contend, organize themselves as the more general resource they can become. They will not feel motivated to become essential elements within the community and an important resource for the quests of individuals impelled to learn a particular something.

Further the museum that is used only on special occasions or for an organized day out will never become the forum, the meeting ground, the crossroads, the town square that we are fond of talking about.

To me, lifting admission fees, even with the attendant risks, beats charging. The major and undeniable problem with charging is that it is a means test. In the current situation only those who can afford the cost, and think the experience is valuable enough to pay for, can have access to the patrimony that belongs to us all. We cannot continue to discuss inclusion if we continue to charge for general admission.

Notes

1 Martin Luther King used this phrase more eloquently and for a much more serious purpose, when he gave his impassioned address on August 28, 1963, in Washington, DC. However, I borrow it with the hope that the importance of according all of our citizens the equal right to access their patrimony would appeal to him as part of the complex fabric of civil rights.

2 There are a number of additional dedicated tax earmarks to offset operating expenditures in local cultural organizations for example, "In St. Louis, a small percentage of property tax millage goes into operating support dollars for arts and cultural organizations. In Pittsburgh, they have a regional sales tax. Montgomery County, Ohio, added a sales tax, and out of that they fund new housing projects and economic development initiatives and support the arts and cultural organizations, as well as many other not-for-profit organizations. The hotel-motel tax is one way many communities provide public-sector funding for the arts." Community Partnership for the Arts and Culture President Thomas Schorgl (*The Plain Dealer* 2002).

3 The current discussion about admissions fees centers on the newly reopened Museum of Modern Art (MOMA) in New York. They charge $20 per person, though they have many discount exceptions (seniors $16, students $12, children with a grown-up free, membership free, and different membership charges depending on how far away the visitor resides or if they are an artist).

4 "...although there has been a rise in visiting among those who might be described as being 'socially excluded', the most significant impact on visiting appears to have been among those groups who traditionally have always gone to museums and galleries" (Martin 2003, p. 10).

5 In a 1995 representative survey, 1,080 Germans were asked by standardized questionnaire to assess the subjective significance of 23 motives and barriers to visiting art museums, history museums, and technology museums on a scale from 1 (very unimportant motive/barrier) to 5 (very important motive/barrier). An analysis of the results of the survey revealed entrance fees to be the only significant subjective barrier (Kirchberg 1998).

6 Such passes exist in Amsterdam, Barcelona, Bologna, Bonn, Brussels, Budapest, Copenhagen, Helsinki, Lisbon, London, Luxemburg, Montreal, Paris, Salzburg, Stockholm, Vienna, and Zurich. There is a North American program entitled Citypass, offered in Boston, New York, Seattle, Chicago, Hollywood, San Francisco, Philadelphia, Southern California, and Toronto (see http://citypass.com). Citypass offers combined admission usually to two to three museums plus some other tourist attractions (such as the Empire State Building in New York or the Hancock Observatory in Chicago) (Ginsburgh and Zang 2001).

7 400 of the 950 Swiss museums can be visited free with the purchase of Swiss Museum Pass. "...The number of people using the museums passport rose by 34 percent in 2003 compared to 2002" (source: Swiss museum passport association).

8 Nearly 6 million more visits to England's formerly charging national museums and galleries took place in 2004, compared to the year before entry charges were scrapped by the government. Three years after the turnstiles were removed visits are up by 75 percent nationally. In London, visits to the Victoria and Albert Museum (V&A) are up by 113 percent, the Natural History Museum by 95 percent, and the Science Museum by 71 percent. Visits to the Royal Armouries in Leeds have risen by 147 percent, to National Museums Liverpool by 94 percent, and to the National Railway Museum in York by 57 percent.

Bibliography

Bailey, S.J. and Falconer, P. (1998) "Charging for Admission to Museums and Galleries: A Framework for Analysis of the Impact on Access," in *Journal of Cultural Economics*, 22:2–3, 167–177.

Choi, B.K. and Beettati, R. (2001) *Endpoint Admission Control: Network Based Approach*, The Twenty-first International Conference on Distributed Computing Systems, Mesa, AZ.

DiMaggio, P. and Pettit, B. (1998) "Surveys of Public Attitudes toward the Arts," in *Grantmakers in the Arts Newsletter*, Seattle, WA, 9:2, 26–30.

Fischer, D. (2005) Museum charges, personal communication.

Ginsburgh, V. and Zang, I. (2001) "Sharing the Income of a Museum Pass Program," in *Museum Management and Curatorship*, Great Britain, 19:4, 371–383.

Jacobs, J. (1961) *The Death and Life of Great American Cities*, New York: Random House.

Kirchberg, V. (1998) "Entrance Fees as a Subjective Barrier to Visiting Museums," in *Journal of Cultural Economics*, 22:1, 1–3.

Lindsay, M. (1994) *Admission Charges – the Issues*, Wellington, NZ: Museum of New Zealand Te Papa Tongarewa.

Martin, A. (2003) *The Impact of Free Entry to Museums*, London: MORI, 10.

The Plain Dealer (2002) "The Quiet Crisis, a Special Report from the Plain Dealer, the Fine Art of Taxing to Support Culture," Cleveland.

Rodríguez, J.P. and Blanco, V.F. (2003) "Optimal Pricing and Grant Policies for Museums." Available http://ideas.repec.org/p/wpa/wuwppe/0309002.html

Part IV

NOODLING AROUND WITH
EXHIBITION OPPORTUNITIES
Examining the process that influences them

Exhibitions are a museum's most visible product. When asked, the public thinks of museums primarily as exhibitions and exhibitions primarily as things in cases. Yet contemporary museum exhibitions are more than that. Some use no collection objects at all, and many incorporate hands-on techniques interspersed with technology. In the end, like all things in museums, exhibition content, design, and production are all rooted in the creators' philosophy – in this case, theories of learning and aspirations on behalf of the intended audience. This section is about the politics of exhibition making, suggesting that the strategies employed leave traces of underlying messages and determine in part how well the visitor will feel served.

14

ANSWERS TO THE TEN QUESTIONS
I AM MOST OFTEN ASKED[1]

A review of exhibitions and learning, 1981

> Every new realization is not just accumulated, but rather causes a
> complete restructure [of] our bank of knowledge. Every process of
> learning, no matter how small or seemingly insignificant, is actually
> a process of unlearning and effects the structure of thought.
>
> (Adelaide Sievert 1994)

This article uses a question-and-answer format and is about museum issues from
a museum educator's point of view. These questions are often asked because they have
no single answer. Reasonable people have answered them all, but each answer has
varied from person to person; and many thoughtful, well-presented answers have
been incompatible with equally well-reasoned replies from other sources. In short,
these are controversial questions that allow one to take a position anywhere along
a continuum. One's choice of answers does much to chart one's career through the
myriad small decisions that are required on a daily basis.

It is pretentious to stand in front of one's peers and sound definitive
about anything. I don't really know you or your problems. I hope they are universal ones.

Question The first question is, of course, "What is a museum?"

Answer The simplest definition is that a museum houses "stuff" – three-dimensional
objects. All other sub-definitions are linked to that.

It is important for each museum to define the nature of its "stuff" and the manner
in which it will be acquired, cared for, and presented. It is very important for
a museum to have a mission and be forthright about it. A museum, in defining its
mission, will make decisions about its "stuff" and its collecting policy. For example,
a fine arts museum that wants to have only the highest quality works will have
a different mission statement than a fine arts museum that wants to have a
comprehensive teaching collection, and each will perform a useful function in the
community. A science museum that wants its visitors to understand scientific
phenomena may use reproductions and nonaccessioned three-dimensional materials
more easily than a science museum that has a greater interest in an authentic presentation of the history of science. A living history museum may use ordinary objects of

the period, whereas a historic house may be interested only in the unique original object.

So it is important for each institution, without bowing to the pressures of fashion or social relevance, to define its mission and therefore define its relationship to "stuff" and ultimately to its audience.

I believe there is a place for some institutions to house and preserve huge collections of unique and rare artifacts, but there are also museums that correctly house ordinary, commonplace, and often nonaccessioned things. Good use can be made of reproductions as well. It does not matter to me whether the institution houses permanent or temporary materials, although I know that organizations housing temporary collections in some countries are called galleries and that technology museums without collections are often referred to as science centers. As long as the institution has clearly defined its purpose and direction, the use of any kind of "stuff" is legitimate.

Question What are the differences and relationships between schools and museums?

Answer It is easier to start with the qualities of learning in a school and then to notice the different qualities that arise in museums.

A school generally has groups of classmates, for example, grade 3. Each group has some amount of homogeneity; that is, they all are approximately in the same reading level or in the same age. They know a lot about each other and spend a great deal of school time learning even more. The class members know whom they like, whom they trust, who is gifted or slow in a variety of subject areas.

The school experience is usually involuntary. A student is obligated to attend, and a great deal of social pressure is exerted for the student to remain. Even in schools for adults, where the initial decision to enter is volitional, there is social pressure to complete the course.

Schools deal with incremental learning. Students, it is hoped, build up knowledge over time during which a teacher has a chance to reinforce and reteach areas that have been misunderstood. Good teachers can adjust the information to particular members of the class because the teacher knows the individual strengths and weaknesses of the class members.

Schools usually are authoritarian systems. The teacher knows more than the student and determines the content, order, and method of instruction. Schools generally use a start-stop method of instruction: "We will all do math for the next 30 minutes." Even in individualized instruction, members of a subgroup are usually learning the same subject for the same period of time. Schools concentrate on printed words, pictures, and other two-dimensional materials for their instruction.

If these attributes of schools are correctly stated, then museums are cousins rather than siblings in the method of instruction. The differences offer museum education its unique opportunity. Individuals learn certain kinds of information best in different kinds of settings. Schools, with their incremental teaching, are excellent for subjects like reading or computational skills, which need incremental reinforcement for mastery. Museums are clearly not schools. Which leads to the next question.

Question What is the nature of museum learning?

Answer Landmark experiences (the "aha!" effect) occur when previously misunderstood, unconscious, or unfocused information gets synthesized into a new, conscious, articulate understanding. It can occur over great or small matters: "I didn't know an elephant was so big," or, "I understand the pressures Martin Luther was under." The synthesis can result from emotional as well as intellectual material and often includes input from the senses. Landmark experiences need happen only once to understand a specific piece of information. Subsequent modification of the "aha" moment builds on rather than erases the original understanding.[2]

As museum people, we cannot orchestrate individual landmark experiences. We can only provide a great deal of raw data so that individual members of our audience have the opportunity to choose for themselves what is meaningful. Museums are not the only venues for landmark learning. All places that deal with reality are excellent locations. Indeed, our first trip to the circus or the zoo often provides that sort of understanding. Similarly, when you interview people about their recollections of museum visits, you will hear a tale of a day filled with sights, with attendant sounds and smells – and the piece of learning that took place. Museums, with their collections of evocative things not ordinarily seen, are remarkable resources for this kind of understanding.

Museums provide the visitor with the raw and often vivid data that I refer to as "unexpurgated mush." These data points get stored away, unassimilated, by individual visitors for synthesis later. I have traveled with my children and heard them tell me about pieces seen years ago in other museums now brought to mind when presented with similar or analogous material. It is like carrying around many single puzzle pieces that fit one day into a completed picture.

This learning makes evaluation difficult in museums (and easier in schools); if schools are about incremental learning, then pre- and posttesting make a great deal of sense. If museums are about landmark learning and banking of raw data for later use, then the learning takes place over such a long period of time, and is so individualized, that pre- and posttesting measure the wrong data. There are evaluation techniques that indicate if anyone has understood anything, but I do not currently know of a way to evaluate the unique educational opportunity that landmark learning presents. I must content myself with countless stories where adults recall important moments in museums in their childhood, with all the details and sensations still fresh in their minds.[3]

Museums can be an occasion for cross-generational learning. Whole families or parts of families can learn together. Strangers can be temporarily bonded. I have seen parents from one family help a child from another when the need for help was apparent. A museum visit is often an opportunity for parents to teach their children, but also for children to demonstrate knowledge their parents didn't know they had.

Because I am fascinated by the unique opportunity that museums offer, where cross-generational volitional learning can occur in the presence of real objects, I am more and more disinclined to focus on museum education as school group touring. Taking a preformed group, doing pre-visit training, keeping the group together, lecturing to it by a knowledgeable teacher, and returning the class to the bus may be

139

the easiest thing to do (and may satisfy the teacher and the department of education), but it makes the museum into a school rather than emphasizing the characteristics that make it a different and valuable learning environment.

Question Who is the museum audience, and what is its motivation for coming?

Answer The audiences of museums can be divided roughly into two segments – the group audience (which I sometimes refer to as a coerced audience, for they do not decide to come to the museum on their own; their leaders decide it would be good for them) and the volitional or general audience, who decide that, given a wide variety of possible choices, a trip to the museum is what they choose to do.

At the Boston Children's Museum, as most everywhere, the group audiences are predominantly children on a school trip.[4] They generally view their visit as a holiday from school. Yet the teacher must justify the trip using an educational rationale. The museum must find a way to satisfy the teacher while making the experience enjoyable enough to encourage a lifelong use of museums in children. We are often not successful in either respect.

The group adult–child ratio is frequently less than the family adult–child ratio, and that lack of supervision puts pressure on museum staffing. The class teacher is often anxious and exerts pressure on the group to behave, to prove to the museum that he or she runs a tidy class. The teacher's anxiety also puts extra stress on the staff. At the Boston Children's Museum, we have, in my opinion, spent too much time trying to please the group leader and placed too much attention on the group audience. By contrast, the general museum audience can provide better clues to the special nature of museum learning.

The general public uses museums during leisure time, requiring museums to compete with other forms of entertainment. Since people do not have to go to museums, they must promote themselves in ways that schools do not. From the museum staff's point of view, this general audience displays no evident history of interests, reading ability, or educational level. They are of various ages and backgrounds. They come when they like, and they leave when they want to. They make an implied contract with the museum in which most of the power is on their side. If they will come, when they will come, why they came, whether they got or did not get what they came for, how long they will stay, and when they will leave – all of this is unknown by staff. Visitors don't articulate the nature of their personal aspirations to the service provider. Feedback and reinforcement for the museum staff is therefore difficult.

We tend to know something about this audience on a statistical basis but not on an individual basis. For example, we know that volitional museum audiences in the United States are relatively well educated, often professional, and middle- to upper-class people (DiMaggio 1996).

To review, if a museum can be defined as a place that houses three-dimensional materials, is visited volitionally by individual and social groups and less voluntarily by groups, is attended by people of all ages, from a variety of backgrounds to a preponderance of a single class, and whose visitors' individual prehistory is unknown, then, with such a mixed group –

Question Where should a museum be located?

Answer Museums are or should be on "neutral turf," that is, on a site that seems safe for all to enter. For example, if the museum focuses on a special Indian population in the United States, then it should be situated in a place that is safe for all members of the tribe to enter. However, if the museum is intended for American Indians and non-Indians alike, then its definition of "neutral turf" may force it to be adjacent to but not on tribal land. In either case, being available and perceived as safe and welcoming to all its intended audience is important.

Question Assuming the museum is interested in augmenting its exhibitions with staff-led (interpreter) programs, and then what kind of programs should be available for the general audience?[5]

Answer There are three categories of staff-led programs.

First, the floor staff can observe visitors within the exhibit, allowing them to use the exhibit any way they choose. The interpreter is trained to interact with visitors on an individual basis and only when they display some confusion or need some additional explanation. Interpreters have to be trained to be observant and patient. They have to be trained to watch all the participants in the space and to feel that they are doing their jobs even when they are doing nothing. It is important to train for this non-intrusive interaction because it allows the visitor to concentrate on the exhibit itself. The effectiveness of an exhibit can easily be hampered by an over-zealous interpreter.

Yet there is often a moment when visitors need assistance. They may want more information or permission to do something; often they look puzzled or hesitant. The interpreter needs to be readily available. At the Children's Museum, we train interpreters where and how to stand in the space so that their body language looks inviting rather than excluding. We role-play ways to enter into conversations and ways to wait until appropriate moments. We call this program Level One because it is the most basic; it is also the most difficult to do correctly.

Level Two programs are ways of changing the traffic flow by calling attention to an element of the exhibit. When an interpreter gives tours, reads selections aloud, or demonstrates an interactive element, the visitor generally focuses on that section. Small groups form, further distorting the normal traffic patterns. This level of program often allows parts of an exhibit that the visitor generally overlooks to be highlighted. It also identifies the interpreter as a helper who might be knowledgeable about other aspects of the exhibit.

Level Three is the introduction of some additional program into the space by using materials that do not remain in the space when an interpreter is not present. This program comes in many forms, including demonstrations, make-and-take activities, boxes of artifacts that can be touched, and costumed role-playing. This form of activity is the easiest to train interpreters for and the easiest for them to do, because it puts something into their hands and allows them to be the focus of the visitors' attention. The interpreter has a clear assignment. This is usually the way our youngest and newest interpreters work. The audience likes these programs because it makes them feel special. They have come upon something that is an addition to the exhibition. Add-on activities allow museums to change the visitors' experience without the capital expense of changing the exhibition itself. The disadvantage of add-on activities is that they tend to be the focus of the visit. The exhibition becomes the backdrop for the program; the audience often experiences the program and then leaves the space without having looked at the walls and objects.

It is important to provide a balanced program for the visitor: some locations where people are free to look around and have help when needed (Level One); some locations where they will have attention focused on specific exhibit elements (Level Two); and some where they will occasionally come across a special add-on program (Level Three). To ensure such a balanced visit for the audience, the educator must train interpreters in the importance of all three levels, for left on their own, many interpreters will concentrate on add-on programs. The programs that they will do most readily will either be product-oriented ones, such as crafts or a cart of touchable material. Additional training is needed for what we at the Children's Museum call orchestration, which allows interpreters and their supervisors to know how and when to change from one level to another and how to achieve program balance in the whole museum at any one time. This issue of "orchestration" is rarely looked at but creates a varied and more interesting program for the visitors.

Question What exhibit technique tends to be the most effective educationally?

Answer First, we must decide whether the exhibit is intended for all people, regardless of previous life history, or for one particular audience segment, for example, scholars. Should we try to communicate to all age groups, all ethnic groups, people who speak our language and those who don't? Can we design for multiple audiences simultaneously – for people who know nothing, those who know a little, and those who know a lot about the subject? Understand that my answers come from a children's museum perspective, and so children and families have a primary importance in the exhibition decisions that I personally make.

If we choose the multiple route, then we must include beginner's information and assume no prerequisite knowledge on the part of the visitor. Yet, understanding that all are not beginners, we need to design ways to give the scholar information without overwhelming or boring the child.

Therefore, the answer is simple: all techniques have their place. While I come from a "hands-on" museum, I am not an advocate of "hands-on" only. Rather, in designing an exhibit I like to concentrate on the following issues.

Can each element of the information be dealt with effectively in an exhibit format? If the answer is that some information will be better understood as a book or a movie, then I try not to put it in an exhibit. This decision is particularly difficult when one is trying to be comprehensive, but information can legitimately be left out if it is better available in a different format.

142

How many strategies do my designers and exhibition developers have at their disposal? I am forever collecting installation strategies used by other museums, commercial shopping locations, and attractions for later use at my own institution (for instance, where are push-buttons effective, how is labeling done, what are the hands-on elements, how are additional resource materials presented?). I am anxious to use the most effective strategy for each exhibit element and feel free to borrow any and all innovative and traditional techniques.

Does the subject matter allow for multiple entry levels so that all visitors can get something from the exhibit? I am most interested in installations that allow for different styles of learning and different levels of interest (Gardner 1983). I am always concerned that we allow the beginning learner to feel comfortable, but I want to include some material for the more advanced learner as well. I pay attention to language levels so that I am not eliminating understanding by using words that are too difficult for children to understand. I like to include many different "sense" entries so that seeing and reading aren't the only gateways to understanding.

I am especially interested in the single exhibit installation that allows for many different outcomes and is considered open-ended. For example, in the exhibit *How Movies Move* at the Boston Children's Museum, visitors draw on strips of paper and place them in a revolving drum. When they look at the paper spinning, the illusion of motion is created. This exhibit works well for a handicapped person just spinning the drum, a young child learning to use a crayon, and an artist making an elaborate cartoon. Each person is rewarded by success, based on his or her experience. Each can utilize the most appropriate artistic next step, and yet the physical element is exactly the same for each. Exhibitions that present water, sand, or bubbles in a way that allows for experimentation are open-ended. Creating such open-ended exhibitions for adults is more difficult but an interesting challenge.

Before building an exhibit at the Boston Children's Museum, we ask ourselves whether we have tried out the individual ideas and whether we can revise what does not work. Trial and revision allow one the freedom to be wrong, and we are often wrong! This approach also gives staff the optimistic knowledge that errors can be corrected. Nothing is more painful than to work daily in an exhibition that does not work, to assess the problem and be unable to correct it. Budgets need to accommodate revision so that all exhibits can have an evolutionary process.[6]

And finally, are there installation techniques that both protect collections and engage the visitor? I am fascinated currently with "hands-off" techniques that allow some audience response, for example, opening drawers and cabinets or installing collections in story or joke form.

Question Can there be fun and learning at the same time, or what is the difference between an amusement center and an amusing exhibit?

Answer I am always annoyed by the question, because it springs, I believe, from a Calvinist notion that fun and pleasure are unworthy. Real learning is itself a pleasurable activity and most of our independent learning has an underlying pleasurable goal (Csikszentmihályi 1990).

Learning to drive a car, learning to do the latest dance, and learning to whistle are all examples of real learning – just as real as learning computational skills. The difference is that the first examples are all volitional learning. For the general audience to come, the museum must be seen as a place of pleasure. Although I hope that everyone is learning something, I am equally hopeful that it is being done with as much joy and humor as possible. It gives me pleasure to hear laughter and excitement in the museum, and I design with that in mind.

Question But if I am content with learning as an amusing activity, will I abandon rigorous accuracy in favor of pap in order to make it more palatable? Or, to put the question another way, what is the difference between simple and superficial? Can accuracy for the beginning learner be other than distorted generality for the more experienced?

Answer This is a very troublesome question, for deciding what to include and what to eliminate is the hardest work of any exhibition or program creation. I have found recently that the most experienced curators have the easiest time with this question. They seem to have come full circle from their own beginning learning, through their interest in complicating nuance, and back to a more generalized synthesis; the more they know and have researched, the more they feel confident to leave out. It is important that exhibits be well researched. It is also advisable that the exhibitions are seen as successful by the visitor without reliance on too much text.

Yet what can the curator do with the rest of the material he or she so passionately knows and wants to share? There is an audience for this more complicated and sophisticated information as well. This audience may know something about the material before visiting the museum or may become interested in the information as a result of the exhibition. They want to learn more. They may even want to teach it to others. I refer to them as "second-layer" learners. If most visitors stay in museum exhibits for an average of one and one-half hours, then the exhibit setting is not the best place to deal with a second layer of learning.

It is important, therefore, to have more in-depth resources available. It can be a place, however defined in your museum, that offers more. Classes, bibliographies, loan materials, training, and access to collections are all examples of second-layer functions. It is important that this layer of material be as available to your audience as the exhibits themselves. Unfortunately, this second layer is often left out of the exhibition process.[7]

There is increasing evidence of exhibitions being created with multiple audiences in mind. I refer to this process as "stripes." A visitor can find varying stripes of objects, text, context, and orientation, "more about" resources, interactivity, current events, opportunity for personalization, and a human interpreter available in the same location at the same time. The visitor can delve into the subject matter at different levels according to interest. The issue of designing with multiple stripes without creating confusion is an intriguing challenge.[8]

Question What is the ideal audience (including those not yet attending) for exhibitions?

Answer It is incumbent on all of us to identify a broad target audience and then experiment with real, not imagined, ways of attracting them. If we want to attract a mix of visitors that range in age and experience, then:

- For families, we must make internal spaces feel comfortable to children.
- For adults with different levels of education, we must think about an appropriate reading level on our labels.
- For ethnic minorities, we must think about involving them directly in policy and planning.
- For the handicapped, we must address accessibility.
- For the elderly, we must make seating and readable signage available.

It is not enough simply to say the museum is for everyone, for there are subtle signs the audience can easily understand when we don't really mean it.

I hope more museums will find it within their missions to serve families. The proliferation of children's museums tends to compete with already-established institutions. Segregating children in their own institutions may seem to alleviate the responsibility of other institutions to deal with them. But many museums would be well served to turn their attention to the beginning learner and to understand that children are only one of the elements of a beginners audience.

Designing for children has good side effects:

- Lower placement of labels works well for the wheelchair visitor.
- Simpler labels work well for the learning disabled or less well educated.
- Hands-on activities work well with the non-English speaking audience.
- Bringing children to learn something allows adults, often surreptitiously, to learn, too.

These few examples remind me that when we include children in our museum thinking, we tend to be more inclusive generally. We also tend to become more humane and more informal in our museum policy. Yet I am not advocating a situation in which chaos ensues. Just as I would like to see all ages feel comfortable in the museum, I understand that we need to protect our property and control the sound and activity levels so that the elderly feel comfortable as well.

Question Do I see this vision of a museum being pursued in other countries?

Answer Yes, there are wonderful museum experiments going on in many different places. I believe a museum that emphasizes three-dimensional materials, beginning learning as well as second-layer learning, that appeals to cross-generational pluralistic audiences, and is set within comfortable neutral space will tend to be a hybrid institution – a cross between a traditional museum, a community center, and resource center – of value within most cultures.

In designing for all ages, interests, and education levels and using a broad-based definition of objects, museums worldwide are experimenting with new models that work well for them and can be instructive for us all.

Question Do I like my job?

Answer I am wild about it. We who work in this field are lucky people, for we can think about something as rich, complex, and unwieldy as museums. However:

- If we fail to collect with foresight and inclusivity, elements of our society will feel alienated and slighted.
- If we fail to preserve carefully, some of our history will be lost.
- If we interpret inaccurately, we will mislead.
- If we interpret boringly, only a few people will come.
- If we interpret flamboyantly (and lots of people come), we will be accused of pandering, or worse.

In an age when schools are under scrutiny, in an age when self education known as lifelong learning is being extolled, in an age when all people are realizing that their traditions and artifacts need preservation, we are sitting here with the "stuff."

Afterword

This essay, written in 1988, seems somewhat quaint in format and idealistic in content. Yet the format is a useful one for teaching and the ideas remain constructive. It might be assigned as a reading for an introductory class in museum education or used in orientation for beginning museum professionals trying to understand the landscape of educational opportunities in museums. It is especially valuable as a grounding for visitor services staff and volunteers in children's museums who have not thought deeply enough about their museums' possibilities.

To augment the intentionally simple approach, I have added a short bibliography of some of my favorite teaching references, which I use to create a clear overview for those in a hurry, for in-service training, or for introductory courses in the process of museum public service. For general grounding in museum education, see Dexter and Lord (1999), AAM (1991), Anderson (1997). For general organizational structures, see Ambrose and Paine (1993), Lord and Lord (2000). For learning theory, see Hein (1998), Csikszentmihályi and Hermanson (1997), Falk and Dierking (2000), Gardner (2004), Dewey (1975, first published in 1938), Hein and Alexander (1998). For evaluation, see (Borun *et al.* (1999), Diamond (1999), McManus (1987). For museum exhibitions, see McLean (1993), Gurian (1991b), Serrell (1996), Dean (1994), Kavanagh (1991), Lord and Lord (2002), Caulton (1998). For program planning and the educational role, see Hooper-Greenhill (1994). For a look at collections, see Gurian (1999b) and for interpreter training, see Cunningham (2004). These books all intentionally explore the museum landscape and would make a useful beginning bookshelf for the museum beginner.

In 1982, as a result of my belief that school group programming took up too much time and turned my staff into teachers rather than museum educators, I abandoned school programming altogether at the Boston Children's Museum. Instead, we offered schoolchildren what they dearly wished: free access to the museum on their own terms, with many staff stationed all over the museum ready to cater to individual interest as it arose. It was a noble effort but failed almost immediately. The teachers hated it because it looked liked chaos and left them with unruly children to take back to school. In today's world of mandatory school testing, it would not be tolerated. More and more museums cater to statewide testing standards in order to attract school field trips of any kind. There must be some middle ground here.

For some children, the school field trip is their only experience in a museum. When the experience is overly prescriptive it becomes a memory of that dank, dark, mysterious place of boredom that forms the basis of the cliché that museums fight against. Yet for others, as it did for me, the school trip leads to a lifelong fascination with the material and the place. The model used routinely for school group visits – guided programs, assignments, handout materials – needs to be rethought. Occasionally, models using theatrical problem solving are brought to my attention. They seem to hold promise, as do the almost daily use of museums that you see as part of the curricula for museum-based schools. The rest is well intentioned, better than no field trip at all, but to my mind, dreary, institutionalized, and in strong need of a brand new rethink.

Notes

1 The initial text of this talk was presented as the keynote speech at the Australian Educator's Museum Conference in Melbourne, Australia in 1981. This is the first formal paper of my professional career. I used subsequent versions in speeches during that and the following year and excerpts were published in Gurian (1982).

2 Museum educators have always had an interest in learning theory as it relates to museums. Whereas this section is written in ordinary language without reference to learning theorists, the reader can see that these writings are a homemade amalgam of some theorists including Jean Piaget, Erik Erickson, Abraham Maslow, Johann Pestalozzi, Friedrich Froebel, Lev Vigotsky, Howard Gardner, and Jerome Bruner.

3 It is clear that since this paper was written some evaluators have taken on just this exercise trying to parse out the long-term learning effects of museum visits. See, for example, Falk and Dierking (2000), Russell (1994), and Kelly (2005).

4 At the time this paper was written, I was the director of the Visitor Center (the public museum section) of the Boston Children's Museum. The references to that institution are used as examples throughout.

5 The Boston Children's Museum had an extensive program of staff (interpreters) who were continuously available in the exhibitions and who conducted various programs in addition to being the evacuation and security force. Separately supervised, the interpreter program included paid staff, volunteers, at-risk teenagers, and student teachers. This was one of the early models of visitor services.

6 Museums are increasingly paying for evaluation of all kinds. The one discussed here is called "front-end" evaluation, but there is appropriate evaluation to be done after the installation is in place as well. Having an on-staff evaluator is more common than it was in the 1980s.

7 More information is indeed available at the exhibition site now with increasing frequency. With the availability of stand-alone computers within exhibition halls, it is now common-place to find resident data banks of information available directly on site. There have been experiments that allow visitors to take additional information home and even check out books before they leave.

8 In the 1980s, Michael Spock experimented with areas adjacent to each other that would allow the visitor to find different levels of engagement within the space. He called that experiment "plum pudding." Much of that work is now ubiquitous. What has not happened yet (and was part of Michael Spock's original conception) is direct connections to appropriate course sign-up sheets in the visitor's neighborhood, and a repository of infor-mation about each visitor's previous visits so that comparative information could be made available to each visitor about individual personal interests.

Bibliography

AAM (1991) *Excellence and Equity: Education and the Public Dimension of Museums: A Report*, Washington, DC: American Association of Museums, Task Force on Museum Education.

Ambrose, T. and Paine, C. (1993) *Museum Basics*, London; New York: ICOM in conjunction with Routledge.

Anderson, D. (1997) *A Common Wealth: Museums and Learning in the United Kingdom*, London: Department of National Heritage.

Borun, M., Korn, R., Adams, R., and American Association of Museums Committee on Audience Research and Evaluation (1999) *Introduction to Museum Evaluation*, Washington, DC: American Association of Museums Technical Information Service.

Caulton, T. (1998) *Hands-on Exhibitions, Managing Interactive Museums & Science Centers*, London: Routledge.

Csikszentmihályi, M. (1990) *Flow: The Psychology of Optimal Experience*, New York: Harper & Row.

Csikszentmihályi, M. and Hermanson, K. (1997) "Instrinsic Motivation in Museums: Why Does One Want to Learn?" in Falk, J.H. and Dierking, L.D. (eds) *Public Institutions for Personal Learning: Establishing a Research Agenda*, Washington, DC: American Association of Museums.

Cunningham, M.K. (2004) *The Interpreters Training Manual for Museums*, Washington, DC: American Association of Museums.

Dean, D. (1994) *Museum Exhibition: Theory and Practice*, London; New York: Routledge.

Dewey, J. (1975, first published in 1938) *The Need of a Theory of Experience. Experience and Education,* 18th edn, Kappa Delta Pi Lecture series, New York: Collier Books.

Dexter, G. and Lord, B. (1999) *The Manual of Museum Planning*, London: The Stationery Office.

Diamond, J. (1999) *Practical Evaluation Guide: Tools for Museums and Other Informal Educational Settings*, Walnut Creek, CA: AltaMira Press.

DiMaggio, P. (1996) "Are Art-Museum Visitors Different from Other People? The Relationship between Attendance and Social and Political Attitudes in the United States," in *Poetics: Journal of Empirical Research on Literature, The Media, and the Arts (special issue on Museum Research)*, 24:2–4, 161–180.

Falk, J.H. and Dierking, L.D. (2000) *Learning from Museums: Visitor Experiences and the Making of Meaning*, Walnut Creek, CA: AltaMira Press.

Gardner, H. (1983) *Frames of Mind: The Theory of Multiple Intelligences*, New York: Basic Books.

Gardner, H. (2004) "What We Do and Don't Know About Learning," in *Daedalus*, Cambridge, MA, 133:1 (Winter), 5–12.

Gurian, E.H. (1982) "Museums' Relationship to Education," in Tage Høyer Hansen, Karl-Erik Andersen and Poul Vestergaard (eds) *Museums and Education: The Museum Exhibition as a Tool in Educational Work*, Copenhagen: Danish ICOM/CECA, 17–20.

Gurian, E.H. (1991b) "Noodling around with Exhibition Opportunities," in Karp, I. and Lavine, S.D. (eds) *Exhibiting Cultures: The Poetics and Politics of Museum Display*, Washington, DC: Smithsonian Institution Press.

Gurian, E.H. (1999b) "What Is the Object of This Exercise? A Meandering Exploration of the Many Meanings of Objects in Museums," in *Daedalus*, Cambridge, MA, 128:3, 163–183.

Hein, G.E. (1998) *Learning in the Museum*, New York: Routledge.

Hein, G.E. and Alexander, M. (1998) *Museums: Places of Learning*, Washington, DC: American Association of Museums/AAM Education Committee.

Hooper-Greenhill, E. (1994) *The Educational Role of the Museum*, London; New York: Routledge.

Kavanagh, G. (1991) *Museum Languages: Objects and Texts*, Leicester; New York: Leicester University Press.

Kelly, L. (2005) *Extending the Lens: A Sociocultural Approach to Understanding Museum Learning*, Sydney: University of Technology.

Lord, B. and Lord, G.D. (2002) *The Manual of Museum Exhibitions*, Walnut Creek, CA: AltaMira Press.

Lord, G.D. and Lord, B. (eds) (2000) *The Manual of Museum Planning*, 2nd Edn, London: AltaMira Press.

McLean, K. (1993) *Planning for People in Museum Exhibitions*, Washington, DC: Association of Science-Technology Centers.

McManus, P.M. (1987) "It's the Company You Keep. The Social Determination of Learning-related Behavior in a Science Museum," in *International Journal of Museum Management and Curatorship*, 6, 263–270.

Russell, T. (1994) "The Enquiring Visitor: Usable Learning Theory for Museum Contexts," in *Journal of Education in Museums*, London, 15.

Serrell, B. (1996) *Exhibit Labels: An Interpretive Approach*, Walnut Creek, CA: AltaMira Press, American Association for State and Local History.

Sievert, A. (1994) *What Is Special About a Children's and Youth Museum?* Fulda, Germany: International conference. Available http://www.hands-on-europe.net/frameset.htm (accessed March 1, 2005).

15

NOODLING AROUND WITH
EXHIBITION OPPORTUNITIES[1]

The potential meanings of exhibition
modalities, 1991

Museum visitors receive far more from exhibitions than just information about the objects displayed. Let me suggest that visitors can deduce from their experience what we, the producers of exhibitions, think and feel about them — even if we have not fully articulated those thoughts to ourselves.

I will explore the notion that we, consciously or unconsciously, impose learning impediments in our exhibitions for some members of our current and potential audiences. We do so because we possess unexamined beliefs about our visitors' capacity to learn and because we want them to act in a style that reinforces our notion of appropriate audience behavior. We continue to do so regardless of our exposure to countervailing theories about learning or examples of experimentation in exhibitions. We often design evaluation tools that measure only those things we wish the audience to learn rather than those the audience is actually learning. We espouse the goal of enlarging our audiences to include underserved populations and novice learners, and yet we continue not to accommodate them: we demand that they accommodate us and then wonder why they do not visit our galleries.

I will argue that it is not content that predetermines the exhibition design, strategies, and installations we use; rather, exhibition content and presentation are separable. Whereas much has been written about the choice of content (and there is still much to explore), very little has been written about choice of style as an expression of intention. Regardless of exhibition content, producers can choose strategies that can make some portion of the public feel either empowered or isolated. If the audience, or some segment thereof, feels alienated, unworthy, or out of place, I contend it is because we want them to feel that way.

It could also be suggested that we, the staff, are partly in collusion with a segment of our audience that wants exhibition presentation to reinforce the aspirations and expectations they have for themselves. This audience of traditional museum consumers does not wish to have others join their company, as that would disrupt their notion of their own superiority and their right to an exclusive domain. Pierre Bourdieu, in the introduction to his book *Distinction: A Social Critique of the Judgment*

150

of Taste, writes:

> A work of art has meaning and interest only for someone who possesses the cultural competence, that is, the code, into which it is encoded.... A beholder who lacks the specific code feels lost in a chaos of sounds and rhythms, colours and lines, without rhyme or reason.... Thus, the encounter with a work of art is not "love at first sight" as is generally supposed.
>
> (1989)

The question we as producers of exhibitions must ask is, why do we participate in this collusion, and what we can do to change if we so desire?

An opportunity for change is provided by the way disciplines such as anthropology, art history, and history are reexamining their foundations and acknowledging that previously held beliefs about the objectivity of research and the impartiality of the investigator were never realistic. By applying these same techniques of self-examination to ourselves as museum professionals, we may gain insights that will enable us to approach our exhibitions – and their audiences – in new, fruitful ways.

Museums and their audiences: identity, politics, and equality

In the catalogue for the National Museum of African Art's exhibition *Images from Barmum*, Christraud Geary writes about the role the viewer plays in the making of a photograph:

> In analyzing photographs, the roles played in the creation process by the photographer, the photographic subject, and the viewer need to be considered. A photograph is a cultural artifact that articulates a photographer's visions, biases, and concerns. It also allows the contemplation of the photographic subject.... In addition to the photographer and the photographic subject, a silent participant – the future viewer – influences the creation of photographs.
>
> (1988)

Changing a few terms in the quote would apply equally well to exhibitions. An exhibition is a cultural artifact that articulates a producer's visions, biases, and concerns. It also allows the contemplation of the exhibition content. In addition to the producer and the content, a silent participant – the audience – influences the creation of the exhibition.

It therefore makes sense to explore the images that museum professionals have of their audiences. Such an exploration needs to consider, among other things, the people who found museums, the people who direct them, and the politics of both groups. Historically, it can be argued that museums have been created to promote the aspirations of their creators. Wealthy patrons and collectors have created art museums to reinforce their status and aesthetic, whereas wealthy merchants have created science-technology centers to enlist the public's concurrence about the progress and future of industry. Historical societies have been founded by people who wanted their personal and class histories to be preserved, and children's museums have been founded by parents and educators who were emboldened by the education theories of Dewey. Finally, counterculture museums have been created by people of all classes who want to preserve a particular viewpoint that has not been expressed in other museums (Alexander 1959).

Thus, a museum's relationship to its audiences might be predicted – regardless of the discipline involved – by determining into which of three roughly delineated political categories it falls: museums that aspire to be established organizations, self-consciously liberal museums, and counterculture museums. The Metropolitan Museum of Art, the New Museum of Contemporary Art, and El Museo del Barrio are examples of museums in the New York art scene that exemplify each of these categories. In political terms, these museums could be positioned right of center, left of center, and on the far left, respectively. Historically, all museums tend to drift toward the right as they become successful; thus, the counterculture museums become less radical, the liberal museums become more mainstream, and the centrist museums tend to protect their elite status.

In addition to the museum's political position, a revealing indicator of the museum–audience relationship might be the personal politics of the director or even the exhibition producer. Directors can consciously alter the museum's political position by force of personality and/or their own personal political convictions. Analysis of their individual political convictions might reveal not only the tone they take toward their audiences but the way in which they construct a work climate for their staffs.

For example, Frank Oppenheimer, director of the Exploratorium in San Francisco from 1968 to 1985, and Michael Spock, director of the Boston Children's Museum from 1962 to 1986, independently but relatively simultaneously produced the unprecedented hands-on exhibitions of the 1960s. They believed themselves to fall into that part of the political spectrum that advocated "power to the people." Each built staff organizations that operated as missionary bands. Oppenheimer's early radical political life[2] may have found expression in his notion that the originators of exhibition ideas should be allowed to realize the exhibition themselves without help (or interference) from designers. In terms of exhibition design practices, his position was unique and radical: if someone only knew how to make his or her exhibition with chewing gum, then gum it was. He believed the audience would feel comforted by exhibitions that looked like they could be reproduced in a home workshop. Oppenheimer did not believe in the need for a uniform institutional style or a consistent aesthetic. He wanted the producer to speak directly to his or her audience. When I first met Frank Oppenheimer, he asked me how much time I spent on the exhibition floor in watching the audience interact with the exhibitions. When I answered "very little," he promptly escorted me to his own exhibition space and taught me how to observe the visitor. He personally spent long hours prowling his own exhibitions, watching visitors struggle with his experiments; then he would modify them accordingly.

To Michael Spock, who grew up dyslexic in a well-known and politically liberal family, learning was understood to be risky business. This led to the use of materials such as wood and cardboard as a matter of museum aesthetics, so that the audience would feel comfortable and "at home." He hoped to give confidence to the learner in order to enable him or her to cope with the world outside of the museum. The subject matter was not his primary interest; enfranchising the learner was. Spock felt that members of the public had something to offer us, the exhibition creators, and one another. I worked for Michael Spock for 16 years.[3] Before we produced an exhibition, we asked the visitors what they wanted to know about the subject. Then we would produce mock-ups and prototypes in order to get feedback from the audience before any exhibition had "hardened." We also produced a series of graphic audience-structured feedback boards on which the audience could write their comments, thereby putting the teachings of the audience beside the teachings of the producers.

The major experiments Oppenheimer and Spock initiated – introducing contextual, direct-experience interactivity to the exhibition floor – changed the face of museums permanently by inviting the audience to participate in their own learning. However, some 25 years after the initial experiments, there is still reluctance in some quarters to adopt Oppenheimer's and Spock's strategies even when they seem appropriate to the subject matter at hand. The reluctance, I propose, comes not from the realistic concern about the additional upkeep and staffing expense that these techniques engender, but rather from these exhibition strategies' inherent inclusionary assumptions about the audience, assumptions that are not universally shared.

Exhibitions such as *Mathematica*, designed by Ray and Charles Eames in 1961, were based on the Victorian tradition of visible storage and on the early cabinets of curiosities. The experience of visual clutter that the Eameses espoused was very liberating for the visitor: visitors instinctively understood that since they could not absorb all the visual information presented, they were free to sort and select. In Eames's productions (and subsequently in Ivan Chermayeff's *A Nation of Nations* at the National Museum of American History, and *The California Dream*, designed by Gordon Ashby for the history section of the Oakland Museum), the previous authoritarianism of the staff member who selected the exhibition objects was replaced by an aesthetic smorgasbord that empowered the audience to select for themselves. Although in an Eames production the staff also chose the objects their strategy resulted in an audience response that was less controlled by the exhibition creators, in contrast to exhibitions done in a "modern" style, in which the audience's attention is focused on single objects highlighted in individual cases. When I met Charles Eames, he was absorbed in his own personal visual investigation, walking around the Boston Children's Museum with a magnifying glass on a chain around his neck in order to see even the smallest detail; he wished out loud that each viewer could be able to orchestrate his or her own visual banquet, independent of either the exhibitor's will or other viewer' choices.

Some parameters of learning in a museum

Chandler Screven, a longtime museum exhibition evaluator, writes, "Museum learning is self-paced, self-directed, non-linear, and visually oriented" (Screven 1987). This statement points out some of the ways in which exhibitions actually work. Museum exhibitions are certainly not school classrooms, which enforce incremental, cumulative learning through authoritarian leadership over rigidly defined, constant social units. Except for school groups, museum audiences are composed of unrelated social units who remain anonymous and display uneven previous knowledge of the subject matter. Exhibitions are places of free choice. Try as we might, the public continually thwarts our attempts to teach incrementally in an exhibition. They come when they want, leave when they want, and look at what they want while they are there. Therefore, linear installations often feel like forced marches.

The audience can understand exhibition content immediately, or reassess and integrate it at some later date, or both. The visitor receives an impressionistic, sometimes indelible, sense of the topic, and in addition creates a mental inventory of items that he or she can bank for later consideration. Michael Spock and others have described the one-time, indelible impression to which all subsequent exposures will be referenced as *landmark learning*. The long-term integration often comes as an "aha" phenomenon when a second trigger is presented that makes the stored items understood in a satisfying way.[4]

Good exhibitions are often conceptually simple. The more complex the verbal message becomes, the less understandable the exhibition turns out to be, since exhibitions are basically nonverbal enterprises. What can be displayed best are tangible materials that can be seen, sometimes touched, and often fantasized about. Exhibition topics deal with both concrete things and abstractions; we display objects that are simultaneously real and emblematic. Objects in exhibitions can elicit emotional responses. The presence of certain artifacts can evoke memories and feelings. Mihaly Csikszentmihályi and Eugene Rochberg-Halton's book *The Meaning of Things* suggests that it is the emotional overlay we place upon impersonal objects that transforms them into objects of meaning (Csikszentmihályi and Rochberg-Halton 1981). If we are interested in changing our exhibitions into exhibitions of meaning, we will have to be prepared to include frankly emotional strategies.[5]

Imposed limits to learning

But we, the producers of exhibitions, have not fully exploited all exhibition tactics that the parameters outlined above suggest. Could this be because we are not entirely comfortable with what certain modes of exhibition might reveal about us? It is not only what we think about our audience that determines the exhibition designs we use; but they are also determined by what we want the audience and our colleagues to think about us. Styles of exhibiting that enhance learning but are sensual and emotive may embarrass us and not conform with our descriptions of ourselves as erudite, intellectual, and respectable.

154

I believe that somewhere in the history of exhibitions, certain nonrational strategies were deemed theatrical. Being in the theater is still not wholly respectable. Museum professionals do not want to be in show business; we want to be in academia. And yet, like it or not, exhibitions are in part public entertainment. Perhaps it was the fate of the first history museum in America, founded by Charles Willson Peale, that reinforced this attitude. Gary Kulik has written:

> Peale's educational vision was lost. His effort to create a museum that was both serious and popular had foundered. By 1850, the building and collections had become the property of Moses Kimball and P.T. Barnum. Barnum and Kimball brought a new meaning to the term museum. Entrepreneurs of the bizarre, they tapped the voyeurism of the American people. Moving far beyond the Peales, they blurred the boundaries between museum and carnival sideshows, between the theater and the circus, between the real and the contrived. Museums of the odd, the curious, and the fake proliferated in antebellum America.
>
> (1989)

Today, our own fascination and ambivalence with Disney theme parks has compounded the problem. Surely the most effective and popular attractions of our time, Disneyland and Disney World, use techniques that may educate while creating enjoyment but, like P.T. Barnum, they have "blurred the boundaries between museum and carnival sideshows," and the museum world would not want to be identified with that!

Another reason why we have not fully exploited the sensory possibilities and opportunities that displaying objects can offer us may be that we have internalized certain cultural preferences for some modes of learning over others. For example, we have been taught that one mark of the civilized person is verbal ability, and so when explicating objects in, say, science or cultural-history museums, we concentrate on producing textual labels. Many producers believe that in exhibitions focusing on aesthetics, the "visually literate" person should know how to use the visual cues provided by the objects without any additional assistance from us, and so we often do not write explanatory labels in art galleries and rarely use auditory, olfactory, or tactile techniques there. Worst of all, appealing directly to the emotions is considered pandering to the mob, so we do not dare to appear enthusiastic. As a result of these internalized preferences, then, exhibitions often become places in which we, the exhibition makers, use certain styles of exhibiting to demonstrate our own mastery of these modes of learning, not only to ourselves but also to our colleagues and our audiences.

Nor do we want to appear friendly, because we believe that informality would reduce the importance of our work. If the audience is having fun, we may be accused of providing a circus and not behaving in a sufficiently reverential manner. If we have a Calvinistic view of our purpose, we will not permit ourselves to be informal. But if we, as exhibition producers, begin to think that playfulness is a permissible part of learning (as learning theorists would have us believe), different exhibition strategies may take over. For example, collections may be placed so that they are not immediately apparent, or objects may be installed in a way that reveals visual jokes. The label will reveal that there is a task of interpretation in the very act of looking. Such an attitude may also make more apparent the humor of artists or cultures, which is often omitted because humor is considered frivolous.

Accommodating different styles and levels of learning

In *Frames of Mind*, Howard Gardner suggests that, regardless of our social history, every individual has his or her own set of gifts or talents and a corresponding set of preferred learning styles (Gardner 1983). He suggests that there are many forms of learning, which can be divided roughly into seven categories: linguistic, musical, logical-mathematical, spatial, bodily kinesthetic, interpersonal, and intrapersonal. These categories are not hierarchical but rather are parallel and have equal value. Most important for exhibition producers is that one form of learning is not necessarily translatable into another; thus, tactile comprehension does not necessarily translate to verbal understanding.

Since, as Gardner suggests, each individual in our audience has a different learning pattern, multisensory exhibition experiences that offer many entry points could facilitate a range of learning experiences, without prejudice. It follows, then, that should we wish all visitors to learn and understand, we must construct a wide palette of exhibition opportunities that utilizes all the senses. There are materials that visitors long to touch. There are many objects that could be better understood if the audience has a chance to participate in a process or an experiment.

In addition to having preferred learning styles, we are all novices about every subject at some time in our lives. It is safe to assume that every exhibition will have novice learners in its audience, and yet most adults do not like to admit publicly their beginner status. It is much kinder for the exhibition producer to accommodate the novice than to assume that the exhibition should work only for the exhibit creator and his or her knowledgeable colleagues. The assumption that novice visitors need to feel welcome suggests the following (not exhaustive) list of obligatory strategies: defining all terms when used, providing an introduction to the social context for all exhibitions, locating all geographical references, and allowing all processes of art production to be understood.

Patterson Williams, Marlene Chambers, and Melora McDermott-Lewis of the Denver Art Museum conducted research for a long time on strategies for including the novice learner in an art museum setting. McDermott-Lewis writes:

> Novices have very mixed feelings about hearing what experts think about art objects. While they acknowledge that the experts know something that might be useful to them in looking, novices are quite adamant that they don't want anyone to decide for them what is good or bad. They don't want someone to tell them that something they really like isn't "good".... They also don't want to be talked down to.... Novices also perceive experts as looking at objects in a very intellectual, unfeeling way.... As novices they

156

tend to have their most pleasurable experience with art when they look at it in a very emotional, feeling-laden way.

(1987)

If we, the creators of exhibitions, think that viewers are inherently smart (though not necessarily well educated or familiar with the subject matter) and that they are entitled to ask questions and receive answers, then we will address questions the audience has rather than tell them what we think they should know. It is logical, then, that the author will have to consult with the public before writing final copy. This assumption implies the time-consuming task of audience interviews before the final installation is done.

Label copy

Even for the writing of label copy there are techniques that can promote inclusion or exclusion. If the label writer believes the audience is composed of receptive students, and the information he or she wants to pass on is genuinely good for them, then the label writer will assume the role of a teacher transmitting information. The audience will be viewed as a passive but obedient recipient. The audience's only choice, then, is to read or not to read, to be willing or to be recalcitrant. However, the audience often perceives failure to read labels as something naughty; consequently, they feel guilty.

The role of teacher is not the label writer's only possible stance. He or she can choose instead to be coconspirator, colleague, preacher, or even gossip columnist. Altering these assumptions about the label writer's role might cause the audience to change its behavior as well. For example, if the writer sees the audience as a partner, then perhaps the audience might participate like a partner. There are also label-writing strategies that encourage interaction between the viewer and the object and between the viewer and members of his or her party. When writing the labels for the opening of the Monterey Bay Aquarium in 1984, Judy Rand set a new standard with a conversational tone. The reader felt like he or she was chatting with a friend rather than being lectured to by a professor. I suspect that this chatty tone encouraged discourse within the visitor's party.

Other label-writing strategies encourage the audience to become the teacher. These strategies, like Spock's talk-back boards, identify the visitor as a resource in addition to the curator and the institution. This approach allows ownership of the exhibition to extend beyond the staff.

A number of museums, including the Decorative Arts Museum at the Louvre, have experimented with text for different reading levels on the same label, which intentionally encourages interaction. Choosing to write label copy at a level that does not exclude children, the less well educated, and those not fluent in the language in which the label is written helps make these groups feel included in a wider sense, whereas writing label copy that requires college-level fluency reinforces the notion that all others have come to the wrong place.[6]

157

Additional sources of information

Some novice members of our audiences will enter the museum as intermediate or even advanced learners, and some will become more knowledgeable within a single museum visit. An object that intrigues the visitor brings out the instantaneous need for more information. Adding information to an exhibition is always a problem because we are mindful of detracting from the object and cluttering up the exhibit. We understand that not everyone wants the same additional information, but the individual who does want more information wants it then and there. Immediate access to information is satisfying to the audience; therefore, the task is to provide information in the exhibition in a manner such that the audience knows it is available without it being intrusive. Putting the catalogue in the gallery is one way to allow the visitor immediate access to more information about the subject at hand. Other strategies include installing computers and interactive media, which have the capacity to hold additional information without cluttering the walls. Embedding a resource center within or next to the exhibition space has been an effective approach in museums, including the Seattle Art Museum and the Denver Art Museum.

Blurring the distinctions between kinds of museums works to the benefit of the audience as well. For the visitor, an object of interest provokes many cross-disciplinary questions; he or she probably is not interested in our museological territorial boundaries. For example, an entire environment about early music has been installed in the Museum of Fine Arts, Boston. The visitor can see the instruments, hear them played either live or on recordings, and study books and facsimile sheet music – all within a climate-controlled space that is itself a storage unit. Information about art, craftsmanship, music history, biography, and social science is available in the same location.

Visual-study storage areas are resources that may provide answers to additional questions from all sections of our audience, including experts. The Corning Museum, the Philadelphia Museum of Art, Jewish Museum Berlin, Te Papa in New Zealand, and the National Museum of Australia have experimented with placing visual-study collections close to the exhibition. Purpose-built activity stations that focus on a variety of subjects and encourage activity or touching without endangering the collection's objects have been successfully used in science centers and children's museums and have now migrated to many natural history and history museums.

Identifying the exhibition creator

An alternative exhibition strategy that also allows the visitor to feel included involves creating an exhibition in which each object has been personally selected by an identifiable source, who self-consciously reveals the decisions surrounding the inclusion of each item. This strategy of making the curator the narrator invites the visitor to become a fellow traveler. The National Gallery in London invites famous artists to select objects for display from the gallery's collections and then explain to the visitor why these objects were chosen and why they are personally important to the chooser. The National Museum of the American Indian (NMAI) has community galleries chosen by members of a specific tribe and all named in the exhibition. An exhibition that is signed, uses the first person in the label copy, and/or reveals the personality of the artist is a personal, creative act analogous to a signed work of art and intentionally becomes an autobiographical exhibition. While visitors expect to see the authors of works of art, music, and fiction identified, they are not used to perceiving exhibitions as the personal work of identifiable individuals. Unsigned exhibitions reinforce the notion that there is a godlike voice of authority behind the selection of objects. But presenting a curator as an individual usefully demonstrates that exhibitions are in reality like signed columns rather than news releases and that each producer, like each columnist, has a point of view. The exhibition *Hispanic Art in the United States*, curated by Jane Livingston and John Beardsley, will probably be credited in the future with widening our perception of modern American art, but the furor caused by the seeming arbitrariness of the show's choices might have been ameliorated if the curators had been an identifiable presence who discussed their choices within the body of the exhibition itself (Beardsley and Livingston 1991).

The museum as gathering place

Ellen Posner writes in the *Atlantic*:

> When museums were thought of primarily as places for the conservation, study, and display of works of art, new structures were designed both to suggest that opportunities for repose and contemplation were available within and to symbolize what were believed to be the uplifting properties of art: hence, the park and suburban settings, the important-looking colonnaded entrances and celestial domes, the exhilarating flights of steps. Now, however, although the art is still there someplace, museums stand at the center of social life. And the buildings themselves are expected to attract and seduce the casual passerby, to deliver glamour, panache, and chic, and to promise a good time to be had by all.
>
> (1988)

This point is reinforced by John Falk's work, which has demonstrated that people visiting any exhibition spend a considerable amount of time in interacting with the people they came with and watching strangers (Falk *et al.* 1985). The need to be in a congregative setting is perhaps much more important than we in the museum business commonly acknowledge. Exhibitions need to support both individual learning and social interactions. Many people do not want to display their ignorance in front of strangers, and so learning opportunities will need to be designed that simultaneously encourage social interaction among members of the visiting party and private contemplation. If we begin to feel that it is within our mission to support sociability, then we will feel more comfortable about promoting seating arrangements that, quite frankly, reinforce social interaction as well as interaction with the objects. For example, despite the conservation problems, cafés in the middle of exhibition spaces, surrounded by the objects, might enhance better learning than cafés separated from these areas. Just go to Te Papa, the National Museum of New Zealand and see how their café operates.

Conclusions

Although we may be reluctant to admit it, the production of an exhibition is more akin to the production of a theater piece than any other form. Like theater, exhibitions are formed by a group of people who have highly individualized visions and styles, in a process in which compromise is the order of the day. The relationship among values, content, and style has to be broadly agreed upon or else the team must be autocratically ruled in order to avoid a cacophony of ideas.

The process of exhibition production and the loci of power within the exhibition team are interesting topics in themselves and deserve further study. For the purposes of this paper, however, I suggest that the resultant product – the exhibition – must have embedded within it either agreed-upon assumptions about the audience or a coherent view of the audience as articulated by a single prevailing power source.

In current practice, however, during production of an exhibition the team members rarely force themselves to reveal and share their views of the visitor. Of course, we can continue to keep our views of the audience hidden even from ourselves, but doing that reinforces messages that I am sure we would be too embarrassed to acknowledge. It follows that if, as part of the initial stages of exhibition formation, we develop tools to allow all of us to articulate our individual assumptions instead, we might be more willing to include strategies that reinforce what we would like to think about our visitors. Then exhibitions may be created that work for the audience, not because we necessarily inherently care about the audience, but because we want to care about the audience and will adjust our behavior accordingly.

As Steven Weil, former deputy director of the Smithsonian Institution's Hirshhorn Museum and Sculpture Garden, writes:

> The real issue, I think, is not how to purge the museum of values – that, in all likelihood, would be an impossible task – but how to make those values manifest, how to bring them up to consciousness for both ourselves and our visitors. We delude ourselves when we think of the museum as a clear and transparent medium through which only our objects transmit messages. We transmit messages too – as a medium we are also a message – and it seems to me vital that we understand better just what those messages are.
>
> (1989)

Notes

1 A version of this article was first published in 1991 in *Exhibiting Cultures: The Poetics and Politics of Museum Display* (Gurian 1991b).

2 See the short biography of Dr Oppenheimer in the Exploratorium website to understand how the Exploratorium was conceived (Exploratorium).

3 I served as director of the Exhibit Center and later as associate director of the Boston Children's Museum from 1971–1987.

4 To see a review of learning theory applicable to museums see Hein and Alexander (1998).

5 For a discussion on emotional intelligence and its uses see Mayer and Salovey (1997).

6 To see more about inclusive label copy strategies see Gurian (1993).

Bibliography

Alexander, E.P. (1959) *The Museum: A Living Book of History*, Detroit, MI: Wayne State University Press.

Beardsley, J. and Livingston, J. (1991) "The Poetics and Politics of Hispanic Art: A New Perspective," in Karp, I. and Levine, S.D. (eds) *Exhibiting Cultures: The Poetics and Politics of Museum Display*, Washington, DC: Smithsonian Institution Press.

Bourdieu, P. (1989) *Distinction: A Social Critique of the Judgement of Taste*, Cambridge, MA: Harvard University Press.

Csikszentmihályi, M. and Rochberg-Halton, E. (1981) *The Meaning of Things*, London: Cambridge University Press.

Exploratorium, biography of Frank Oppenheimer, Available http://www.exploratorium.edu/frank/bio/bio.html (accessed February 22, 2005).

Falk, J.H., Koran, J.J., Dierking, L.D., and Dreblow, L. (1985) "Predicting Visitor Behavior," in *Curator*, 28:4, 326–332.

Gardner, H. (1983) *Frames of Mind: The Theory of Multiple Intelligences*, New York: Basic Books.

Geary, C.M. (1988) *Images from Bamum: German Colonial Photography at the Court of King Njoya, Cameroon, West Africa*, Washington, DC: Smithsonian Institution Press and National Museum of African Art.

Gurian, E.H. (1991b) "Noodling around with Exhibition Opportunities," in Karp, I. and Lavine, S.D. (eds) *Exhibiting Cultures: The Poetics and Politics of Museum Display*, Washington, DC: Smithsonian Institution Press.

Gurian, E.H. (1993) "Adult Learning at Children's Museum of Boston," in Strand, J. (ed.) *Selected Reprints from Museums, Adults, and the Humanities, a Guide for Educational Programming*, Washington, DC: American Association of Museums.

Hein, G.E. and Alexander, M. (1998) *Museums: Places of Learning*, Washington, DC: American Association of Museums/AAM Education Committee.

Kulik, G. (1989) "Designing the Past: History Museum Exhibitions from Peale to the Present," in Leon, W. and Rozensweig, R. (eds) *History Museums and Historical Societies in the United States*, Urbana, IL: University of Illinois Press.

McDermott, M. (1987) "Through These Eyes: What Novices Value in Art Experience," *Museum Program Sourcebook*, Washington, DC: American Association of Museums.

Mayer, J.D. and Salovey, P. (1997) "What Is Emotional Intelligence?" in Salovey, P. and Sluyter, D. (eds) *Emotional Development and Emotional Intelligence: Implications for Educators*, New York: Basic Books.

Posner, E. (1988) "The Museum as Bazaar," in *Atlantic*, 262:2, 68.

Screven, C. (1987) *Museum Learning and the Casual Visitor: What Are the Limits?* Conference on Museum Evaluation, University of Toronto.

Weil, S.E. (1989) "The Proper Business of the Museum: Ideas or Things?" in *Muse*, 12:1, 31.

16

LET'S EMPOWER ALL THOSE WHO HAVE A STAKE IN EXHIBITIONS

About the uses, meaning, and failings of the team approach, 1990

The time has come for audience advocates to take their rightful place within museums.

After decades of struggle, museum educators can claim considerable progress. Their work is increasingly respected. They have been assisted in this transformation by various external forces: an increasing dependence on earned income from admissions in many places, the generous array of visitor services provided by our nearest competitors (for-profit attractions), and the publication of professional association white papers such as *Excellence and Equity* in the United States and *A Common Wealth: Museums and Learning in the United Kingdom*.[1]

In the past, museums tended to act as if they collected, preserved, and studied objects and only then, to a lesser degree of importance, educated their audiences. Even though mission statements had conjoined education to these other activities, museums behaved as if they were stuck in a zero-sum game, forced to choose one element of their mission over another. Now, these same institutions generally affirm the coexistence of multiple missions, allowing attention to audiences and scholarship to live side-by-side (though some curators would argue – in a time of declining budgets – that their role of scholarship is in danger of being slighted).

In many museums, the last two decades have been an invigorating time for educators. Internal and external pressures to diversify audience, to make the interpretation of museum collections more representative, and to broaden the palette of exhibition strategies – all elements that fell most naturally to museum educators – elevated their role. There was increased recognition that to accomplish these goals, spokespersons for the audience would need to be present within the decision-making hierarchy of museums.

Encouraging evidence of the acceptance of multiple missions could be seen in the creation of senior positions – assistant directors for public programs – alongside their existing counterparts for research and curation within numerous museum hierarchies. Toward the end of the 1980s at the Smithsonian Institution, there was a policy change in job descriptions and promotion schedules that placed the assistant directors for public programs and curatorial research at the National Museum of Natural History at equal rank and pay, recognizing that these two essential thrusts of the institution were equivalent. It was, at that time, a difficult achievement. Today that structure is more common, mirrored in more than one of the Smithsonian's museums and many other institutions around the world. Although not perfect, when this structure works, it is because each of the offices acknowledges the importance of the other, and each respects the different perspectives represented.

Assistant directors find that they can advocate more robustly for their respective positions if they know that the director feels passionate about both elements – audience and content. This situation is less often the case than educators would like but more widespread now than in earlier times.

Of course, change in management structure at the top does not, in and of itself, improve the product that is delivered to the public. A long-standing argument has been that in order to include the concerns of the visitor in the most visible part of the museum – its exhibitions – the process of exhibition creation itself would have to change. Toward that end, a new form of exhibition creation was promoted in the late 1970s. The Boston Children's Museum and the Field Museum of Natural History in Chicago "are widely credited with originating the models that led to what we now call the team approach to exhibit design" (Roberts 2000).

The team approach maintained that three equal advocacy positions – content, design, and audience – needed voice within the exhibition process from the onset. This seemingly innocuous change was essentially political. The team approach attempted to break the then closely held monopoly of curators and designers over exhibition creation. What was new was the insertion of the educators' role right from the start, not waiting for the exhibition to harden by allowing curators and designers to work alone, as had been common in the past. The argument underpinning this change was that too many exhibitions were esoteric, understood only by the most knowledgeable, and audience needs were superimposed on completed products as an afterthought. The counter-argument made by curators was that a firm foundation of scholarly accuracy was needed first before "dumbing down" was added. It was then, and remains now, a lively debate.

Some variant of the team approach is increasingly used worldwide. Placed within the team at its inception, the audience advocate is not a token representative but a player of importance. To prevent the unbalancing of the representation, each advocate formally acts on behalf of fellow colleagues and advisors in their field of concern, all of whom have a stake in seeing that their interests are addressed. The formality of their roles – plus this equality of representation – distinguishes the team.[2]

If the advocates are to enjoy equal access to plead their case, they must report to be a neutral supervisor. In many institutions, this position is an ombudsman, known as the broker or project manager, who in turn reports to the client, usually the museum director.

Museums now using the team approach have modified the structure or the nomenclature slightly to fit the traditions of their own institutions. But the major component – a three-pronged advocacy – remains essential and consistent. In some cases a fourth advocate has been added to represent the object – dividing exhibition content from collections care. And in other permutations, marketing and external affairs have been added as the fourth player. However, these remain a rarer occurrence.

The content advocate is usually but not always the curator (Chicago's Field Museum of Natural History uses a "developer"); the design advocate is usually but not always the actual designer (sometimes the in-house designer, sometimes a contractor); and the audience advocate is usually but not always a museum educator.

The audience advocate's training

To make the system more effective, what do audience advocates need to know, and how should they be trained? It is clear that a knowledge base can be outlined: an audience advocate should be familiar with, in part, developmental theory, learning theory, handicapped accessibility requirements, evaluation techniques, history and culture of divergent groups, and curriculum development processes. In addition, an audience advocate must have the ability, experience, and sensitivity to work with representatives of many communities.

This as-yet-uncodified syllabus is a tall order for anyone to master and especially hard for already employed staff with overfilled plates. Although many museum educators know some of the material, very few practitioners know the whole batch. Happily, there are experienced audience advocates who help by mentoring. In addition, there are publications and conferences that disseminate the information needed.

Because the position of audience advocate is more recent and therefore less familiar, unlike that of the design and content advocates, the museum community must continue to provide learning opportunities for museum educators that fit within an already crowded and productive work life. For example, from 1997 to 2003, the now-closed Antorchas Foundation in Argentina funded in-service exhibition training that radically altered the exhibition process in a broad segment of the country's museums, allowing many museum educators to participate in the team approach for the first time.

Issues and opportunities

The team approach was originally designed for in-house personnel. Now, with increasing use of contractor design teams, many of which bring along their own content and educational specialists, museums must modify the system to represent the knowledge base of the in-house museum personnel without negating the input of the exhibition contractor. This new circumstance – the relationship between contractor and staff – has not been well addressed. A new variant of the team may be needed to balance the expertise of the contractor with the aspirations and creativity of the in-house staff.

In 2000, *Exhibitionist* (the publication of NAME, the National Association of Museum Exhibitions) issued an entire volume on the assessment of the team approach (NAME 2000). For it, Jay Rounds and Nancy McIlvaney created a survey on the effectiveness of the approach. "Respondents to this survey strongly favored the team approach over linear methods of exhibit development," they report. "Nonetheless, they acknowledged that intra-team conflict is often a problem and that

many teams have difficulty in establishing workable methods for decision making"
(Rounds and McIlvaney 2000).

Dan Spock, director of exhibitions at the Minnesota Historical Society, commenting
online about the survey, related the team approach to increased museum visitation:

> *Museum News* estimates an increase of nearly 200 million visitors to American
> museums in the last 10 years – 678 to 865 million. Though some of this rep-
> resents a building boom, could it also be related to the fact that museums
> have become more engaging? And might this be correlated to the increased
> preponderance of exhibitions developed by teams? Perhaps the inclusion of a
> wide variety of skills and perspectives in development also generates a more
> multivalent and attractive visitor experience in the finished product.
>
> (McIlvaney 2000)

As suggested, the major evidence of team approach influence may be the broad
palette of exhibition modalities that is now ubiquitous within the museum field.

The team approach has not run its course. The current arguments about its use
revolve around who should make the decisions, who should hold the vision, how
teams should work together more amicably and efficiently, and how creativity can
be supported and encouraged. It is evident that creative vision is not a collective
activity, but it is an essential ingredient for successful exhibitions.

Others have indicated that successful group process must be learned and that
insufficient training is available. Further, with increased input from community
advisory boards, the integration of their wishes with those of the team need better
orchestration. Like all teamwork, this is also complex.

I often remind museum staff that the exhibition process is not meant to be smooth
and passionless and that tensions within the group are not necessarily indications of failure or inappropriate methods. There may be an inbuilt tension present in all advocacy
situations. Working out the tensions of the group may be part of the natural process.

On balance, I would submit that the introduction of the team approach as
a method of exhibition creation has had very positive consequences. The process is
not perfect and remains a center of debate. The solution, however, does not lie in
a return to the curator as the sole arbiter, but rather in further experience and
fine-tuning to balance and incorporate the creativity of the each individual.

Afterword

A version of this chapter was originally published in *Museum News* in 1990. At that
time, I was deputy assistant secretary for museums at the Smithsonian Institution. Part
of my responsibility was to increase the role and power of the Smithsonian's public service staff and to increase the diversity of subject matter and audience in its exhibition
and program elements. The team approach to exhibition design was then still new. I
had come from the Boston Children's Museum which is among those credited with its
creation, so I was very familiar with it. When I arrived, it was not being practiced in

the Smithsonian. Twenty years later, the team approach is used widely throughout the profession, but it remains both revolutionary and problematic. This new version of the original paper attempts to place the origins of the team approach in historic context and to establish its continuing relevance today (Gurian 1990).

Notes

1 Both of these white papers had a great influence on increasing emphasis on public service found within the museum sector (Anderson 1997), (AAM 1992).
2 In order to manage the rough edges of this messy process, museums are increasingly codifying the rules of engagement now leading to a new debate that structure increases rigidity and reduction of creativity in the process. See NAME (2002).

Bibliography

AAM (1992) *Excellence and Equity: Education and the Public Dimension of Museums*, Washington, DC: American Association of Museums.

Anderson, D. (1997) *A Common Wealth: Museums and Learning in the United Kingdom*, London: Department of National Heritage.

Gurian, E.H. (1990) "Let Us Empower All Those Who Have a Stake in Exhibitions," in *Museum News*, March/April.

McIlvaney, N. (2000) "Rethinking the Exhibit Team: A Cyberspace Forum," in *Exhibitionist*, 19:1, 8–15.

NAME (2002) "Formalizing Exhibition Development," in *The Exhibitionist*, Spring.

Roberts, L.C. (2000) "Educators on Exhibit Teams: A New Role, a New Era," in Hirsch, J.S. and Silverman, L.H. (eds) *Transforming Practice*, Washington, DC: Museum Education Roundtable.

Rounds, J. and Mcilvaney, N. (2000) "Who's Using the Team Process? How's It Going?" in *Exhibitionist*, 19:1, 4–7.

17

RELUCTANT RECOGNITION OF THE SUPERSTAR

A paean to individual brilliance, and how it operates, 1992[1]

It is by logic that we prove, but by intuition that we, discover.
(Henri Poincaré in *Sparks of Genius* (2000))

I was wrong! The team approach to exhibition production is not the only way to go.

The team approach, for those unfamiliar with the concept, is a political and administrative model in which the exhibition organizing group is made up of advocates for content, design, and audience. Each of these advocates has say and status in the process in order to create a product that reflects multiple levels of ideas and information and multiple viewpoints. There are variations on the team approach, but each was designed in part to break the perceived hold on exhibitions by just one person – most often the curator. It was said that this fictitious individual often (but not always) exerted his or her controlling viewpoint to create exhibitions that were boring for the ordinary visitor because they were designed primarily for the enjoyment of the producer's colleagues. The resulting mythical exhibition was said to be obscure, wordy, object driven, full of professional jargon, and preachy in tone.

Now, face to face with the talent of Jeshajahu Weinberg – the director of the United States Holocaust Memorial Museum, where I serve as deputy director – I reluctantly admit that under certain circumstances there is a place in the exhibition production firmament for the single vision of a person, who I refer to as the superstar. In fact, looking back on the most notable exhibitions I have visited, I find it is often the superstar who has broken with tradition and allowed the rest of us to reassess our assumptions about exhibitions and the learning that can take place there. Contemplate, for example, some of my own favorite superstar-created exhibitions: Alexander Girard's installation of his own collection of folk toys, *Multiple Visions: A Common Bond* in the Museum of International Folk Art in Santa Fe; Ray and Charles Eames' traveling exhibition *Mathematica*; Ivan Chermayeff's *A Nation of Nations*, installed in the National Museum of American History; or the small gem of an exhibition, *Mining the Museum*, created for the Maryland Historical Society by Fred Wilson. I am sure that each of us has such a list of favorites.

Superstars have certain characteristics that exempt them from the rules made for the rest of those who wish to control exhibitions. It goes without saying that superstars have extreme talent in the exhibition medium and create products that are – to use an overused word – unique.

Superstars, like choreographers and playwright-directors, think of their products as works of art, though not necessarily consciously. (In fact, this resemblance between the exhibition process and performing arts productions would bear more scrutiny.) Superstars wash every decision through an internal process that judges the feel of the product – almost the taste – against a set of personal criteria. For them, developing an exhibition is an aesthetic, intuitive process rather than an intellectual one.

This is not to say that the people surrounding the superstar are not valued for their necessary contributions or are mere serfs acting out the decisions of the master. Quite the contrary, the work is very much an interactive process among colleagues. But there is a shared belief that the result will be a work of art rather than a didactic lesson. The team members believe that they are in the presence of a rare talent who, like the artist in the atelier, is worth working for, and has final authority. With the voluntary permission of the group, the content of the exhibition is shaped by a single intelligence. The group's acquiescence resembles the eagerness of actors in a repertory company.

Jeshajahu Weinberg belongs in the superstar group. Shaike (as he prefers to be called) was the founding director-general of the Museum of the Diaspora in Tel Aviv, another one of my personal favorites. Prior to his inadvertent entrance into the museum field, he was the director of the Cameri Theater, the municipal theater company in Tel Aviv, for 15 years.

Shaike, like other superstars, defies acknowledged wisdom. He has had a lifelong suspicion of broadly based decision-making processes, though he is a very good listener. And I cannot believe that he would put much credence in formative evaluation as part of the exhibition development process. Both things I held dear and often preached about before I met him.

Shaike believes in the creation of linear storytelling exhibitions in which the artifact is the contextual illustration of any idea.[2] In fact, the Museum of the Diaspora does not have a single authentic artifact. He loves technology and mediated presentations. He is a shameless borrower of the techniques of commercial display. He assumes that we, the audience, have such interest in the story he is going to tell that we will devote hours rather than minutes to a single exhibition. Everything he believes runs counter to thoughtful audience research, yet his wildly successful exhibitions work just as he predicts.

The permanent exhibition at the United States Holocaust Memorial Museum (opened in April 1993) continues his tradition. It is told via a circular route that covers three floors. Visitors begin with an elevator ride to the fourth floor and proceed as if captive for the duration until they reemerge on the second floor, 35,000 square feet later. The permanent exhibition about the Holocaust contains 3 movies, 70 video monitor programs, endless texts, and real and facsimile artifacts. Even a short visit will last more than 40 minutes.

168

I believe that most powerful element in this production will prove to be the synchronicity between the forced march imposed on the visitor and the terror of the content. The audacity of this approach seems quite natural to Shaike. In fact, he would do it in no other way. He has no hesitation about the chosen strategy – only endless worry about individual parts.

While I continue to recommend that the rest of us mortals work within the team approach, it is the exhibitions created by superstars that remain most memorable for me. Perhaps the presence of the underlying artistic temperament (aided by the fact that each of these people was a successful practicing artist in some non-museum field before entering the exhibition business) somehow illuminates the exhibition from within and provides the secret but necessary incentive for the visitor to learn. The process may be analogous to having a superb teacher, rather than our own inherent curiosity, as the catalyst for developing a lifelong interest in a subject.

As museum professionals we should think more about superstars and the gifts they have shared with us all. We should give more credence to the likelihood that when the superstar is author and teacher, visitors will have an indelible experience. We need to spend more time deciphering the importance of direct communication between the exhibition developer and the audience. It may be that this model differs from the older, often-maligned curator-led approach because there is no presumption of objectivity. Instead, the superstar's personal vision is clearly communicated.

Whatever the magic is, I wish to thank those remarkable individuals who created exhibitions that brought me such indelible unexpected memories.

Afterword

This paper, written in 1992, just before the opening of the United States Holocaust Memorial Museum anticipates its success and tries to make sense of the experience even before the public had seen the results. I was the deputy director at that time and worked for Shaike Weinberg for three years, an opportunity for which I remain deeply grateful.

With over a decade to reflect on the museum and its impact, I am even more persuaded than before that exhibitions are, in part, works of art. Indeed many of the most talented exhibit creators are trained either as visual artists or in the performing arts, most notably the theater. The relationship between the artist and the exhibition needs further study and understanding.

I trust that the reader will understand that this paper is not only about an extraordinary man – Shaike Weinberg – but also documents a privileged exception to the usual team process of creating exhibitions.

I continue to be fascinated by the "superstar," who conceptualizes and creates indelible exhibitions that change the form itself. I believe we find them only rarely. I treasure among my friends some of the most respected producers of exquisite and profound exhibitions. They are the best of their profession. But the superstar, like all stars, passes through one's life with a luminescence that is of another quality altogether.

Notes

1 A version of this article was first published in 1992 in *Journal of Museum Education* (Gurian 1992b).
2 To learn more about how Shaike Weinberg thinks read Weinberg and Elieli (1995) and Linenthal (1995).

Bibliography

Gurian, E.H. (1992b) "Reluctant Recognition of the Superstar," in *Journal of Museum Education*, Washington, DC, 17:3, 6–7.

Linenthal, E.T. (1995) *Preserving Memory: The Struggles to Create America's Holocaust Museum*, New York: Viking Press.

Root-Bernstein, R. and Root-Bernstein, M. (2000) *Sparks of Genius*, Boston, MA: Houghton Mifflin, p. 379.

Weinberg, J. and Elieli, R. (1995) *The Holocaust Museum in Washington*, New York: Rizzoli International Publications.

18

A BLURRING OF THE
BOUNDARIES, 1994[1]

Fantasy works inwards upon its author, blurring the boundary between
the visioned and the actual.... The creative imagination works
outwards, steadily increasing the gap between the visioned and the
actual, till this becomes the great gulf fixed between art and
nature.

(Dorothy Sayers 1941)

In twenty-five years, museums will no longer be recognizable as they are now known.
Many will have incorporated attributes associated with organizations that now are
quite distinct from museums; hence, the "blurred boundaries" of the title. The
process is and will continue to seem gradual and inevitable.

The change will come slowly and maybe not overtly, though the museum
community will embrace a new expanded definition of museums and these emerging
hybrids. These many new museums are to be welcomed; there is the opportunity for
the changed museum to make a more relevant contribution to our society.

The museum's relationship to its collections and their ownership and care will
change, and in some instances already have changed. The distinct edges of differing
function among libraries, memorials, social service centers, schools, shopping malls,
zoos, performance halls, archives, theaters, public parks, cafes, and museums will
blur, and in many cases have already begun to.

On the content side, museums will become more comfortable with presentations
that contain a multiplicity of viewpoints and with the interweaving of scientific fact
and what is considered by some, but not by others, to be myth. On the interpretive
side, museums will rely less on collections to carry the story and more on other forms
of expression, such as stories, song, and speech and the affective, dramatic, and
psychological power that their presentations can contain. They will be less apologetic
about including emotional and evocative messages. These changes will help
museums to become more effective storehouses of cultural information.

Rather than the collecting of objects defining museums, museums will be seen as
aligned with other entities in new classifications. One important grouping – the one
concentrated on here – is those institutions of memory that store and transmit our

171

collective human and earthly past. Not surprisingly, this group of institutions will include libraries, archives, and schools but also technologically based storehouses such as databases, distance-learning sites, film, video, and recording storage facilities. Institutions of memory will include, for example, religious centers and language class.

Whereas some will collect three-dimensional materials, others will house songs, ritual, music, dance, and stories. The defining element for this classification will be the storing and passing on of evident markers of culture and cultural transmission.

The United States Holocaust Memorial Museum

Significant trends in museums lead to the conclusion that museums will become more closely aligned with such other institutions of memory. Let us explore aspects of the United States Holocaust Memorial Museum (founded in 1993) and the visitor behavior that can be observed there.[2] The team that produced that place hoped to create a quality museum. They had no idea that they were creating an artistic masterpiece or that they were creating more than a museum. The museum has become an icon, a symbol for the contemplation of personal responsibility, and a place to reflect on the excesses of government (even as it sits in the shadow of the US federal buildings).

The architecture and the permanent exhibition work so well together they seem to be a single unified environment. The linear route the visitor has to traverse occupies space on three different floors. The exhibition contains 3 films, nearly 70 different video programs, over 5,000 individual items, which range in size from a railcar to a toothbrush; a few large castings of in situ historic monuments; lots of text; and thousands of photographs.

The museological implications are interesting and puzzling. Visitor behavior contradicts what is normally to be expected. Is this the exhibition that proves the rule? Or is it the exhibition that opens all rules to reevaluation?

Rather than the usual one and one-half hour visit that people usually engage in, regardless of the size of the museum, visitors here stay much longer. Rather than conversational interactions with each other, they are quiet and almost reverential. Rather than ignoring their fellow visitors who are strangers, they show concern for each other's well-being. In the absence of research, one can only surmise that the visitor believes that this sojourn is more like a pilgrimage to a church, a gravesite, or a memorial than a museum visit and is therefore not to be entered into lightly. Could it be that the visitors' kindness stems from their desire to distance themselves from the behavior of the Nazi perpetrators they see depicted?

The exhibition is linear. Visitors can either follow the route offered or jettison the whole experience; they cannot alter their path. Conventional wisdom about the design of exhibitions for a democratic society suggests that successful exhibitions should offer visitors freedom of choice so that they can decide the order in which they will experience the elements and choose to skip some altogether.[3] At the Holocaust Museum, that is certainly not the case. There is a fixed order. Does the willingness of the crowd to participate in this directed march suggest that whenever one produces what the director called a "narrative exhibition," visitors will not feel oppressed by being led? Alternatively, is this exhibition successful because the forced march that was part of the actual Nazi history is emotionally echoed by the viewers' optionless route?

The exhibition artifacts were chosen and positioned for their illustrative value, quite like pictures in a children's book, even though some of them are extremely noteworthy. They are rarely placed there for their unique quality but to add credence to the overall story. Likewise, the photographs are there as evidence rather than as singular images. From the moment you enter the elevator to the time you exit two stories below the starting point, you are inescapably surrounded by the story. Is it this atmospheric surround that brings such power to the experience? Has the museum become a three-dimensional theater with a play containing crescendos, respites, and resolution?

There is seemingly endless text. We all know that visitors do not read. Yet at the Holocaust Museum, many visitors read everything even though the typeface is small, the text is long, and the reader needs a sophisticated vocabulary. Why does the audience read this lengthy group of texts? Is it the nature of the topic, the embedding within the environment, or a style of writing that is stark and without judgmental modifiers? Has the text become a novel, and like a good mystery, too engaging to put down?

The exhibition engages adolescents, the hardest age group for any museum to reach, especially when they come in groups of peers. Why is this so?[4]

Museum professionals quizzed immediately after their visit say that they cannot integrate what they have just seen and need some time to reflect. Most people cannot immediately reengage with their normal life. During the next week or so, they say that the images and ideas invade their thinking at odd moments. Is this because of the power of the story? Or because this narrative is presented in an encompassing multisensory environment that takes time for people to integrate?

Or because, according to Howard Gardner, the different modes of intelligence needed to experience the exhibition do not have easy integrative pathways to one another?[5]

People revisit this exhibition, contrary to the expectation that it would be a single, though indelible, experience. They say they return so that they can read more about areas that they did not fully explore in their previous visit. Are we to believe that if you fill an exhibition with too much information, rather than defeating visitor interest, it serves as an impetus to return?

And what about the subject matter! This is an exhibition about horrific news. Yet, we do not see the voyeuristic behavior or hear sounds of titillation that were feared before the opening. Visitors emotionally prepare themselves to come and take on the visit as a journey of personal introspection. In their internal dialogue, they decide not only how they would have behaved in the past but also how they wish to behave in the future when confronted with issues of racism or government excess. This is not to suggest that the exhibition by itself is a change agent, creating a more concerned public out of its visitors. However, if museum professionals are interested in the role exhibitions can play within a civil society, visitors to this exhibition are worthy of long-range study to ascertain if exhibitions can be contributing factors in attitudinal change.

Further, the museum is used as metaphor in public debate by national and world leaders who assume in their discourse that their listeners have seen the museum. Members of the museum's governing council are asked to comment publicly on national policy and to appear at historic occasions at the side of the president of the United States. It is interesting that visiting heads of state feel obliged to visit the museum if they have not already done so.

Taking these elements together, the United States Holocaust Memorial Museum has blurred the boundaries between museum and theater, between museum and religious memorial, and has become a national icon and public metaphor. Visitor experience in this museum should cause the museum community to rethink audience behavior, stay length, and exhibition technique.

Indigenous peoples

In 1994, the George Gustav Heye Center of the National Museum of the American Indian opened in the Alexander Hamilton US Customs House in New York.

It is the first branch of the National Museum of the American Indian to open; two additional sites are planned.[6] Native Americans (and, by extension, other indigenous peoples) wish to have a profound effect on the shaping of museums in the future. In the United States, Canada, Australia, and New Zealand, many museum professionals now concede that native people are the legitimate spokespersons for the use and display of "their" artifacts within the museum. New laws and museum policies state that material such as human remains, associated grave goods, and secret/sacred objects are possible subjects for repatriation, regardless of the clarity of the provenance, if the acknowledged spokespersons of the applicable tribes so request (NAGPRA 1990). Thus, the exclusive right of museum personnel to decide what shall be included or excluded in their public exhibitions will end, and in some cases already has. The display of any object without consultation with the native group and, by extension, with any group importantly affected, I predict, will become obsolete.

At the three opening Heye Center exhibitions, all label text includes native first-person narrative, sometimes alone and sometimes with anthropological and curatorial voices. Who can or should speak for the object are questions that have now been broadened. Upon reflection, the resolution of the controversy over the Enola Gay exhibition at the National Air and Space Museum relies on the same premise – that is, the users of the object in question (in this case, the veterans who flew the plane) assert that they have the primary right to control the narrative voice.[7]

The involvement of native peoples in the business of museums goes much deeper than mere presentation. They propose to change many of the most basic tenets of our profession regarding care of the collections made by their ancestors. Museums that hold native material are increasingly allowing those objects to be used during ceremonies to which the object is related. Using objects, of course, may affect their condition and is anathema to those who feel they are charged with preservation at all costs. Sending out objects for use and subsequent return makes museums more like lending libraries than storage vaults. In some museums, the analogy to an American process called "self-storage" is more apt. The native family or tribe need not cede ownership at all and withdraws the object whenever it is needed; the museum houses, preserves, and even displays the object at other times with the permission of the owners. The Queen of England's access to her jewels held in the Tower of London is no different.

In addition, because for some American Indians the boundary between animate and inanimate things is translucent, how an object is to be housed and preserved interests them. Some objects need to be "fed," some need to be separated from their neighbors, and some cannot be visited by women or by the uninitiated. Objects of one tribe should not sit next to objects of their traditional enemies, and most objects cannot be wrapped in such a way as to prevent them from "breathing." The demand to treat objects in storage in accordance with native wishes supersedes the increasingly technological methods of collection care that have been taught as good practice.

This insistence by native peoples has caused conservators to reappraise more traditional conservation methods, and interest in the benefits of these older, less costly, methods is growing.

The case of the Zuni War Gods is perhaps the most dramatic example in which the preservation of objects is not seen as the ultimate good. Zuni War Gods were funerary figures of the Zuni tribe that were supposed to remain with the above-the-ground corpse until both had disintegrated. The Zuni Tribe argued successfully in the courts that their graves had been desecrated and the War Gods stolen. Therefore, the objects should be returned and should be allowed to disintegrate as originally intended. The Zuni position was sustained, and most museums that held these objects have returned them. The War Gods were placed in a secure vault open to the elements, where they are now disintegrating. Museums, through their care of collections, have had a key role in conserving the artifacts of many cultures, but preservation is no longer seen as an absolute good, and the decisions on what to preserve are no longer ours alone to make.

Museums that hold ethnological collections most commonly face these questions, but these issues do not relate only to natural history and history museums. When faced with requests to balance information arrived at by the scientific method and by the differing explanations of natural phenomena arising from alternate world views, what stand should museums take? How, for example, does one reconcile the current scientific explanation of the arrival of the American Indian in North America via the Bering Strait land bridge with the emergence from the Fourth World seen by some tribes as the creation explanation? Is one to be referred to as "science" and one as "myth?" Should both be presented in the same exhibition as explanations of equal value? Does displaying both with equal weight open the door to the Flat Earth Society and the Creationists? Do we care? This is not a theoretical discussion, but one that many museum people of good will are struggling with – some with frustration and some in a spirit of optimism, but all feeling that they are wandering in an unconventional and uncharted environment.

Native colleagues are not very interested in object display as the principal method of cultural transmission. They feel their culture is more aptly transmitted and understood through association with environments, language, dance, song, music, smell, and storytelling; and they wish the public display of Indian material to include those methods. They do not seem alone in that position. Other sections of our society, African American people, for example, wish to have their history publicly told but find there are few readily available preserved artifacts, and so must look to other methods of presentation. They feel that much of their culture has been preserved as stories, songs, food, and speech and are interested in creating appropriate forms of presentation. It may be that the notion of museum as primarily display of objects fits best within a very few cultures. As the world's population continues to migrate and intermingle, institutions called museums that include more active methods of cultural transfer will be created. Sound, smell, and environmental setting will gain ascendancy as methods of interpretation; and objects will become not the raison d'etre, but rather just one element in a complex presentation. In this regard, the multiple exhibition strategies of the United States Holocaust Memorial Museum and the preferences of indigenous people coincide.

The changing view of authenticity

Jeshajahu Weinberg, director of the Holocaust Museum, was previously the founding director of the Museum of the Diaspora in Tel Aviv. When faced with no available collection and the desire to tell the history of the migration of the Jews, which extends over more than 5,000 years, he made a decision to create a "museum" that used all the most interesting technological presentational methods available at that time and reproductions of all the three-dimensional objects needed. There was not a single "authentic" object in the entire presentation. That institution is now considered a museum, but whether it qualified as one was debated at its inception.

Science museums have had a long tradition of creating purpose-built tactile stations to illustrate scientific phenomena and, at least in the United States, many science museums have few or even no collections. Yet, science centers are called "museums" even though we continue to talk about museums as the place where the authentic object can be found.

As we move to a time in which we are increasingly reliant on the most modern means of communications, these methods will have a great impact on presentations within the institutions we currently call museums. Whereas the central tenet of museums has until now been the holding of material evidence, the major modern means by which we communicate with each other (telephone, Internet) either leave no material trace of that event – or, like computer printouts, faxes, photos, movies, CDs, tapes, and computer discs, the "original" evidence can come in large runs of multiples. Except for the production of the visual and craft artist and the occasional handwritten letter, we are creating a plethora of evidence for which there is no unique object and, in many cases, no object at all.

Now, as we no longer produce much of the unique thing, we may be becoming much more comfortable with the idea and use of reproductions and copies. Uniqueness is losing its importance, and the definition of authenticity is broadening. Except in rare instances, we believe that all copies made from a photo negative are real enough, and it is the image that becomes the object. We will all have to struggle with what in the future constitutes the real object and what environments or parts thereof can be honorably replicated. Though not a new struggle (many of the dinosaur bones on display have long been castings), it becomes more complicated with the advent of easy digital manipulation of images.

Next steps

So what can be made of these examples? This is not a recitation intended to deconstruct museums. Rather, the desire is to review and then recombine. Out of these and other new threads may come the likelihood of producing institutions that use a multiplicity of "meaning-making" processes that fit better with people's natural learning and cultural-transference styles.

The Holocaust Museum has demonstrated that out of the fixed narrative can come enough points of empathy so that each visitor can find compelling relevance. The visitor has become engaged not only in information gathering, but also in an attitudinally and emotionally provocative process. The native people have helped redefine the place of collections within a rich complex of cultural transmission methods. "Institutions of memory" store the collected past. Some of these institutions are individuals (storytellers, for example), some collect ephemeral material (song, for example), and some collect tangible material (museums, libraries, and archives, for example). The boundaries between these institutions are blurring as we discover that we need, in some cases, to replace older and no-longer-functioning forms of cultural transmission and, in others, to take on the task of storing new kinds of material. Museums with their broadened definition can become important, even central, institutions of memory.

Violence and acrimony seem to be increasing worldwide. Whereas some of this violence is caused by the breakdown of community, in other cases group coherence is maintained by hate of and violence toward others. Institutions of memory have been used both to foster healthy and positive group recognition and to justify aggression.

Thus museums and their kindred institutions can be used for either peaceable or aggressive ends and are not a priori institutions of good or evil. Citizens must, therefore, pay remedial attention to the fostering of those institutions that are seen as agents of civilizing behavior and more peaceful coexistence. New and important research is helping to explain the importance of family, neighborhood, church, and other institutions, that complex of cultural transmission methods. Boundaries have been blurred, and a different way of focusing begins to emerge.

In the past, museums have been defined as belonging to a number of institutional categories; for example, as one of a number of cultural organizations that contribute to our quality of life. In addition, they have been placed in a category with other informal education institutions. They have been further identified as part of a small group that acts as protectors of the original object. The suggestion here is that we create *new* categories and in doing so acknowledge the more central role these institutions play in our collective well-being. One of these groups in which museums can claim membership could be called "institutions of memory."

As we begin to dissect the elements that make up civil behavior, we discover that organized consensual rules of interaction help us humans, who tend to be violent and aggressive, live relatively peaceably within our own groups. These rules of behavior are transmitted in many forms by a wide variety of affiliative associations – family, religious, cultural, ethnic, and class – each of which helps to define us. These groups need methods and structures for collecting their past in order to study, alter current understandings accordingly, and pass accumulated wisdom on to the future. When combined, these groups could help us become individually safer, more disciplined and productive, and more communally responsible. Our collective opportunity is to ascertain how to create, restore, or re-create systems and organizations that can bring us a greater measure of nonviolent human interaction. As boundaries blur, museums can and should be counted among them.

Notes

1 The original version of this text was presented at the Education for Scientific Literacy Conference held at the Science Museum in London, England, in November 1994. A revised version was published in 1995 (Gurian 1995a). This version has been updated further.
2 For a full discussion of the creation of the United States Holocaust Memorial Museum by the founding director, see Weinberg and Elieli (1995).
3 For an interesting review of research on various exhibition techniques and their consequences, see Bitgood (2002, p. 11).
4 For an interesting review of adolescents uses of museums, see Kelly *et al.*:

> Youth audiences had quite particular interests and expectations when it came to museums. This age group tended to be seeking involvement in relevant areas, becoming aware of cutting edge developments and were looking to build upon their identity and role in society.

(2002)

5 Howard Gardner's theory of multiple intelligences has been very influential in exhibition design, facility most especially in children's museums (Gardner 1983).
6 The Cultural Resource Center, a storage and community outreach, opened in Suitland, Maryland in 1998, and on September 21, 2004, the National Museum of the American Indian opened on the Washington, DC, mall. All three form the National Museum of the American Indian (NMAI) which is part of the Smithsonian Institution.
7 To read a further discussion on the Enola Gay controversy, see Linenthal and Engelhard (1996) and Harwit (1996).

Bibliography

Bitgood, S. (2002) "Environmental Psychology in Museums, Zoos, and Other Exhibition Centers," in Bechtel, R. and Churchman, A. (eds) *Handbook of Environmental Psychology*, New York: John Wiley & Sons.

Gardner, H. (1983) *Frames of Mind: The Theory of Multiple Intelligences*, New York: Basic Books.

Gurian, E.H. (1995a) "A Blurring of the Boundaries," in *Curator*, 38:1, 31–39.

Harwit, M. (1996) *An Exhibit Denied: Lobbying the History of Enola Gay*, New York: Copernicus Springer-Verlag.

Kelly, L., Barlett, A., and Gordon, P. (2002) *Indigenous Youth and Museums: A Report on the Indigenous Youth Access Project*, Sydney: Australian Museum.

Linenthal, E.T. and Engelhard, T. (1996) *History Wars: The Enola Gay and Other Battles for the American Past*, New York: Holt.

NAGPRA (1990) *Native American Graves Protection and Repatriation Act*, 101 Congress, US. Available http://www.cr.nps.gov/nagpra/SITEMAP/INDEX.htm (accessed January 15, 2005).

Sayers, D.L. (1941) "The Mind of the Maker," in Andrews, R., Biggs, M., and Seidel, M. (eds) *The Columbia World of Quotations*, New York: Columbia University Press, 1996.

Weinberg, J. and Elieli, R. (1995) *The Holocaust Museum in Washington*, New York: Rizzoli International Publications.

19

THE UNITED STATES HOLOCAUST MEMORIAL MUSEUM

History or metaphor?[1] 1993

> Not unlike the fair-minded author who serves up ideas to readers only
> to have them march off in any direction and for any purpose with the
> ideas in their grasp, exhibit curators offer up the past with no control
> or ownership over the consequences of their creations. There is no
> anticipating all personal and collective memories that an exhibit
> might trigger – that is, after all, what is desired.
>
> (William Lang 2003)

On April 22 of this year, the United States Holocaust Memorial Museum (USHMM)
will be dedicated and become part of official Washington. Along with the Capital's
other museums, monuments, memorials, and historic landmarks, the Holocaust
Museum will become one of the shared experiences of millions of Americans who
journey to Washington on an almost reverential civic pilgrimage.

The museum is directed by Jeshajahu Weinberg (the creator of the Museum of
the Diaspora in Tel Aviv). The staff is talented, dedicated, cohesive, intelligent, and
committed. The brilliance of their work will be self-evident; their personal sacrifice
of time and anxiety will not show. I am proud to be among them.

The Holocaust Memorial Museum, given its location at the foot of the Washington
Monument, next door to the highly visited Bureau of Printing and Engraving (where
they print our money!), and on the edge of the National Mall that contains the
Smithsonian and the US Capitol, will be in the thick of the tourist ambulation.

So, what is the United States Holocaust Memorial Museum? Why is it in
Washington DC? And what is it about?

Rising on a plot of land between 14th Street and Raoul Wallenberg Place stands
a seven-story building designed by James Ingo Freed of Pei, Cobb, Freed, and
Partners. The exterior brick and granite make the building blend well with
its neighbors, whereas the interior shapes and materials eerily remind the visitor of
concentration camp buildings. The architecture of the building and the mood it
evokes will be worth the trip alone.

However, visitors will soon understand that they are surrounded by an institution
of unusual depth when they begin to explore the permanent exhibition, traverse its

three floors, visit two additional galleries housing temporary exhibitions, and encounter a technological state-of-the-art interactive learning center, an education center with a separate teacher's resource center, two theaters, and an academic research institute housing five separate archival collections (documents, film and video, oral history, photographs, and a registry of American Holocaust survivors), plus a library of 20,000 volumes. At the end of their visit, visitors will come upon a skylighted six-sided memorial whose interior is lit with candles. What is opening to the public is a nearly fully formed institution. I think every visit, no matter how casual, will leave the visitor in some way changed.

The permanent exhibition occupies 36,000 square feet and is organized in a linear fashion over three descending floors. The exhibition will portray a comprehensive story of the events between 1933 and 1945, perpetrated by Nazi Germany, which came to be known as the Holocaust. The exhibit uses authentic artifacts, which include a Polish railcar and a Danish fishing boat as well as castings of prominent but unmovable artifacts such as a portion of the Warsaw ghetto wall and the chillingly ironic gateway to Auschwitz, which reads "Arbeit Macht Frei (Work Will Set You Free)." Large-scale photographs will be used prominently, along with 70 separate video programs and 3 small movie theaters. This exhibition is not gratuitously horrific. Nevertheless, its material is so insistent and unremitting that we suggest it be limited to visitors above the age of 11. I believe the synchronicity of the linear "forced march" style of the exhibition with the subject matter it depicts will be chilling.

The visitor will learn about the history of the perpetrators, the suffering of the victims, the heroic efforts of the resisters and rescuers, and the moral dilemma of the bystanders. Visitors will undoubtedly question themselves as to what role or combination of roles they would have chosen had they been faced with the circumstances presented.

At the end of the visit to the permanent exhibit, the visitor is offered three choices: to enter the candlelit memorial and contemplate what one has just seen; to go to the Learning Center to find out more about the time period through a computerized touch screen that integrates text, maps, photos, film, music, chronologies, and oral histories; or to go downstairs through the rotunda called the Hall of Witness to return to the outside world and one's current life.

The United States Holocaust Memorial Council, established by authorization of Congress in 1980, was charged with overseeing the creation of the museum. The story (apocryphal or not) is that President Jimmy Carter had watched the television docudrama *The Holocaust* and decided that America should not be allowed to forget this devastating chapter in history in which the United States played a complex (some would even say complicit) role. In 1978 he initiated the President's Commission on the Holocaust whose charter reads in part, "The Commission shall submit a report...containing its recommendations with respect to the establishment and maintenance of an appropriate memorial to those who perished in the Holocaust" (Carter 1978).

This commission was headed by Elie Wiesel, who was not only the subsequent winner of the Nobel Peace Prize but is clearly, to many Americans, a Holocaust survivor and author of legendary stature.

In 1979, the commission issued a report that recommended the establishment of the USHMM and further stated, "The museum must be of symbolic and artistic beauty, visually and emotionally moving in accordance with the solemn nature of the Holocaust" (Weisel 1979).

The commission also recommended that the three components of such a living memorial be a memorial/museum, an educational foundation, and a Committee on Conscience.

Over the following decade many questions were framed, debates initiated and continued, tentative answers reached, and compromises struck to bring the project to its current state. The issues have had to do with the following dilemmas, each requiring an answer that would satisfy the immediate question while leaving room to revisit and refine in the future.

- Was the institution to be mainly a memorial or a museum?
- Are the events of the Holocaust to be described as a Jewish tragedy with other victims, or a human tragedy with many victims, primarily Jews?
- Is the Holocaust so singular an event as to defy comparison, or is it emblematic of the atrocities and cruelties that man is capable of?
- What is the relevance to Americans of this historic event that took place on foreign soil?
- Why should this memorial be in the United States capital city and operated, in part, by government funds?

And finally, and (to me) most interestingly:

- Is this to become a history museum documenting one particular place and era, or an institution that uses history as metaphor and therefore discusses the whole panoply of previous and subsequent inhumane acts we visit upon each other?

The debate over these questions continues – within the council, the staff, the community of survivors and witnesses to the event, and every member of the potential public who stops to reflect on these questions.

It is perhaps in the small daily decisions that one begins to discover what position one actually holds on these issues. The following are questions that our staff and council have had to wrestle with. In confronting the same issues, readers will begin to see their own preferred answers emerging within the spectrum of possible positions.

- All federal museums are closed only for Christmas Day. In memory of and out of respect for the majority of victims, should the USHMM be closed on Yom Kippur as well?
- Jews were numerically, by far, the largest group of victims of the Holocaust. Further, only the Gypsies shared with the Jews the dubious distinction of being

a people who were murdered because of national or racial affiliation. Would you describe the Holocaust as primarily a Jewish event?

- There were other victims. Besides the Gypsies, homosexuals, political dissidents (primarily socialists and communists), the handicapped and mentally ill, Jehovah's Witnesses, and the political and intellectual leadership of the Polish people were interred and murdered. How would you portray these victims? Would you refer to them as "non-Jewish victims," as "other victims," or just as "victims"?

- Much as we would like to think otherwise, the American liberation of the concentration camps was a ragged affair with soldiers happening upon camps unprepared. Some of these liberators were African Americans and some were Japanese Americans, though their numbers were small compared to the other liberating troops. Would you call attention to the fact that some of our liberators were Americans of color?

- Should this museum take an official public stand on current events? What, if anything, would you suggest the museum say about Haitian boat people; ethnic cleansing in Bosnia; deportation of Gypsies by Germany; vandalization of Jewish schools, cemeteries, and Holocaust memorials in Europe and South America; antihomosexual ballot propositions in Colorado and Oregon; or the starvation of civilians in Somalia?

- Where should subject-matter boundaries be drawn for public programs, research, collections, and exhibit topics? Should they be restricted to the Holocaust event itself, or should they be expanded to include current issues that arise in the lands that were affected by the Holocaust, to specific Holocaust victim groups, or to events that have parallels within the Holocaust (e.g. the refusal of sanctuary for the Haitian boat people and the turning back of the SS *St Louis*)?

- Other groups use the word "holocaust" when describing their own people's history. Should the museum provide a forum for their story as well? Should it help tell the story of the Armenians, African Americans, American Indians, Biafrans, or Somalians?

- Should the museum look at generic issues raised by the Holocaust? Should we address genocide, medical ethics, or the rule of law in condoning racism, or the effects of religious intolerance on ethnic strife throughout the modern world?

- In order to do the job well, which of the following must the next director of the museum be: a Holocaust scholar, an experienced museum director, and/or a person with family connections to the events or a member of one of the victim groups?

In my informal survey, I have come to believe that the position one takes on these issues has primarily to do with one's age and one's country of origin. If born after the Second World War and/or born in America, I have found one tends to favor of broadening the museum's focus to use its history to teach lessons for the future and engage with other instances of human tragedy. The problem inherent in this position is that to do so consistently will, in due course, blur the definition and original mission of the institution.

On the other hand, if one participated in the historical events and/or was born abroad, one tends to believe that the singularity of the Holocaust needs to be emphasized and the museum kept as close to a memorial and history museum as possible.

As one can imagine, the truce between proponents of these two differing positions is hard to keep, especially when many parties to the debate feel a certain entitlement about their position, where even entering into the debate itself is viewed as disloyalty. It is therefore with some trepidation that I offer my own sense as a museum veteran, a first-generation American born of German-Jewish immigrant parents, and a relative newcomer to the USHMM staff. In brief, I think the long-term importance of this new museum lies precisely in the tension between the historical particularity of the Holocaust and the universality of the human condition.

Having said that, I recognize that the mission of the museum, simply put, has been and must continue to be an inclusive one, one of "and." It must be both history and metaphor, not an either/or. The founders and current leadership of the museum have striven to preserve these inherent tensions by including as many aspects of opinion as possible. Thus, even the name of the institution, for example, contains both "memorial" and "museum."

The permanent exhibition is unashamedly about the Holocaust itself, with few digressions into historic precedents. Yet in telling this one story fully and dramatically, the exhibit should serve as both a historic recounting and a universal tale. The exhibition presents a predominance of Jewish material, but with notable inclusion of other victims. The exhibition has a subtheme about what Americans knew and when they knew it, to make concrete the US aspect of the story. In addition, external niches of the building contain quotes from several US presidents about the event and the need to memorialize it forever.

A sincere balance between all factions and a legitimization of the needs of all parties remain a difficult task. More than any other museum I have been associated with, the USHMM continuously debates its basics – with the attendant possibility that it might someday reinvent itself. The danger that the USHMM will become the captive of one element of the argument is always present. If that happens and the tension is eliminated, I believe the institution will fail some of its important constituencies.

We have been fortunate to have a director who could envision a clear path that makes peace with all factions. The continuing challenge will be to maintain empathy for all segments of the argument, credibility among all detractors, and the ability to steer an inclusive programmatic course.

Afterword

I was serving as the deputy director of the USHMM in charge of operations and public programs when I wrote this paper and presented it in 1993, just before the opening. I had not been part of the exhibition team but watched from the next office as the director headed up its creation. We staff did not know at the time that the Holocaust Museum would cause such a stir in the museum and foreign policy worlds. We were slightly overwhelmed by the crowds that rushed to see it. But we already knew that we had participated in creating an artistic triumph and felt extremely fortunate to have had the opportunity to work with our director, a true genius – Jeshajahu (Shaike) Weinberg.

The lessons I learned while working for Shaike would last from that time forward. Most important I began to understand that an exhibition can function as a history lesson while viewers are transforming it into their own analogies to illuminate issues pertinent to their own lives. Such transformations are often personal and private; sometimes they inspire new perspectives on contemporary events, and even encourage corresponding actions.

If one were to eavesdrop today at the Holocaust Museum's exit door, I am certain one could hear patrons talking to each other about the current Iraq war and current issues of atrocities and genocide such as Darfur. These events were, of course, not foreseen when the exhibition was created. But the dialogue the exhibition provokes makes it of continuing relevance to all manner of public and personal events.

Many of the questions I posed in this essay have been answered by the museum's actions over the last ten years. I recommend a periodic review of its Web site, which is comprehensive, adventuresome, and interesting. It can be found at www.ushmm.org.

The transformational quality of exhibitions is not often contemplated by their creators at the time of conception, or much written about in museum literature. Historians interested in memorializing do investigate exhibitions and look at the interaction between audience and memorial, for example. In some cases it is precisely due to this interactive quality of exhibitions that they are chosen over the more passive and static memorial statues of the past.[2]

If exhibition creators would pay more attention to the personalizations that occur when visitors confront exhibitions, they would understand that museums are much more than an educational venue or social setting. They are simultaneously places for daydreaming, introspection, and attitudinal change.

Museums, because of their particular ingredients – environmental surround, three-dimensionality, evidence in the form of diverse objects and media, and temporality as the visitor traverses the space – may have an unexplored power to influence, as well as the power to educate.

A slight change in opinion, a small shift in worldview, a tiny change in mindset in the presence of the exhibition artifact are not easily measured. The potential for these changes dwells within the individual, based on personal experience, as triggered (or not) by the material we present. The producers of exhibitions can only be mindful that some of these outcomes are possible.

Of course, exhibition producers are often tempted to preach overtly. By contrast, the power of the permanent exhibition of the USHMM, I am convinced, lies in its insistence to be neither emotive nor overtly judgmental. It is, instead, the unadorned, unbearable facts that force the visitor to think and to ponder.

While "History or Metaphor?" is about a particular museum and its internal debates at the time it was about to open, I hope I have provided a glimpse of the unexpected transformation of an entire institution into a universal and useful metaphor (in this case, about personal responsibility in the face of organized evil) and its implications for future exhibition production in other museums and on other subjects.

Shaike's mantra at the time was, "If we tell the particular history truthfully and dispassionately, the public will transform it." At the time, we did not believe in the transformational quality of one set of specific facts into metaphor, and we, myself included, believed we needed to be more explicit and more specific about many of the horrific events that were happening around us. In retrospect, Shaike was right, and I learned a lesson that has been with me since.

Notes

1 The initial text of this talk was presented at the conference "Intolerance and Toleration," Mary Washington College, Fredericksburg, Virginia, 1993, just before the museum's opening. A later version was presented at the opening of a new wing at the Norton Museum of Art, Palm Beach, Florida, in the mid-1990s. The version in this book has been shortened slightly.
2 For a look at some historians interested in memorials see Linenthal (1995) and Young (1993).

Bibliography

Carter, J. (1978) *Executive Order 12093, President's Commission on the Holocaust*: The White House.

Lang, W.L. (2003) *Museum Teams: Two Exhibits and Their Lessons*, Anchorage, AK: Anchorage Museum.

Linenthal, E.T. (1995) *Preserving Memory: The Struggles to Create America's Holocaust Museum*, New York: Viking Press.

Weisel, E. (1979) *United States Holocaust Memorial Commission Report to the President of the United States*, Washington, DC: Holocaust Memorial Commission.

Young, J.E. (1993) *The Texture of Memory: Holocaust Memorials and Meaning*, New Haven, CT: Yale University Press.

Part V

SPIRITUALITY
The end of the age of the rational

Museums were created from a desire to present both emotional evocations and the results of rational inquiry. So a tension of purpose appeared in museums right from the beginning. In recent times, museums have generally thought of themselves as more rational than expressive. Now indigenous and religious peoples worldwide are demanding that museums reestablish a better balance, diminishing the preoccupation with explaining and educating in order to embrace the legitimacy of spiritual responses. Fundamental changes in museum practice have and will continue to result.

20

A JEW AMONG THE INDIANS[1]

How working outside of one's own
culture works, 1991

I have the privilege of attending Indian pow wows[2] now, an activity I would not have imagined in the past.[3] At a recent pow wow, an Indian member of our delegation, as a gift to her hosts, stood up and said:

> My name is _____. I am a member of the _____ tribe, and I will speak to you in my native tongue. In that language my name is _____, and now I will sing you a song of joy at our being together, a song of my people.

I thought: if they call on me, I will be able to say the same thing and in the same order.

> Let me introduce myself. My name is Elaine Heumann Gurian, I am a member of the tribe of Israel, and I will speak to you in my native language – Hebrew. In that language, my name is Mara-Tov bat Hanach vie Hannah, and I will sing you the prayer of joy at our gathering – the Shehecheyanu.

But they did not call on me, for I am not an Indian, I am a Jew.

My position on staff offers me an opportunity to view the formation of an ethnically focused museum from a particular vantage point – that of the inside/outsider. As a person deeply attached to my ethnicity, I feel I can connect to other groups in a sympathetic way.

Yet I'm clear that I am not of these people. I am also not a "wannabe." The Indian passions and their deeply held feelings are not mine. I am empathetic but not involved.

Whenever I am the focal point of an Indian's anger, or witness to behaviors I do not approve of and which are antithetical to my belief systems, I am – for the first time in my life – curiously dispassionate. This isn't my fight, I remind myself. In the most fundamental respect this is not my museum. I am a mercenary, a hired gun. I refer to myself as the museum's auto mechanic. Make no mistake about it, I take pride in my ability to be a good auto mechanic, and I work hard to make this Indian institution the best place possible. But I am clear about what is, and what is not,

189

my role. I suspect that this position – of curious detachment – is even truer of the nonrelated visitors to our ethnic museums and should be remembered when we seek to explain ourselves to them.

I am, however, neither immune nor anesthetized. My feelings get hurt when I am treated as a nonperson sitting invisibly in a room, or when I am thought to be an even pushier broad than usual. Nevertheless, I find that my continued presence, my ongoing "thereness," eventually makes me a real person for my colleagues – no larger, no smaller, no more fallible or infallible, and no more dismissible than anyone else. I work in a real-life environment. I have become part of the team – warts and all. I am now among colleagues and friends. However, I cannot travel without an Indian companion to clear the way, to apologize for or to legitimatize my presence. I must begin again every time I go out among strangers.

I love my job; it is fascinating. But in order to do it successfully, I must remain clear about who I am and who I am not. I am not the arbiter of the cultural material; I am one of the facilitators. It is a professional position that has its own value and many rewards.

The National Museum of the American Indian

The National Museum of the American Indian is poised on the edge of doing business not-as-usual. In fact, our rhetoric says that we will be "the museum different." We have pledged to interview our constituency – the Indians of this hemisphere – and to ask them what kind of museum they wish to have. In answer to the questions we have already asked, we heard that museums are irrelevant institutions to many Indian people, that museums have portrayed Indians inaccurately, and that Indians need to tell the story of their ongoing history to their own children. There is no "the Indians." There are many independent sovereign nations that need to save their material and their intangible culture for their own needs and descendants. In some deeply held way, some Indians believe that a national museum is not only irrelevant; it is, frankly, none of our business. They wish to have their materials returned to use for their own purposes, ceremonies, and education. They wish us to help them document their existing traditions but not for the edification of others – only for themselves and their offspring.

I wonder what would happen if Jewish museums asked their own community what it is they wanted. Would Jewish museum professionals find that the Jewish population wishes the notion of museum itself to be redefined in order to be more relevant?

The Indians have told us that if we must have a museum, they wish it to focus on the multisensory spiritual aspect of the individual Indian cultures. They wish the sounds, smells, and environment inherent in their traditions to be as present as the artifacts they have produced. This focus on other-than-objects makes producing exhibitions a new and relatively uncharted adventure.

The National Museum of the American Indian is prepared to rewrite or expand the definition of museum as currently understood. The staff is not tied to the Heye Foundation's[4] previous history, nor are we tied to the history of museums within the

Western tradition. However, I am not sanguine – even as well intentioned as we are – that we know how to rewrite these definitions, or that we will be successful in creating the new structures that would most help our constituency.

I do not know yet how to respond to the various things we are hearing in our consultations out in Indian country, but I am intrigued and pledge to try to understand deeply enough for the resulting museum to be, in fact, responsive. I am sure that our museum – when completed – will not look as radical as we would wish because we cannot imagine an altogether new institution. But I am also clear that we will create incrementally fresh structures and that the amalgam of these small but inventive departures will, in the long run, create an interesting and maybe prototypical new institution. If we can remain open in our thinking, realistic but radical in our solutions, unmired in the aspirations of traditional museology, and not too limited by the wishes of funders, we may be able to move the whole field forward.

When I was last involved in such an endeavor, it was when the Boston Children's Museum was small, insignificant, and unselfconscious. The National Museum of the American Indian has none of these attributes, and working issues out in the full glare of media and public funding accountability makes the task much harder. But I am confident that we will, at least in part, succeed.

Worries

That having been said, let me tell you what I am worried about – both for my project and for you. I worry that:

- In our zeal to redress past omissions in historic presentations, we will create new distortions or fail to illustrate balance and perspective by telling a one-sided story. We must be careful to include multiple perspectives and a sense of scale. No decision was ever unanimous, nor was its effect as decisive as storytellers would like. However, the people we represent are often hesitant to include such nuances lest they muddy the issue or make the event seem less heroic.
- Romance colors our vision. Every constituency wishes their people to be presented as beautiful, honest, visionary, and uncomplicatedly pure. But life was never like that for anyone. Do we have an obligation to present pride of past deeds with the warts showing, or can we, in complicity with our people, present "history" that is intentionally idealized and humanly unattainable?
- We, the museum facilitators, can become both the victims and the perpetuators of re-creationism – not only of history but also of traditions. We cannot forget that all things change, have always changed, will continue to change, and that we are only participants in a much larger process.
- When we become intentionally or inadvertently the modelers of artifact production and the instructors of technique, will the re-creation of artifacts be used for purposes that the originators might find offensive – not just the glorious continuation of unbroken arts production? Do we need to show only the best objects so that only great material will serve as the primer for others?

- Our sources may not be representative or accurate, but we use their information because we are naive, the speaker is powerful or insistent, the information is currently politically "correct," it fits within our own current notion of what should have taken place, or all other sources are dead or unavailable. Are you an elder if you are merely old? Anthropologists worry about the authenticity of the informant, but the problem becomes even more difficult when you are working from the inside, because each voice must be considered as authentic as any other. How do you choose between voices without being accused of elitism or of representing one clique over another?

- Spike Lee uses the quip, "You wouldn't understand," meaning, outsiders simply by virtue of being outsiders are unable to comprehend. I believe the statement to be both true (in that members of an ethnic group do have basic shared assumptions that are unspokenly understood) and false (in that this remark is sometimes used to keep the outsider unquestioning and defensive when the thinking presented is unclear or unbalanced).

- The museum will not sufficiently provide for nor respond to "outsider" audiences, who need ways of understanding information that is implicitly understood by the insider.

- The definition of who is and who is not "one of us" is too restrictive and unnecessarily rigid in its application. Having grown up and being afraid of the Nazis' belief in Aryan purity, how can I now listen to Indian conversations about blood quanta?

- In recognizing that each ethnic and cultural group has an internalized and coherent aesthetic – one that is different from the Eurocentric tradition that has controlled museum choices in the past – will we be able to set up and apply a culturally consistent aesthetic when selecting objects for display? Or will we become indiscriminate in order to be widely representative?

- Exhibition formats as we understand them – even newly invented multisensory ones – cannot adequately convey other peoples' interactions, motivations, and emotions. Does this render the museum's principal goal unachievable?

- Norms of behavior that are objectionable in one society are tolerated or even encouraged in another. One group's notion of violence, abuse, or chauvinism is another group's sense of business-as-usual. It takes a long time even to explain ourselves to each other, a much longer time to be sympathetic to each other, an even longer time to like each other. To know each other is not to forgive each other – immediately.

- In our rush to redefine who should and should not have access to collections and who should control and own them, we will have violated a trust placed on us implicitly by future members of the very same groups.

- When redefining museums and cultural centers in currently new and useful ways, we will have invented institutions that will be useful only in transitory ways while the world moves along with some other need.

- The pride and self-esteem born of knowing one's past can simultaneously breed intolerance for others and justification for future violence against them.

- Differences – racial, national, or cultural – have been used in the past to justify war and aggression. Are we emphasizing the commonalities among all of us enough?

Summary

Worries aside, I feel as though I am participating in a great adventure, out of which the next generation of relevant social institutions may be born. And part of my effort and attention is devoted to trying to prevent it from becoming a justification for cultural isolation and the creation of renewed grounds for hate.

My hope is, and has always been, that to be responsible we must support all kinds of institutions simultaneously. We need focused institutions that explore the many facets and interrelationships of a specific culture or subject, as well as institutions that concentrate on integrative overviews. We each personally need to know our particularized stories and yet live and work together in a heterogeneous world with respect and acceptance of the other. Our well-being depends on the pride and exploration of our own patrimony and on a belief in tolerance for others and the importance of the common good.

Rational men and women will have to prevail, people who believe in balance, in complexity, and in the belief that each of us is entitled to take up equal space, time, and attention. Without a concurrent commitment to the integrated and harmonious, as well as to the separate and glorious, all can be lost.

Notes

1 This paper was given in New York City at the Jewish Museum Association Meeting on January 27, 1991. Parts of it appeared in Gurian (1999a).
2 A pow wow (sometimes powwow or pow-wow) is a gathering of Native Americans. Typically, a pow wow consists of people (Native American and non-Native American alike) meeting in one particular area to dance, sing, socialize, and generally have a good time (Wikipedia).
3 I attended pow wows as a member of the National Museum of the American Indian consultation team between 1990 and 1991 when I was deputy director for public program planning.
4 Through a series of negotiations, the Museum of the American Indian, Heye Foundation, in New York City became part of the Smithsonian Institution through an Act of Congress in 1989. Its successor organization became the National Museum of the American Indian.

Bibliography

Gurian, E.H. (1999a) "Thinking About My Museum Journey," in Pitman, B. (ed.) *Presence of Mind: Museums and the Spirit of Learning*, Washington, DC: American Association of Museums.

Wikipedia *Pow Wow*, Wikipedia Foundation, Inc. Available http://en.wikipedia.org/wiki/Powwow (accessed February 10, 2005).

21

REPATRIATION IN CONTEXT

The important changes brought to museums by
indigenous communities, 1991[1]

Collecting things, I believe, is an impulse locked within the human genetic code. This tendency is the prelude to the creation of museums. Hoarding is just a potentially maladaptive extension of the human need to accumulate things in order to survive.[2] Because human beings do not come equipped with protective outer coverings, we must make our homes, clothes, implements, medicines, and tools. We make them from pieces of our environment that we find, store, and combine. We are (and always have been) on the lookout for "bits and bobs" that might help us live more comfortably, or at all.

People of real – or hoped-for – influence have attempted to impress their contemporaries by collecting and then displaying objects that might be considered rare and therefore valuable. In addition, they have attempted to amass many more things than their compatriots do. With these objects, these individuals have had a tangible way of demonstrating their superiority and elevated status. People within every culture have created storehouses and/or display units of some kind. Museums, as we know them, while relatively recent Western creations, fit within the continuum of these treasure storehouses.

The display of individual power has always been – and continues to be – one motivation for the establishment of museums. Princes, presidents, and popes have founded and continue to establish museums. Today, as in the past, people with a surfeit of assets – but an insufficient hold on societal approbation – collect things and establish or endow museums.

George Gustav Heye's urge to collect fits within that long and continuing tradition. George Heye wanted things, and lots of them. He wanted more and "better" things than his peers. His decision to collect Indian things might have been more a convenient and incidental motif rather than an intentional interest. His collection is the basis today for the National Museum of the American Indian.

In addition to the conjecture that people are innately acquisitive and that museums are an outgrowth of that need, I believe that human beings have an innate need to decorate. Why else would people – in every age, in every culture, no matter how spare or uncomfortable the surroundings – embellish the things they have made? Why would they do so when decorating an object takes longer and does not necessarily improve its function? Ordinary folk have, I believe, invented decoration for their own pleasure. These objects please them and sometimes please others. In all societies, being acknowledged best at decoration leads to social distinction for the producer.

Obtaining embellished objects has often been the focus of the collector, even when, and sometimes because, the culture and the context are a mystery. Collectors have sometimes been uninterested, or only minimally interested, in the meaning of the object within its own society, while explicitly pleased that the object is both odd and rare in their own right. Over time, they have valued foreign objects not by applying the artistic norms used by the object's producer, but on the basis of the aesthetic choices prevalent in the culture where the object "finds itself."

People of power have also wanted to solidify their positions by being surrounded in life or death by such excesses as castles and pyramids. They have decorated their persons by wearing ornate jewelry and intricate clothes. Their status is measured by the volume of rare things in their possession that require intricate and unusual skill to produce. This might be considered hoarding in another context.

Following conquests and colonial occupation, the victors bought, brought, and stole objects from the conquered culture, en masse, and moved them to their own land. There has always been a tradition of the triumphal relocation of "the spoils of war."

If one accepts the thesis that these two inherent desires – acquisitiveness and embellishment – were expanded and distorted in the exercise and concentration of power, it is easy to understand how museums that contain vast storehouses of ornamented materials – without regard to the creators of the objects, their uses, or their meaning – came to be.

It is then also easy to appreciate how descendants of the makers of the objects – understanding their original uses and meanings and wanting to reestablish a sense of historical continuity or to reconnect with their culture's spiritual life – might want the objects either back in their own care or presented quite differently in their current location.

The American Indian tribal claims for the return of some of their objects mirror the same claims that other formerly conquered peoples have made elsewhere. Objects taken by the more powerful from the less powerful provoke a yearning for their return, claims for which have been made at different times and by many peoples.[3] Put in that context, American Indian claims are not new; they are part of the organized assertion for the return of materials throughout the world.[4]

Such claims by native peoples – in their persistence and their reliance on the law[5] – have been powerful catalysts for the worldwide reappraisal of museums as social institutions.[6] For this, all of us, even in our most fearful and anxious of states, should be grateful.

Because in response, I believe museums will change in ways that in the future will seem logical and preordained. I predict we will scarcely be able to remember or reconstruct what the fuss was all about. Museums will evolve from the safe deposit boxes they are now to the lending libraries of the future.

Each of these organized services – safe deposit boxes and lending libraries – has its usefulness. They are fundamentally different by design and one might say even oppositional in intent. It is unusual for one kind of institution to voluntarily transform itself into its opposite. Thus this prediction that museums will voluntarily reformulate some of their fundamental structure goes against pattern. Yet, a growing list of examples suggests that requests for object use are made, seriously considered, negotiated, and sometimes acceded to.

Looking ahead, it is impossible to forecast the full consequences of all the repatriation legislation and resulting policies and procedures. It is unlikely that museums will be forced to "give everything back" to those that suggest they will "back moving trucks to the cargo bay door." It is this extreme prediction that causes so much fear, inaction, and hardening of positions on both sides. Yet, to be fair, none of the players really can predict the ultimate range of outcomes. We will all have to repeatedly take small steps and look around and see where we are in order to decide what to do next. We will have to have patience. We will need to declare that measured change is evidence of good will rather than of intractability. We must become inventive and excited about the creation of new avenues of interconnectedness. Now is no longer business-as-usual.

While the situation is often cast as either "I own it" or "you own it," I do not believe these are – or will be – the only models for repatriation. There are already different models of ownership, and more may be contemplated: "we both own it," "I own it and lend it to you for as long as you want it," "I own it and lend it to you whenever you need it," "you own it and lend it to me to keep safe for you," "someone else owns it and we both have reproductions of it," "we all have all the information and images of it and we can access them whenever we want to," "I give it back and you return it to the elements," "I give it back and you keep it, but no one but the initiated can ever come in contact with it," etc. This long list – and other permutations – will likely become the future norm when talking about objects in museums.

This means, of course, that life will be more complicated for the professionals who care for museum collections. Every permutation of ownership will suggest a slightly different contract of care. "I own it and I take care of it," "I own it and you take care of it," "You own it and I take care of it," "You withdraw it, you use it, and then I care for the returned – and thereby changed – object," "I take care of it according to your instructions," "You take care of it according to my instructions," etc.

The complications will come from the variety of care museums will agree to, not in the difficulty each object's care will present. Museums will no longer be able to put out manuals of generalized optimum care, nor will the material composition of the objects be the sole determinant of care. Schools will not train all collections managers to respond the same to every item. Professionals will become more interested in and more respectful of "traditional" care, and "traditional" conservation. These will take their place alongside modern technical care. Everyone will become more invested in "appropriate technology" – the natural and time-honored ways of repairing and storing each object – not as a curiosity but as a legitimate method of doing business. Our collections care staff will have increased interest in culturally appropriate storage design just as they now have for the culturally specific object (Flynn 2001).

This is a new and exciting era. In 1991, in a conversation I had with Steven Weil, former deputy director of the Hirshhorn Museum and Sculpture Garden and one of the best thinkers in our profession, he pointed out that there are time-honored, and therefore acceptable, models within the European museum tradition for each and every one of the new permutations of collections sharing.

It is, therefore, useful to examine and to acknowledge these models' existence so that the onus of inventiveness does not fall exclusively on the native community. For example, the English crown jewels sit on public display in the Tower of London. Every one can see them except when the Queen wants or needs to wear them. Aren't we, therefore, accustomed to lending ceremonial material for use at appropriate times? Similarly, most collections of old musical instruments have organized occasions when the instruments are played. It is done not only because seeing an instrument without hearing it makes little sense, but also because the instrument itself loses its vibrancy if it is not played. Its "soul" resides in its use, not its inanimation. What, then, is new about allowing, or even requiring, that some objects are used, rather than only stored and/or looked at?

In the case of native objects, determining which objects may be used may not be up to the museums alone. In fact they are not as startled by such a request as they once were. In many cases, museums have procedures in place to send the piece out and welcome it back. The leadership in other museums can find museological precedent for acceding to such requests and might not reflexively refuse or feel acute discomfort in response.

There are models that can be adapted for long-term loan, for shared ownership, for joint documentation, for objects that return to their owners for a short term, and for displayed objects that retain their individual ownership,[7] all within standard museum practice. Further, there are examples of appropriate cultural care and restoration and of the approximation of appropriate climates and surroundings, in specialized collections of nonnative objects.

There isn't anything new being asked for here, and therefore we could – if we put our minds to it – search for and adopt appropriate models now. Doing so will exact a change in the power structure of museums as institutions. It is no longer we – museum specialists – who will exclusively control the use and care of certain objects. Increasingly it will be the descendants of the producers. This sharing or transference of ownership is, I suspect, what makes us profoundly uncomfortable. We believe those who have chosen museum employment as their life's work have been charged in perpetuity with the preservation of humankind's material culture. Therefore, it feels as though we are abrogating our responsibility when we change. Instead, we can share it with new and worthy compatriots.

Without being rich ourselves, we came to think we owned the stuff. Now – with feelings of some loss and regret – we will have to learn to share. Each of us managed that – painfully – in childhood. All of us can learn it – one hopes less painfully – again.

Notes

1 This paper was was originally written as a speech in 1991.
2 According to Frost and Gross,

> Saving allows the hoarder to avoid the decision required to throw something away, and the worry which accompanies that decision (worry that a mistake has been made). Also, it allows hoarders to avoid emotional reactions which accompany parting with cherished possessions, and results in increased perception of control.
>
> (1993)

3 The request by the Greek government for the return of the Elgin Marbles from the British Museum is a long-standing debate. This and other requests by one government for the return of material from major museums has led some museums to take the position that they are "universal museums." For their declaration and some discussion, see ICOM (2004). This white paper, as one would imagine, is controversial.
4 The demand by descendants of Holocaust victims for the return of objects stolen by the Nazis joins this issue. Because of these demands, museums have provided information about their collections in a much more transparent way in order to expedite information about what might have been stolen. See, for example, AAMD (2001).
5 In the United States,

> NAGPRA provides a systematic process for determining the rights of lineal descendants, Indian tribes, and Native Hawaiian organizations to certain Native American human remains, funerary objects, sacred objects, and objects of cultural patrimony with which they are affiliated, and for the disposition of discoveries on Federal and tribal land.
>
> (NAGPRA 1990)

6 Many interesting Web sites describe the collections policy of specific museums as regards their material belonging to the first peoples of their land. To sample a few go to any search engine and type in "museum collections policy" or "human remains policy" for Australia, Canada, and New Zealand. See also the NAGPRA site, http://www.cr.nps.gov/nagpra/SITEMAP/INDEX.htm
7 The West Vancouver Museum and Archive is an interesting example of a nonnative museum concerned with local history, becoming a lending library with the owners as lenders. "The museum's Community Collections program allows people to register their willingness to lend historically significant objects to the museum, while continuing to enjoy them in their own setting" (WVMA 2003).

Bibliography

AAMD (2001) *Art Museums and the Identification and Restitution of Works Stolen by the Nazis*, Association of Art Museum Directors. Available http://www.aamd.org/pdfs/Nazi%20Looted%20Art.pdf (accessed January 16, 2005).

Flynn, G.A. (2001) *Merging Traditional Indigenous Curation Methods with Modern Museum Standards of Care*, Washington DC: The George Washington University Museum Studies Program. Available http://www2.gwu.edu/~mstd/flynn_paper.pdf (accessed January 16, 2005).

Frost, R.O. and Gross, R.C. (1993) "The Hoarding of Possessions," in *Behaviour Research and Therapy*, 31:4, 367–381.

ICOM (2004) *ICOM News* 2004–1, Paris, France: International Council of Museums. Available http://icom.museum/pdf/E_news2004/p4_2004-1.pdf (accessed January 20, 2005).

NAGPRA (1990) *Native American Graves Protection and Repatriation Act*, 101 Congress, US. Available http://www.cr.nps.gov/nagpra/SITEMAP/INDEX.htm (accessed January 15, 2005).

WVMA (2003) *WVMA Collections*, West Vancouver, Canada: West Vancouver Museum and Archives.

22

SINGING AND DANCING AT NIGHT[1]

A biographic meaning to working in the spiritual arena, 2004

During many of my 35 museum years, I have had the privilege of working with indigenous and minority groups who wished to have their story told in a museum setting.[2] Working with colleagues in this way has changed my personal and professional life. Personally, I have come to reunite my spiritual world with my rational self. Professionally, I have come to appreciate that museums can become places where a synthesis between factual and emotive material might be made evident. Furthermore, because of this work, I now firmly believe that public spaces, especially museums, can be sites of reconciliation between strangers who are wary of, but curious about, each other.

Let me begin with a short autobiography. I was born in the United States in the 1930s, the child of an immigrant German-Jewish couple. My early childhood was completely colored by the Second World War and the war's aftermath – ending in the 1950s with the final settlement of refugees – that allowed the last of my surviving extended family to arrive in the United States.

Immigrant Jewish adults who found themselves in the United States – intentionally or by accidental good fortune – developed an overlay of concerns. They worried about their trapped families in Holocaust Europe; they felt both guilty and relieved at being in the United States; and they were constantly fearful that every Christian they met, at any activity, could become an irrational enemy in the blink of an eye. Like many, my family did not permit any of us to speak German in public, lest strangers become alarmed. For my mother, especially, entering public spaces populated by strangers was a trial. She did not voluntarily go to libraries, museums, or concert halls and even a trip to the supermarket had a certain aura of danger.

My parents and their friends thought that their seemingly legitimate concerns were shielded from their children, who spoke English without an accent; went to public, non-parochial schools; and who, they thought, could pass as "regular" Americans. My parents often wished for the prevailing cultural aspiration of the time: assimilation and majority conformity. The norms of beauty, dress, and behavior that my parents wanted for me were accepted by the white Christian world that they simultaneously feared.

Contrary to the hopes of our parents, our childhood was totally and irrationally consumed by the fear that the surrounding adults exuded. It seemed impossible to resolve the instructions of our parents, to "pass" as Americans, while staying alert to the possibility of immediate danger at every turn.

Like all religions, Judaism has a spiritual dimension that is based on faith, and a set of customs that does not bear the test of rational scrutiny. Like many Jews in the United States during the 1940s and 1950s, my family tried to resolve the fear of "the other" by rejecting the ancient Jewish ways in order to appear modern. They divorced the spiritual part of Judaism, which they rejected, from the cultural and familial part, which they embraced. They identified themselves as culturally Jewish while remaining nonreligious.

Like all people who occupy peripheral status in majority cultures, I learned to live in two worlds – gingerly in the American one and more comfortably in the Jewish one.

This autobiography, while particular in detail, is comparable to the American childhood of others born within a minority culture and with immigrant parents. It is analogous to the experience of African American children whose immigration story happened forcibly generations ago. And many would argue that the tale is the same for Native American children, born in their own country from a lineage of ancient people, but isolated and marginalized on reservations.

Social scientists, finding themselves in contemporary polyglot America, keep trying to describe a situation that will allow people with specific cultural heritages to remain true to their values and worldviews, while uniting in harmony in a larger society. They wish for all of us to extol our particular strengths, while sharing peaceful coexistence. Over the years, we have grown accustomed to new, sometimes overlapping, and even competing theories – assimilation, pluralism, Americanization, integration, inclusion, "melting pot," "salad bowl," "ethnic stew," multiculturalism, and "cultural mosaic" – which, through proposals to amend social policy, are offered to promote national well-being. Yet the truth remains that this country is always slightly agitated with itself, and a wholesale peaceable reconciliation within our heterogeneous cultural mélange continues to be an unresolved national aspiration.

Over the last half-century, museums have paid attention to these varying sociological theories, and continuously, through a series of self-conscious adjustments, have tried to reflect the current thinking most in vogue. In the main, during this period, the premise underlying museum display started from the supposition that the majority culture was superior. What followed was a tentative and then more widespread recognition that the descendants of the makers of the objects have a right to share authority in museum display, collections care, and museum management.

Historically, the makers of objects in museums have been asserting their rights to the disposal and interpretation of their own material for a long time. But only in the last 50 years have the stars aligned worldwide, allowing the voices of minority peoples to become loud enough, and their power to coalesce enough, to cause actual change in museum policies. Museums are learning, in small and sometimes large ways, to share control over their objects.

Sharing authority almost always turns out to be more difficult than anticipated because the parties in question do not have entirely congruent value systems. Sharing authority means understanding, and then accommodating to, an often fascinating, sometimes exasperating, competing worldview. Indeed, upon encountering museums that hold their objects, native peoples often demand that their materials are presented in accordance with belief systems that are an anathema to the institutions' existing policies.

Most native people acknowledge that they are animists who believe that things/objects have emanations and power beyond that which can be seen with the eye. They make no apology for combining their passionate, spiritual worldview part of their thinking with their more factually based, daily selves.

Not unlike my own family, most museums are dedicated to maintaining a clear separation between the knowable and factual and the spiritual part of life. Museums have traditionally presented material, even religious material, as inanimate and interesting, but without power. Scientific thinking and seemingly fact-based impartiality are held in such high status in museums that veneration of objects of any religion is generally not accommodated within museum displays. Veneration is safely relegated to the place where such behavior is expected – the church, the synagogue, the mosque. To overtly embrace the passion inherent in or the ritual prescribed by the objects within a museum setting is to acknowledge the nonrational aspect of thinking.

But things are changing for museums, and for me. When the United States Holocaust Memorial Museum (USHMM) opened in Washington, DC, in 1993, the memorial space was designed to allow people to light candles, and the Dalai Lama, who was the first public visitor to enter the museum, immediately created a ritual there. Yet, as people began to say the Jewish prayer for the dead in a federally funded museum, I, the museum's then deputy director, became alarmed about the constitutional separation of church and state, and sought to have a sign made saying something ludicrous, like "No Praying." Fortunately my director had no such qualms and sent me to my office to reconsider this request. A similar conflict arose for me when the board determined that the museum would be closed on Yom Kippur. I pointed out that, as a federal museum, we could not determine the closing dates based on the religious practice of a victim group. Again, the director prevailed and, again, I understood that the integration of spiritual practices into a museum setting was beginning to happen. There is now a historic church placed within the European history section of the Canadian Museum of Civilization, which is comfortably used for services, just as the Maori Marae[3] is used inside Te Papa, the National Museum of New Zealand. So things have begun to change.

The tone of most curated labels during much of the past century intentionally distances the writer from the maker by use of third-person references: "They believe...." This disassociation presumably allows the writer to be perceived as rational and objective, while the maker of the objects is cast as a believer and, perforce, inferior and misguided. The explanatory information associated with the objects in question is presented as myth.

This belief, in the higher order of nonemotive, factually based thinking, does not stop curators (the writers of such labels) from participating in their own personal religious observances. Nor does it stop their churches from insisting on belief in their articles of faith. However, the curator separates the Friday, Saturday, or Sunday worship from the job at hand the rest of the week. The separation is not necessarily easy or free from ambiguity. Traditional civic practice includes many customs and rituals that originate in religion. The tradition in the United States of opening each congressional session with a prayer (a practice which is deemed not to violate the separation of church and state) is a notable example.

I am not naive enough to think that all native peoples have fully realized and satisfying lives. Nor do I believe that individual or societal attempts to integrate spiritual nonrational thinking and evidentiary scientific thinking make all edges of contention disappear. On the contrary, new edges appear, and these new edges make it very interesting for those of us in museums to operate and negotiate.

These edges raise intriguing questions for which museum administrators, I among them, are not prepared to answer. Questions like: "What is the appropriate storage system for an object that needs to sing and dance at night?" Or, "If the spirit of an old destroyed object is passed along to a newer one, how old is the new object?" Or, "If the story my elders have told me about this object is discordant with scientific information, which information shall we use in the records?"[4] Fascinating and unresolved questions such as these are on the negotiating table whenever museums work to reach mutual accommodation with representatives of the cultures that made the objects.

As with all complex questions, contradictory views often have equivalent justification, no matter what the opposing proponents might assert. Therefore, the only way to resolve conflict and reach a common ground is to keep working together, over and over, with people of conscience and tenacity, on an individual-to-individual basis, with good will and an open mind. Complex negotiated settlements are difficult to reach and contrary to a Western presumption of "winner take all." Yet over the last half-century, negotiations on matters of native material have successfully occurred in many museums and in many countries. The outcome has often been accompanied by the emergence of increased respect on all sides.

Take the issue of human remains. It is true that when skeletal remains are reburied, bones will decay and forensic scientists will permanently lose access to more scientific information. But the issue of reburial is really one of balancing sets of priorities, and those priorities involve more than science. The proponents of reburial almost always cite a belief in the spirit and the afterlife – notoriously nonscientific issues. And indeed, for almost everyone, the deciding argument (regardless of whose bones are in question) becomes, in the end, a spiritual one: we want our loved ones to repose in peace.

If we, museum workers, truly believe that bones are inanimate, as we often assert, what difference would it make? Not surprisingly, at the beginning of the NAGPRA[5] negotiations, most museum staff took a position in favor of science. The issue was seen as one of science against religion (and so it remains in the legal arguments about the disposition of Kennewick Man) (Lepper 2001).

Yet, in Western societies, it is often in matters of death and funerary practice that our underlying belief in the power of inanimate materials (e.g. bones, the sites where deaths occurred, the memorials in remembrance of dead people) becomes evident. Why else do people make small, spontaneous shrines by the side of a road to mark a fatal automobile accident? Why else do people leave talismans recalling lost soldiers at the Vietnam Veterans Memorial, where nobody is buried? I find it interesting that some museums are now considering burying their "white" skeletons in order to give them a "Christian burial" (Epps 2004).

For museums, the ongoing dialogue about ownership, shared authority, secret wisdom, and so-called myth involves, of course, much more than bones and funerary objects, and continues as the descendants of the makers of the materials and the museums who care for those materials keep on negotiating. Museums have become slightly more comfortable about keeping native materials in accordance with descendants' wishes and are beginning to present both scientific and spiritual information on an equal footing for the visitor to contemplate in exhibitions.

When I first began negotiating with individual native people over such matters, I was at first disbelieving, next skeptical and intrigued, and finally comfortable with the different frames of reference I encountered. In the process I learned a great deal, and I found in that dialogue an approach to research and exhibition that museums also have begun to pursue as a way of enriching their work.

Museums, no matter their subject matter, have begun to look at issues originally brought to the table by native people as being relevant to all the materials they hold. Thanks to prompting from indigenous peoples, museum staff are reconsidering such emotive questions as: "Why do people stand hushed and overwhelmed when faced by pictures of sublime beauty?" "Why did people flock to museums right after September 11?" "Do performance, music, and speech, which evoke emotional responses, need to be separated from the spaces where objects are presented?" "Can we allow religious or spiritual services inside our museums?" "What is the real reason visitors care about seeing (and often long to touch) the real thing?"

All humans, no matter their background, have a range of emotions, beliefs, and spirituality in their lives. In the past, most Westerners, while valuing spirituality, compartmentalized it, relegating its practice to settings clearly removed from daily life. In addition to places of worship, emotional responses of many sorts were permitted in certain other civic spaces – crying at the movies, cheering at athletic events, applauding at concerts. Native people have demonstrated that museums can be added to the list of places where emotional and spiritual responses are both appropriate and welcome.

Museums do not yet know quite how to realize all aspects of spiritual inclusion in their policies, practices, and public spaces. This is not particular to the native material in their collections. Quite the contrary, many museums informed by faith struggle with the same issues. Because the rules of observance demand that desecrated Torahs are to be buried, the presentation of a Torah desecrated during Kristallnacht in the USHMM required consultation with both religious leaders and scholars to ensure that the display would not violate religious practice. I predict that soon every artifact once created for any religious ceremonial use and now displayed in a museum will require new presentation skills that respect the underlying spiritual information as well as the more dispassionate content. We have indigenous peoples to thank for introducing us to this profound new dimension of possibilities.

I left the National Museum of the American Indian to work at the USHMM.[6] I went, albeit reluctantly, because my American Indian colleagues taught me that[7] "When the elders ask you to come home to help, it is your obligation to go." Had it not been for that teaching and the encouragement of my Native American teachers, I would not have been able to face up to my own past and work in a museum that helped bring my own family's story to public view. I want to thank my native colleagues for showing me a way to reconcile my own nonrational heritage with my life in public. This gift from elders, not my own, would surprise my ancestors. I hope it makes their spirits more tranquil.

Notes

1 This chapter was originally published in *Stewards of the Sacred* in 2004 (Gurian 2004).

2 I have been a consultant to the following museums and have worked with the indigenous, minority, or culturally specific group that were part of the constituency of each of these museums: National Museum of Australia; Te Papa, National Museum of New Zealand; Canadian Museum of Civilization First Peoples Hall; reinstallation of the Native American collection of the Denver Art Museum; National Museum of the American Indian, Smithsonian Institution; Agua Caliente Museum; Mashantucket Pequot Museum; National African American Museum Project, Smithsonian Institution; African American Museum of Art and Culture; National Underground Railroad Freedom Center; United States Holocaust Memorial Museum; Jewish Museum Berlin; Japanese American National Museum; and Cirma (the National Archives of Guatemala).

3 The purpose of Maori Marae is described here:

> The Marae offers a unique experience within Te Papa and is also unique within New Zealand. It is Te Papa's response to the challenge of creating an authentic yet inclusive marae (communal meeting place) for the twenty-first century.... It is also a living exhibition that interprets for visitors the meaning of the marae experience, and acts as a showcase for contemporary Māori art and design.... Like other marae, this Marae is about identity – here, it is our nation's bicultural identity that is addressed. The Marae embodies the spirit of bicultural partnership that lies at the heart of the Museum and is based on the idea that Te Papa is a forum for the nation. All people have a right to stand on this Marae through a shared whakapapa (genealogy) and the mana (power) of the taonga (treasures) held in Te Papa Tongarewa's collections. All cultures can feel at home on this marae.
>
> (Te Papa 1998)

4 These sentences are paraphrases of actual questions put to me during the 12 consultations I attended for the planning of the National Museum of the American Indian in 1990.

5 NAGPRA (1990) is the US federal law that governs the disposition of Native American human remains, secret and sacred material, and grave goods held in museum repositories.

6 From 1990 to 1991, I served as deputy director for public program planning of the National Museum of the American Indian. From 1991 to 1994, I was deputy director of the USHMM.

7 These Native American guides and colleagues include George Horse Capture, Suzan Shown Harjo, Rick Hill, Rina Swentzell, Lisa Watt, Dave Warren, and W. Richard West Jr.

Bibliography

Epps, P. (2004) "Museum Mull Re-Burial of Historic Bones". *Reuters*, January 6, 2004. Available http://today.reuters.com/news/

Gurian, E.H. (2004) "Singing and Dancing at Night," in Sullivan, L.E. and Edwards, A. (eds) *Stewards of the Sacred*, Washington, DC: American Association of Museum in cooperation with Center for the Study of World Religions, Harvard University.

Lepper, B.T.L. (2001) "Kennewick Man's Legal Odyssey Nears an End," in *Mammoth Trumpet*, 16:4, 1–2, 15–16.

NAGPRA (1990) *Native American Graves Protection and Repatriation Act*, 101 Congress, US. Available http://www.cr.nps.gov/nagpra/SITEMAP/INDEX.htm (accessed January 15, 2005).

Te Papa (1998) *Maori Marae*, National Museum of New Zealand Te Papa Tangarawa. Available http://www.tepapa.govt.nz/TePapa/English/WhatsOn/LongTermExhibitions/TheMarae.htm (accessed January 25, 2005).

BIBLIOGRAPHY

AAM (1991) *Excellence and Equity: Education and the Public Dimension of Museums: A Report*, Washington, DC: American Association of Museums, Task Force on Museum Education.

AAM (1992) *Excellence and Equity: Education and the Public Dimension of Museums*, Washington, DC: American Association of Museums.

AAMD (2001) *Art Museums and the Identification and Restitution of Works Stolen by the Nazis*, Association of Art Museum Directors. Available http://www.aamd.org/pdfs/Nazi%20Looted%20Art.pdf (accessed January 16, 2005).

Alexander, C. (1964) *Notes on the Synthesis of Form*, Cambridge, MA: Harvard University Press.

Alexander, C. (1987) *A New Theory of Urban Design*, New York: Oxford University Press.

Alexander, E.P. (1959) *The Museum: A Living Book of History*, Detroit, MI: Wayne State University Press.

Ambrose, T. and Paine, C. (1993) *Museum Basics*, London; New York: ICOM in conjunction with Routledge.

Anderson, C. (1990) "Australian Aborigines and Museums, a New Relationship," in *Curator*, 33: 165ff.

Anderson, D. (1997) *A Common Wealth: Museums and Learning in the United Kingdom*, London: Department of National Heritage.

Anderson, D. (2000) "Museum Education in Europe," in Hirsch, J.S. and Silverman, L.H. (eds) *Transforming Practice: Selections from the Journal of Museum Education, 1992–1999*, Washington, DC: Museum Education Roundtable.

Anderson, G. (2004) *Reinventing the Museum: Historical and Contemporary Perspectives on the Paradigm Shift*, Walnut Creek, CA; Oxford: AltaMira Press.

Andrews, R., Biggs, M., and Seidel, M. (eds) (1996) *The Columbia World of Quotations*, New York: Columbia University Press.

The Association of Children's Museums (2001) *Strategic Framework*. Available http://www.childrensmuseums.org/strategic_framework_2001.htm (accessed Janauary 27, 2005).

Association of Children's Museums (2004) *Mission*, Washington, DC: Association of Children's Museums.

Baeker, G.G. (1981) *The Emergence of Children's Museums in the United States 1899–1940*, Toronto: University of Toronto.

Bailey, S.J. and Falconer, P. (1998) "Charging for Admission to Museums and Galleries: A Framework for Analysis of the Impact on Access," in *Journal of Cultural Economics*, 22:2–3, 167–177.

Beardsley, J. and Livingston, J. (1991) "The Poetics and Politics of Hispanic Art: A New Perspective," in Karp, I. and Levine, S.D. (eds) *Exhibiting Cultures: The Poetics and Politics of Museum Display*, Washington, DC: Smithsonian Institution Press.

Bitgood, S. (2002) "Environmental Psychology in Museums, Zoos, and Other Exhibition Centers," in Bechtel, R. and Churchman, A. (eds) *Handbook of Environmental Psychology*, New York: John Wiley & Sons.

Blais, J.-M. (2000) "Museum-Related Education in Quebec: An Historical Survey," in *Musées*, Montreal: Société des musées québécois. Volume 22, issue December.

Borun, M., Cleghorn A., and C. Garfield (1995) "Family Learning in Museums: A Bibliographic Review," in *Curator*, 39:2, 123–138.

Borun, M., Korn, R., Adams, R. and American Association of Museums Committee on Audience Research and Evaluation (1999) *Introduction to Museum Evaluation*, Washington, DC: American Association of Museums Technical Information Service.

Bourdieu, P. (1989) *Distinction: A Social Critique of the Judgement of Taste*, Cambridge, MA: Harvard University Press.

Burghart, T. (2002) *Children's Museum Invites Youngsters to Step Inside Contemporary Art*, Naples, Florida.

Carter, J. (1978) *Executive Order 12093, President's Commision on the Holocaust*, The White House.

Casey, D. (2001) "Museums as Agents for Social and Political Change," in *Curator*, 44:3, 230–236.

Caulton, T. (1998) *Hands-on Exhibitions, Managing Interactive Museums Science Centers*, London: Routledge.

Chew, R. (2002) "In Praise of the Small Museum," in *Museum News*, March/April, 36–41.

Choi, B.K. and Beettati, R. (2001) *Endpoint Admission Control: Network Based Approach*, Mesa, AZ: IEEE Computer Society.

Cooke, A. (1979) "Eternal Vigilance by Whom?" in Cooke, A. (ed.) *The Americans*, New York: Berkeley Books.

Csikszentmihályi, M. (1990) *Flow: The Psychology of Optimal Experience*, New York: Harper & Row.

Csikszentmihályi, M. and Hermanson, K. (1997) "Intrinsic Motivation in Museums: Why Does One Want to Learn?" in Falk, J.H. and Dierking, L.D. (eds) *Public Institutions for Personal Learning: Establishing a Research Agenda*, Washington, DC: American Association of Museums, pp. 67–77.

Csikszentmihályi, M. and Rochberg-Halton, E. (1981) *The Meaning of Things*, London: Cambridge University Press.

Cunningham, M.K. (2004) *The Interpreters Training Manual for Museums*, Washington, DC: American Association of Museums.

Cuno, J. (ed.) (2004) *Whose Muse? Art Museums and the Public Trust*, Princeton, NJ, Cambridge, MA: Princeton University Press and Harvard University Art Museums.

Davis, J., Gurian, E.H., and Koster, E. (2003) "Timeliness: A Discussion for Museums," in *Curator*, 46:4, 353–361.

Davis, P. (1999) *Ecomuseums: A Sense of Place*, London; New York: Leicester University Press.

The Dead Mall Competition Web Page. Available http://www.laforum.org/deadmalls/index.html (accessed December 14, 2004).

Dean, D. (1994) *Museum Exhibition: Theory and Practice*, London; New York: Routledge.

Dean, T.L. (2001) "Children's Museums Exhibit Attendance Leap over Decade," *Chicago Tribune*, Saturday, May 5, 2001.

Deasy, C.M. (ed.) (1985) *Designing Places for People, a Handbook for Architects, Designers, and Facility Managers*, New York: Whitney Library of Design.

Dewey, J. (1975, first published in 1938) *The Need of a Theory of Experience. Experience and Education,* 18th edn, Kappa Delta Pi Lecture series, New York: Collier Books.

Dewey, J. (1977) in Peters, R.S. (ed.) *John Dewey Reconsidered*, London: Routledge and Kegan Paul.

Dexter, G. and Lord, B. (1999) *The Manual of Museum Planning*, London: The Stationery Office.

Diamond, J. (1999) *Practical Evaluation Guide: Tools for Museums and Other Informal Educational Settings*, Walnut Creek, CA: AltaMira Press.

DiMaggio, P. (1996) "Are Art-Museum Visitors Different from Other People? The Relationship between Attendance and Social and Political Attitudes in the United States," in *Poetics: Journal of Empirical Research on Literature, The Media, and the Arts (special issue on Museum Research)*, 24:2–4, 161–180.

DiMaggio, P. and Pettit, B. (1998) "Surveys of Public Attitudes toward the Arts," in *Grantmakers in the Arts Newsletter*, 9:2, 26–30.

Drucker, P.F. (1998) "Introduction: Civilizing the City," in Hesselbein, F. (ed.) *The Community of the Future*, San Francisco, CA: Jossey-Bass.

During, S. (1993) "Introduction," in During, S. (ed.) *The Cultural Studies Reader*, London: Routledge.

Epps, P. (2004) Museum Mull Re-Burial of Historic Bones. *Reuters*, January 6, 2004. Available http://today.reuters.com/news/

Exploratorium, biography of Frank Oppenheimer. Available http://www.exploratorium.edu/frank/bio/bio.html (accessed February 22, 2005).

Falk, J.H. and Dierking, L.D. (2000) *Learning from Museums: Visitor Experiences and the Making of Meaning*, Walnut Creek, CA: AltaMira Press.

Falk, J.H., Koran, J.J., Dierking, L.D., and Dreblow, L. (1985) "Predicting Visitor Behavior," in *Curator*, 28:4, 326–332.

Fischer, D. (2005) Museum charges, personal communication.

Flynn, G.A. (2001) *Merging Traditional Indigenous Curation Methods with Modern Museum Standards of Care*, Washington, DC: The George Washington University Museum Studies Program. Available http://www2.gwu.edu/~mstd/flynn_paper.pdf (accessed January 16, 2005).

Foucault, M. (1970) *The Order of Things: An Archeology of the Human Sciences*, London: Tavistock.

Franklin, U. (1998) "Le Bistro Des Idées," in *Muse*, 15:4, 9.

Frost, R.O. and Gross, R.C. (1993) "The Hoarding of Possessions," in *Behaviour Research and Therapy*, 31:4, 367–81.

Fulton, W. (1996) *New Urbanism: Hope or Hype for American Communities?* Lincoln, MA: Lincoln Institute of Land Policy.

Gallup, A.B. (1907) *The Work of a Children's Museum*, Washington, DC: American Association of Museums.

Gardner, H. (1983) *Frames of Mind: The Theory of Multiple Intelligences*, New York: Basic Books.

Gardner, H. (2004) "What We Do and Don't Know About Learning," in *Daedalus*, Cambridge, MA, 133:1 Winter, 5–12.

Geary, C.M. (1988) *Images from Bamum: German Colonial Photography at the Court of King Njoya, Cameroon, West Africa*, Washington, DC: Smithsonian Institution Press and National Museum of African Art.

Ginsburgh, V. and Zang, I. (2001) "Sharing the Income of a Museum Pass Program," in *Museum Management and Curatorship*, 19:4, 371–383.

Gurian, E.H. (1982) "Museums' Relationship to Education," in Tage Høyer Hansen, Karl-Erik Andersen, and Poul Vestergaard (eds) *Museums and Education: The Museum Exhibition as a Tool in Educational Work*, Copenhagen: Danish ICOM/CECA, 17–20.

Gurian, E.H. (1990) "Let Us Empower All Those Who Have a Stake in Exhibitions," in *Museum News*, March/April.

Gurian, E.H. (1991a) "The Opportunity for Social Service," in *ICOM-CECA. Annual Conference, The Museum and the Needs of People / Le musée et les besoins du public*, 1991, Jerusalem.

Gurian, E.H. (1991b) "Noodling around with Exhibition Opportunities," in Karp, I. and Lavine, S.D. (eds) *Exhibiting Cultures: The Poetics and Politics of Museum Display*, Washington, DC: Smithsonian Institution Press.

Gurian, E.H. (1992a) "The Importance of 'And'," in Nichols, S. (ed.) *Patterns in Practice: Selections from the Journal of Museum Education*, Washington, DC: Museum Education Roundtable.

Gurian, E.H. (1992b) "Reluctant Recognition of the Superstar," in *Journal of Museum Education*, 17, 6–7.

Gurian, E.H. (1993) "Adult Learning at Children's Museum of Boston," in Strand, J. (ed.) *Selected Reprints from Museums, Adults, and the Humanities, a Guide for Educational Programming*, Washington, DC: American Association of Museums.

Gurian, E.H. (1995a) "A Blurring of the Boundaries," in *Curator*, 38, 31–39.

Gurian, E.H. (1995b) "A Draft History of Children's Museums," unpublished, Cleveland Children's Museum.

Gurian, E.H. (1995c) "Offering Safer Public Spaces," in *Journal of Museum Education*, 20, 14–16.

Gurian, E.H. (1996) *A Savings Bank for the Soul*, Seattle, WA: Grantmakers in the Arts, 7:2, 6–9.

Gurian, E.H. (1998) "Continuous, Unexpected Joy and Fascinating, If Demanding Work," in *Museum News*, 77:4, 36–37.

Gurian, E.H. (1999a) "Thinking About My Museum Journey," in Pitman, B. (ed.) *Presence of Mind: Museums and the Spirit of Learning*, Washington, DC: American Association of Museums.

Gurian, E.H. (1999b) "What Is the Object of This Exercise? A Meandering Exploration of the Many Meanings of Objects in Museums," in *Daedalus*, Cambridge, MA, 128, 163–183.

Gurian, E.H. (2001) "Function Follows Form: How Mixed-Used Spaces in Museums Build Community," in *Curator*, 44:1, 87–113.

Gurian, E.H. (2002) "Choosing among the Options: An Opinion about Museum Definitions," in *Curator*, 45:2, 75–88.

Gurian, E.H. (2004) "Singing and Dancing at Night," in Sullivan, L.E. and Edwards, A. (eds) *Stewards of the Sacred*, Washington, DC: American Association of Museum in cooperation with Center for the Study of World Religions, Harvard University.

Gurian, E.H. (2005) "Threshold Fear," in Macleod, S. (ed.) *Reshaping Museum Space: Architecture, Design, Exhibitions*, London: Routledge.

Gurian, E.H. and Tribble, A.D. (1985) *Children's Museums, an Overview*, unpublished manuscript.

Gypsies and Travelers in Belgium – an Online Interview. Available http://home2.pi.be/tmachiel/educati2.htm (accessed August 14, 2004).

Harwit, M. (1996) *An Exhibit Denied: Lobbying the History of Enola Gay*, New York: Copernicus Springer-Verlag.

Heath, C. and Vom Lehn, D. (2002) *Misconstruing Interactivity, Interactive Learning in Museums of Art and Design*, London: King's College.

Hein, G.E. (1998) *Learning in the Museum*, New York: Routledge.

Hein, G.E. and Alexander, M. (1998) *Museums: Places of Learning*, American Association of Museums/AAM Education Committee.

Hill, T. and Nicks, T. (1992) *Turning the Page: Forging New Partnerships between Museums and First Peoples: Task Force Report on Museums and First Peoples*, 2nd edn, Ottawa: Assembly of First Nations and Canadian Museums Association.

Hogan, T.E., Editor (1995) in *ICOM News*, 48:3, 1.

Hoggart, R. (1957) *The Uses of Literacy*, Harmondsworth: Penguin.

Hood, M. (1983) "Staying Away: Why People Choose Not to Visit Museums," in *Museum News*, Washington, DC: American Association of Museums, 61:4, 50–57.

Hooper-Greenhill, E. (1994) *The Educational Role of the Museum*, London, New York: Routledge.

Hooper-Greenhill, E. (1998) "Cultural Diversity, Attitudes of Ethnic Minority Populations Towards Museums and Galleries," in *BMRB International, commissioned by the Museums and Galleries Commission, GEM News*, 69, 10–11.

ICOM (2004) *ICOM News 2004–1*, Paris, France: International Council of Museums. Available http://icom.museum/pdf/E_news2004/p4_2004–1.pdf (accessed January 20, 2005).

The International Ecotourism Society (2003) *Ecotourism Statistical Fact Sheet*, http://www.ecotourism.org/index2.php?research/stats (accessed February 26, 2005).

Jacobs, J. (1961) *The Death and Life of Great American Cities*, New York: Random House.

Jeffrey, K.R. (2000) "Constructivism in Museums: How Museums Create Meaningful Learning Environments," in Hirsch, J.S. and Silverman, L.H. (eds) *Transforming Practice: Selections from the Journal of Museum Education, 1992–1999*, Washington, DC: Museum Education Roundtable.

Katz, P. (1994) *The New Urbanism: Toward an Architecture of Community*, New York: McGraw-Hill.

Kavanagh, G. (1991) *Museum Languages: Objects and Texts*, Leicester; New York: Leicester University Press.

Kelly, L. (2005) *Extending the Lens: A Sociocultural Approach to Understanding Museum Learning*, Sydney: University of Technology.

Kelly, L., Barlett, A., and Gordon, P. (2002) *Indigenous Youth and Museums: A Report on the Indigenous Youth Access Project*, Sydney: Australian Museum.

Kirchberg, V. (1998) "Entrance Fees as a Subjective Barrier to Visiting Museums," in *Journal of Cultural Economics*, 22:1, 1–3.

Klemm, M.S. (2002) "Tourism and Ethnic Minorities in Bradford: The Invisible Segment," in *Journal of Travel Research*, 41, 85–91.

Konigsburg, E.L. (1972) *From the Mixed-up Files of Mrs. Basil E. Frankweiler*, New York: Simon & Schuster.

Koster, E. (2002) "A Disaster Revisited," in *Muse*, 20:5.

Koster, E. and Peterson, J. (2002) "Difficult Experiences: A Museum Forum on the Lessons of September 11," in ASTC *Dimensions*, May/June.

Kulik, G. (1989) "Designing the Past: History Museum Exhibitions from Peale to the Present," in Leon, W. and Rozensweig, R. (eds) *History Museums and Historical Societies in the United States*, Urbana, IL: University of Illinois Press.

Kunstler, J.H. (1996) *Home from Nowhere: Remaking Our Everyday World for the Twenty-First Century*, New York: Simon & Schuster.

Lang, W.L. (2003) *Museum Teams: Two Exhibits and Their Lessons*, Anchorage, Alaska: Anchorage Museum.

Lepper, B.T.L. (2001) "Kennewick Man's Legal Odyssey Nears an End," in *Mammoth Trumpet*, 16:4, 1–2, 15–16.

Lindsay, M. (1994) *Admission Charges – the Issues*, Wellington, NZ: Museum of New Zealand Te Papa Tongarewa.

Linenthal, E.T. (1995) *Preserving Memory: The Struggles to Create America's Holocaust Museum*, New York: Viking Press.

Linenthal, E.T. and Engelhard, T. (1996) *History Wars: The Enola Gay and Other Battles for the American Past*, New York: Holt.

Lord, B. and Lord, G.D. (2002) *The Manual of Museum Exhibitions*, Walnut Creek, CA: AltaMira Press.

Lord, G.D. and Lord, B. (eds) (2000) *The Manual of Museum Planning*, 2nd edn, London: Altamira Press.

McDermott, M. (1987) "Through These Eyes: What Novices Value in Art Experience," *Museum Program Sourcebook*, Washington, DC: American Association of Museums.

McIlvaney, N. (2000) "Rethinking the Exhibit Team: A Cyberspace Forum," in *Exhibitionist*, 19:1, 8–15.

McLean, K. (1993) *Planning for People in Museum Exhibitions*, Washington, DC: Association of Science-Technology Centers.

McManus, P.M. (1987) "It's the Company You Keep. The Social Determination of Learning-related Behaviour in a Science Museum," in *International Journal of Museum Management and Curatorship*, 6, 263–270.

Martin, A. (2003) *The Impact of Free Entry to Museums*, London: MORI.

Mayer, J.D. and Salovey, P. (1997) "What Is Emotional Intelligence?" in Salovey, P. and Sluyter, D. (eds) *Emotional Development and Emotional Intelligence: Implications for Educators*, New York: Basic Books.

Museum of Science (2005) *Corporate Sponsorship*, Boston. Available http://www.mos.org/doc/1026 (accessed March 1, 2005).

NAGPRA (1990) *Native American Graves Protection and Repatriation Act*, 101 Congress, US. Available http://www.cr.nps.gov/nagpra/SITEMAP/INDEX.htm (accessed January 15, 2005).

National Association for Museum Exhibition (2002) "Formalizing Exhibition Development," in *The Exhibitionist*, NAME, National Association for Museum Exhibition, Spring.

Oldenburg, R. (1989) *The Great Good Place*, New York: Paragon House.

Pacific Island Museum Association (2001) *Constitution (Charitable Purpose)*. Available http://edtech.mcc.edu/~mfulmer/pima/cst-intro.html (accessed March 3, 2005).

Pitman, B. (1992) "Excellence and Equity: Education and the Public Dimension of Museums, an Introduction," in Nichols, S. (ed.) *Patterns in Practice: Selections from the Journal of Museum Education*, Washington, DC: Museum Education Roundtable.

The Plain Dealer (2002) "The Quiet Crisis, a Special Report from the Plain Dealer, the Fine Art of Taxing to Support Culture," Cleveland.

Posner, E. (1988) "The Museum as Bazaar," in *Atlantic*, 262:2, 68.

Potok, C. (2005) United States Holocaust Memorial Museum. Available http://www.facinghistorycampus.org/Campus/Memorials.nsf/0/DE9B4E8C4798B95385256ECF0070413E? OpenDocument (accessed January 18, 2005).

Putnam, R.D. (1995) "Bowling Alone: America's Declining Social Capital," in *Journal of Democracy*, 6, 65–78.

Putnam, R.D. (2000) *Bowling Alone: The Collapse and Revival of American Community*, New York: Simon & Schuster.

Ricketts, A. (2001) "Ingenious Panache," in *Spectator*, December 7, 2001.

Roberts, L.C. (2000) "Educators on Exhibit Teams: A New Role, a New Era," in Hirsch, J.S. and Silverman, L.H. (eds) *Transforming Practice*, Washington, DC: Museum Education Roundtable.

Robinson, J. and Quinn, P. (1984) *Playspaces: Creating Family Spaces in Public Spaces*, Boston, MA: Boston Children's Museum.

Rodríguez, J.P. and Blanco, V.F. (2003) "Optimal Pricing and Grant Policies for Museums." Available http://econwpa.wustl.edu/eps/pe/papers/0309/0309002.pdf (accessed February 20, 2005).

Root-Bernstein, R. and Root-Bernstein, M. (2000) *Sparks of Genius*, Boston, MA: Houghton Mifflin, p. 379.

Rounds, J. and Mcilvaney, N. (2000) "Who's Using the Team Process? How's It Going?," in *Exhibitionist*, 19:1, 4–7.

Russell, T. (1994) "The Enquiring Visitor: Usable Learning Theory for Museum Contexts," in *Journal of Education in Museums*, 15.

Sayers, D.L. (1941) "The Mind of the Maker," in Andrews, R., Biggs, M. and Seidel, M. (eds) *The Columbia World of Quotations*, New York: Columbia University Press, 1996.

Schwartz, A. (ed.) (1967) *Museums, the Story of America's Treasure Houses*, New York: E.P. Dutton and Co., Inc.

Screven, C. (1987) *Museum Learning and the Casual Visitor: What Are the Limits?*, Conference on Museum Evaluation, 1987, University of Toronto.

Seattle Art Museum Holocaust Provenance, Research on World War II History of Ownership, Seattle, WA: Seattle Art Museum. Available http://www.seattleartmuseum.org/Collection/holocaustProvenance.asp (accessed February 3, 2005).

Serrell, B. (1996) *Exhibit Labels: An Interpretive Approach*, Walnut Creek, CA: AltaMira Press, American Association for State and Local History.

Sharp, D. (1995) "Welcoming Minorities in Cities Coast to Coast," in *USA Today*, September 19, 1995, p. 8D.

Sievert, A. (1994) *What Is Special About a Children's and Youth Museum?* Fulda, Germany: International conference. Available http://www.hands-on-europe.net/frameset.htm (accessed March 1, 2005).

Sola, T. (1992) "Museum Professionals: The Endangered Species," in Boylan, P. (ed.) *Museums 2000: Politics, People, Professionals and Profits*, New York: Routledge.

Spencer, H. (1897) "The Principles of Sociology," in Goffman, E. (ed.) *Relations in Public*, 1971, New York: Basic Books, Inc.

Taborsky, E. (1982) "The Sociostructural Role of the Museum," in *The International Journal of Museum Management and Curatorship*, 1: 339–345.

Te Papa (1998) *Maori Marae*, National Museum of New Zealand Te Papa Tangarawa. http://www.tepapa.govt.nz/TePapa/English/WhatsOn/LongTermExhibitions/TheMarae.htm (accessed January 25 2005).

Tirrul-Jones, J. (1995) "Regional Museums Serve Their Communities," in *ICOM News*, 48:3, 3.

Tortolero, C. (2004) Executive director, the Mexican Fine Arts Center Museum, *Group Conversation*, personal communication.

Weil, S.E. (1989) "The Proper Business of the Museum: Ideas or Things?," in *Muse*, 12:31.

Weil, S.E. (1990) *Rethinking the Museum and Other Meditations*, Washington, DC: Smithsonian Institution Press.

Weil, S.E. (1999) "From Being About Something to Being for Somebody: The Ongoing Transformation of the American Museum," in *Daedalus*, Cambridge, MA, 128:3, 229–258.

Weil, S.E. (2002) "Your Paper," personal e-mail. January 23, 2002.

Weinberg, J. and Elieli, R. (1995) *The Holocaust Museum in Washington*, New York: Rizzoli International Publications.

Weisel, E. (1979) *United States Holocaust Memorial Commission Report to the President of the United States.*

Wikipedia (January 19, 2005) *Pow Wow*. Wikipedia Foundation, Inc.

WVMA (2003) *WVMA Collections*, West Vancouver, Canada: West Vancouver Museum and Archives.

Young, J.E. (1993) *The Texture of Memory: Holocaust Memorials and Meaning*, New Haven, CT: Yale University Press.

Zervos, C. (2002) *Children's Museums: Edu-Tainment for Young Learners*, Adelaide. Available http://www.museumsaustralia.org.au/conf02/Papers/zervosc.htm (accessed February 17, 2005).

INDEX

Related titles from Routledge

Reshaping Museum Space
Edited by Suzanne Macleod

At no other point in their modern history have museums undergone such radical reshaping as in recent years. Challenges to create inclusive and accessible spaces open to appropriation and responsive to contemporary agendas have resulted in new architectural forms for museums, inside and out.

Reshaping Museum Space pulls together the views of an international group of museum professionals, architects, designers and academics highlighting the complexity, significance and malleability of museum space and provides reflections upon recent developments in museum architecture and exhibition design. The problems of navigating the often contradictory agendas and aspirations of the broad range of professionals and stakeholders involved in any new project are discussed in various chapters that concentrate on the process of architectural and spatial reshaping.

Contributors review recent new build, expansion and exhibition projects questioning the types of museum space required at the beginning of the twenty-first century and highlighting a range of possibilities for creative museum design.

Hb: 0–415–34344–5
Pb: 0–415–34345–3

Available at all good bookshops
For ordering and further information please visit:
www.routledge.com

Related titles from Routledge

The Engaging Museum
Developing Museums for Visitor Involvement
Graham Black

'*The Engaging Museum* charts a logical path from audience development to interpretation in the gallery, synthesising much thinking of the last 20 years into a textbook of practical value to the student and museum professional.' – *Simon Knell, University of Leicester*

'As an academic textbook it serves us well, fully developing each topic, and is replete with supporting information and quotes by reputable sources recognized as being on the cutting edge of visitor studies and museum educational curriculum and evaluation.' – *David K. Dean, Museum of Texas Tech University*

'Graham Black gets to the core of what a museum might aspire to in visitor-centred experience, including interpretive planning based on research, a defined audience and multi-layered opportunities for visitors. He has put into print our goals and aspirations – a truly inspirational read.' – *Adera Causey, Hunter Museum of American Art, Chattanooga*

This very practical book guides museums on how to create the highest quality experience possible for their visitors. Creating an environment that supports visitor engagement with collections means examining every stage of the visit, from the initial impetus to go to a particular institution, to front-of-house management, interpretive approach and qualitative analysis afterwards.

This holistic approach will be immensely helpful to museums in meeting the needs and expectations of visitors and building their audience base and includes:

- chapter introductions and discussion sections
- supporting case studies to show how ideas are put into practice
- a lavish selection of tables, figures and plates to support and illustrate the discussion
- boxes showing ideas, models and planning suggestions to guide development
- an up-to-date bibliography of landmark research.

The Engaging Museum offers a set of principles that can be adapted to any museum in any location and will be a valuable resource for institutions of every shape and size, as well as a vital addition to the reading lists of museum studies students.

Hb: 0–415–34556–1
Pb: 0–415–34557–X

Available at all good bookshops
For ordering and further information please visit:
www.routledge.com